THE SONG OF SOLOMON

AN INTRODUCTION AND COMMENTARY

by

THE REV. G. LLOYD CARR,
B.TH., B.A., B.D., TH.M., PH.D.
*Professor of Biblical and Theological Studies,
Gordon College, Wenham, Massachusetts*

INTER-VARSITY PRESS
LEICESTER, ENGLAND
DOWNERS GROVE, ILLINOIS, U.S.A.

Inter-Varsity Press
38 De Montfort Street, Leicester LE1 7GP, England
Box 1400, Downers Grove, Illinois 60515 U.S.A.
© *G. Lloyd Carr 1984*

First Edition 1984

Inter-Varsity Press, England, is the publishing division of the Universities and Colleges Christian Fellowship (formerly the Inter-Varsity Fellowship), a student movement linking Christian Unions in universities and colleges throughout the United Kingdom and the Republic of Ireland, and a member movement of the International Fellowship of Evangelical Students. For information about local and national activities write to UCCF, 38 De Montfort Street, Leicester LE1 7GP.

InterVarsity Press, U.S.A., is the book-publishing division of Inter-Varsity Christian Fellowship, a student movement active on campus at hundreds of universities, colleges and schools of nursing. For information about local and regional activities, write
IVCF, 233 Langdon St., Madison, WI 53703.

Text set in 10/10pt Baskerville
Phototypeset by Input Typesetting Ltd., London SW19 8DR
Printed in the United States of America

British Library Cataloguing in Publication Data
Carr, G. Lloyd
    The Song of Solomon. – (The Tyndale Old Testament Commentaries)
    1. Bible. O.T. – Song of Solomon – Commentaries
    I. Title   II. Series
    223'.907   BS1485.3

    ISBN 0-85111-638-8 Hardback
    ISBN 0-85111-839-9 Paperback

Library of Congress Cataloging in Publication Data
Carr, G. Lloyd, 1930-
    The Song of Solomon.

    (The Tyndale Old Testament commentaries; 17)
    Includes bibliographical references.
    1. Bible. O.T. Song of Solomon - Commentaries.
    1. Title. 11. Series.
    BS1485.3.C37   1983   223'.907   83-22651
USA ISBN 0-87784-918-8 (hardback)
USA ISBN 0-87784-268-X (paperback)
USA ISBN 0-87784-880-7 (set of Tyndale Old Testament Commentaries, hardback)
USA ISBN 0-87784-280-9 (set of Tyndale Old Testament Commentaries, paperback)

99 98 97 96 95 94
17 16 15 14 13 12 11 10 9 8

The Tyndale Old Testament Commentaries

General Editor:
PROFESSOR D. J. WISEMAN, O.B.E., M.A., D.Lit., F.B.A., F.S.A.

THE SONG OF SOLOMON

For
GWENDOLYN
'My sister, my bride,
my beloved, my companion,
my friend'

GENERAL PREFACE

THE aim of this series of *Tyndale Old Testament Commentaries*, as it was in the companion volumes on the New Testament, is to provide the student of the Bible with a handy, up-to-date commentary on each book, with the primary emphasis on exegesis. Major critical questions are discussed in the introductions and additional notes, while undue technicalities have been avoided.

In this series individual authors are, of course, free to make their own distinctive contributions and express their own point of view on all controversial issues. Within the necessary limits of space they frequently draw attention to interpretations which they themselves do not hold but which represent the stated conclusions of sincere fellow Christians.

Dr Carr brings a wide understanding and sympathetic insight to this new study of a unique and brief part of the Old Testament. He is cognizant of the variant interpretations and applications of its story and message which abound; yet he provides us with such detailed, and often original, views, that the elucidation of the text and thus of the study and teaching of the Song makes it freshly relevant to any reader today.

In the Old Testament in particular no single English translation is adequate to reflect the original text. Dr Carr has chosen to base his commentary on the Revised Standard Version, but like other contributors to this series he quotes freely from many versions, or gives his own translation in the endeavour to make the more difficult passages or words meaningful today. Where necessary, words from the Hebrew Text underlying the study are transliterated. This will help the reader who may be unfamiliar with Hebrew to identify the word under discussion and thus to follow the argument.

Interest in the meaning and message of the Old Testament continues undiminished and it is hoped that this series will thus further the systematic study of the revelation of God and his will and ways as seen in these records. It is the prayer of the editor and publisher, as of the authors, that these books will help many to understand, and to respond to, the Word of God today.

D. J. WISEMAN

CONTENTS

AUTHOR'S PREFACE

THE believing Christian comes to the Bible with the faith that it is God's Word to mankind. But we are more than merely 'spiritual' beings; we are human. If God is concerned about our human condition – and the incarnation makes it plain that he is – his revelation will be concerned with every aspect of that condition. And that includes human sexuality. The Christian mind recognizes the paradox that the whole person, professionally, privately, intellectually, physically, emotionally, spiritually, is brought to that place of freedom and fulfilment only as a slave of Jesus Christ, who is Lord of all.

The commentator's primary task is not one of application; he is to clarify the text and get to its *meaning*, so that the reader can grasp its principles and apply them in life and experience. The things we handle here are sacred. They need to be handled fearlessly, intelligently and critically, but also with that reverence that springs from the constant awareness that the text before us is part of Holy Scripture. Once the meaning of the text is discovered, that meaning stands; we dare not condemn the Word as reasonable or unreasonable, acceptable or unacceptable. The Christian stands under the judgment of the Word of God and must lead every thought captive in obedience to Christ. It is this perspective I have endeavoured to maintain throughout this book.

The unique features presented by the Song of Solomon will be apparent to many. The whole question of its overall interpretation is unparalleled in the Old Testament, while a glance at the many translations available will show that the actual text, with its many unusual words and expressions, presents an exceptionally large number of problems of vocabulary and syntax. The latter require frequent technical discussion, making the Commentary proper unusually technical for this series. This factor has also prompted the unusual step of basing the Commentary initially (though by no means exclusively) on one English version. Conversely, material of more general interest is to be found in the Introduction and in the four Subject Studies.

The translation followed is the Revised Standard Version, with constant reference to other versions in common use. The standard Hebrew-English lexicons by Brown, Driver and Briggs, by Köhler and Baumgartner and by Holladay have been my constant companions, as also have been the concordances of S. Mandelkern (Schocken, Jerusalem, 1964) and of George V. Wigram (Bagster).

I want to express my thanks to the Faculty Senate and the Faculty Development Committee of Gordon College whose programme, financed in part by the Kellogg Foundation, made it possible for me to spend a sabbatical working with Professor D. J. Wiseman and the faculty and staff of the School of Oriental and African Studies, University of London. Much of my preliminary work on ancient Near Eastern love poetry was done there.

The invitation of the President and faculty of Atlantic Baptist College, Moncton, N.B., Canada, to deliver the 1979 Guptill Lectures gave me an opportunity to share an early draft of part of this material with the college community. The task of bringing the manuscript from chaos to order was performed by my two typists: my daughter-in-law, Mrs Rose Marie Carr, and Mrs Madeline MacDonald. Much thanks to both these colleagues in the work.

Finally, I want to acknowledge the patience and understanding of Professor Wiseman and of the editorial staff of Inter-Varsity Press, Leicester, without whose support and encouragement this work would never have been undertaken.

G. LLOYD CARR

CHIEF ABBREVIATIONS

AJSL	*American Journal of Semitic Languages*
ANEP	*The Ancient Near East in Pictures* edited by J. B. Pritchard (Princeton, ²1969)
ANET	*Ancient Near Eastern Texts* edited by J. B. Pritchard (Princeton, ³1969)
ASV	American Standard Version, 1901
AV	Authorized (King James) Version, 1611
BA	*Biblical Archaeologist*
BASOR	*Bulletin of the American Schools of Oriental Research*
BDB	*Hebrew and English Lexicon of the Old Testament* by F. Brown, S. R. Driver and C. A. Briggs (OUP, 1906)
Bib.	*Biblica*
CBQ	*Catholic Biblical Quarterly*
CT	*Christianity Today*
Douay	Douay (Roman Catholic) version of the Bible (1609)
GK	*Hebrew Grammar* by Gesenius and Kautzsch (OUP, ²1910)
Holl.	*A Concise Hebrew and Aramaic Lexicon of the Old Testament* by William L. Holladay (Eerdmans, 1971)
IBD	*The Illustrated Bible Dictionary* (IVP, 1980)
JAAR	*Journal of the American Academy of Religion*
JAOS	*Journal of the American Oriental Society*
JB	Jerusalem Bible, 1966
JBL	*Journal of Biblical Literature*
JBR	*Journal of Bible and Religion*
JEA	*Journal of Egyptian Archaeology*
JETS	*Journal of the Evangelical Theological Society*
JSS	*Journal of Semitic Studies*
JTS	*Journal of Theological Studies*
KB	*Hebräisches und aramäisches Lexicon zum Alten Testament* by L. Köhler and W. Baumgartner (Brill, ³1967).

CHIEF ABBREVIATIONS

LXX	The Septuagint (Greek version of the Old Testament)
MT	Massoretic Text
NEB	New English Bible, 1970
NIV	New International Version, 1978
PAPhS	*Proceedings of the American Philosophical Society*
PEQ	*Palestine Exploration Quarterly*
PTR	*Princeton Theological Review*
RB	*Revue Biblique*
RSV	Revised Standard Version, 1952, ²1971
TB	*Tyndale Bulletin*
TDNT	*Theological Dictionary of the New Testament* edited by G. Kittel and G. Friedrich (Eerdmans, 1964–76)
TDOT	*Theological Dictionary of the Old Testament* edited by G. J. Botterweck and H. Ringgren (Eerdmans, 1974–)
SVT	Supplements to *Vetus Testamentum*
UT	*Ugaritic Textbook* edited by C. Gordon (Pontifical Bible Institute, 1965)
VT	*Vetus Testamentum*
Vg.	The Vulgate (the late fourth century Latin translation of the Bible by Jerome)
WTJ	*Westminster Theological Journal*
ZAW	*Zeitschrift für die alttestamentliche Wissenschaft*

SELECT BIBLIOGRAPHY

THE literature published on the Song is incredibly vast. Many of the books and articles are highly technical and deal with specific texts. Others are more general, touching on many aspects of the Song. I have quoted or referred to nearly 150 separate items. Some authors have written several articles which I have quoted; for all those, bibliographical data can be found in the footnotes of the Commentary. Books listed here are referred to in the Commentary simply by the author's surname.

Dahood, M., *Psalms, Anchor Bible* vols. 16, 17, 17a (Doubleday, 1965–1970).

Delitzsch, F., *Commentary on the Song of Songs and Ecclesiastes* (T. & T. Clark, 1885).

Fuerst, W. J., *The Song of Songs, Cambridge Bible Commentary* (CUP, 1975).

Gaster, T. H., *Thespis* (Harper & Row, 1950).

Gordis, R., *The Song of Songs and Lamentations* (KTAV, [2]1974).

Hirschberg, H. H., 'Some additional Arabic etymologies in Old Testament lexicography', *VT* 11, 1961.

Kidner, D., *Psalms, Tyndale Old Testament Commentaries* (IVP, 1973, 1975).

Kramer, S. N., *The Sacred Marriage Rite* (Indiana U.P., 1969).

Lambert, W. G., 'The problem of the love lyrics' in H. Goedicke and J. M. M. Roberts (eds.) *Unity and Diversity* (Johns Hopkins U.P., 1975).

Lehrman, S. M., 'The Song of Songs' in A. Cohen (ed.) *The Five Megilloth* (Soncino Press, 1946).

Lys, D., 'Notes sur le Cantique', *SVT* 17 (Brill, 1969).

Pope, M. H., *Song of Songs, Anchor Bible* vol. 7c (Doubleday, 1977).

Rabin, C., 'The Song of Songs and Tamil Poetry', *Studies in Religion* 3, 1973.

SELECT BIBLIOGRAPHY

Rowley, H. H., 'The interpretation of the Song of Songs', *JTS* 38, 1937. Revised and expanded in *The Servant of the Lord and Other Essays on the Old Testament* (Blackwell, [2]1965).

Seerveld, C., *The Greatest Song* (Trinity Pennyasheet Press, 1967).

Simpson, W. K., *The Literature of Ancient Egypt: An Anthology of Stories, Instructions and Poetry* (Yale U.P., [2]1973).

Wolff, H. W., *Anthropology of the Old Testament* (SCM Press, 1974).

Yadin, Y., *The Art of Warfare in Biblical Lands* (McGraw Hill, 1963).

Young, E. J., *An Introduction to the Old Testament* (Eerdmans, [2]1960).

INTRODUCTION

A MONG the books of the Bible, the Song of Solomon is one of the smallest, most difficult, yet one of the most popular with both Jews and Christians. Over the centuries hundreds of books and commentaries have been written and unnumbered sermons preached on these 117 verses.[1] The book has attracted the attention of some of the best intellects and spiritual minds of the believing community, and, in spite of its apparent simplicity, poses a great number of major interpretative difficulties.

For this reason, it is essential that careful attention be given to the material in this extended introduction. This section is not just unnecessary filler, but is crucial to an understanding of the problems the book raises as these relate to a comprehension of the commentary on the individual texts in the Song. The commentary itself should not be read in isolation, but with regular attention to and comparison with the Bible itself.

I. THE PLACE OF THE SONG IN HOLY SCRIPTURE

The Song of Solomon is part of the third section of the Hebrew Bible, the *Kethubim* or Writings (Heb. *keṯuḇîm*).[2] These Writings are a rather diverse collection including such works as the prophecy of Daniel, the historical books of Chronicles, Ezra and Nehemiah, the poetry of Job, Psalms and Proverbs, and the so-called 'Five Scrolls' (Heb. *meḡillôt*, 'Megilloth'), the Song of Solomon, Ruth, Lamentations, Ecclesiastes and

[1] Pope contains a fifty-five page bibliography with over a thousand entries. Even this is a selective list with notable omissions and no entries later than 1975.

[2] See 'Bible: III. The Old Testament', *IBD*, p. 195, and 'Canon of the Old Testament: IV. The evolution of the second and third sections', *IBD*, pp. 236f.

15

THE SONG OF SOLOMON

Esther, which were read publicly at the major Hebrew festivals.[1] Of these, Job, Proverbs, Ecclesiastes, and often the Song of Solomon and some Psalms, are classified as 'Wisdom'.

'Wisdom' is a literary genre, common throughout the ancient Near East, which shows many similar characteristics all across the region in various time periods. Although there is a wide variety of definitions, most simply, Wisdom is the closest thing to 'philosophy' the ancient peoples had. For the most part, even though Wisdom is not presented in carefully-structured philosophical treatises like those of the ancient Greeks, the more homely literature of the ancient Near Eastern Wisdom wrestles with the same basic philosophical questions: Where did I come from? Where am I going? What is the meaning of life? How is the universe ordered? Is there life after death? Can I know God? How? What is life all about? What is the nature of love? *etc.* These are universal human questions and it is not surprising that the ancient Hebrews found it necessary to address them.

Many scholars argue that the Wisdom Literature, especially the Song of Solomon, was a late addition to the Hebrew canonical Scriptures, noting that as late as AD 90 the rabbis were still debating whether or not the Song should remain in the Canon. It was in the context of this debate that Rabbi Aqiba's famous dictum was uttered: 'No man in Israel has ever contested that the Song of Solomon defiles the hands.[2]

[1] The Song was read at Passover, the most important Hebrew festival, celebrating the deliverance from Egypt (Ex. 12); Ruth, at the Feast of Weeks (Pentecost, 50 days after Passover), celebrating the barley harvest in late May (Ru. 2 – 3); Lamentations, on the ninth of Ab (late July), for the anniversary of the destruction of Jerusalem in 587 BC (2 Ki. 25:1–12); Ecclesiastes, at the Feast of Tabernacles (15 – 21 Tishri, late September or early October), the annual harvest festival, recalling the wilderness experience by a week spent in temporary shelters ('booths' or 'tabernacles'. Lv. 23:33–43); and Esther, at the Feast of Purim (14 – 15 Adar, late February), to celebrate the deliverance of the Jews from the genocidal intent of Haman (Est. 9:16–22). The use of a particular book at a specific festival is an ancient Hebrew tradition, but the connection of the Song and Ecclesiastes with their respective festivals is not obvious. Perhaps there is a reflection of the common Hebrew idea of teaching by contrast. Thus the love/death juxtaposition in Song 8:6 takes on fresh poignancy in the shadow of the tenth plague on Egypt (Ex. 12), and the pessimism of Ecclesiastes contrasts with the joyous celebration of harvest.

[2] To 'defile the hands' is the standard rabbinic expression used to describe holy things, especially the holy (canonical) books. This unusual expression meant that the person who handled these books had to wash his hands before

For in the entire world there is nothing to equal the day on which the Song of Solomon was given to Israel. All the Writings are holy, but the Song of Songs is most Holy, and if there has been dispute, it is only about Ecclesiastes.'[1] While the preservation of this saying is evidence of opposition to the inclusion of the Song in the Canon, the remark itself makes it clear that the Song was not being considered for inclusion in an enlarged canon, but rather was being re-examined to verify its canonical status. The decision was positive, the deciding factor being that it had not been disputed previously.

II. THE DATE OF THE BOOK

This is a complex question with no unanimity on the answer. Any decision depends on how various lines of evidence are evaluated, and as is so frequently the case in biblical studies, different conclusions are reached according to the presuppositions which the commentator brings to the materials. Specifically, questions of vocabulary, grammatical constructions, historical references, personal and place names, themes, and traditional understandings of particular items all need careful attention.

Taken at face value, the title (1:1) would suggest that Solomon was the author of the book (but see below, pp. 19–21 and commentary). That would set the date for composition sometime about the middle of the tenth century BC. There are several examples of this sort of title on love poem collections from Egypt in the late second millennium BC, so no argument can be made for a late date for the Song on the basis of the title.[2] More critical scholarship argues that the poems were

---

touching anything else (*e.g.* food, *etc.*) because the sanctity of the book would otherwise be transmitted via the hands to common or unworthy objects. (*Cf. Mishnah, Yadaim* 4:6.) The origin of the expression is obscure, but Delitzsch, p. 13n., notes that the Torah scrolls (written on leather) and the food offerings (Lv. 7:11–14), especially the cakes, were considered holy and placed in the temple. 'It was discovered that the sacred books were thereby exposed to damage by mice; and hence to prevent their being brought any longer into contact with the *Theruma* [food], the Rabbins decided that they were henceforth to be regarded as unclean, and they gave forth the decree, "All Holy Scriptures pollute the hand." This decree was applicable only to *holy* or *inspired* books' (his italics).

[1] *Mishnah, Yadaim* 3:5.

[2] For details, see G. L. Carr, 'The love poetry genre in the Old Testament and the ancient Near East', *JETS* 25, 1982, pp. 489–498.

written perhaps as late as the fourth or third centuries BC. The presence of four fragments from the Song among the Dead Sea Scrolls from Qumran warn against opting for too late a date.

Some scholars who identify the Song as an ancient cult-ceremony (see below, pp. 32–34) date the original composition during the second or even the third millennium BC during the Canaanite period before the patriarchs ever arrived in Egypt.

In any event, it appears as if the book has a long history, and in the form in which we now have it gives at least some indication of being an early poem on which editorial work was done over an extended period of time. The position adopted in this commentary is that the poem, essentially complete, probably originated in the time of Solomon or shortly thereafter, and was preserved and updated during the time of the divided monarchy in much the same way as the Proverbs and other Writings were.[1]

This conclusion is based in part on the variety of linguistic phenomena in the book. Detailed discussion would be redundant here, since the commentary treats these questions as they arise in the text. However, it is fair to say here that there is enough evidence of archaic (pre-tenth century) grammatical and linguistic forms in the Song – *e.g.* so-called 'single word' parallelisms, 1:2b–3a; 2:15; 6:8, *etc.* which are a feature of twelfth and eleventh century poetry; the presence of the relative particle *še*, instead of the more common *ʾašer* which in the Song occurs only in the title; and numerous verbal parallels with the Ugaritic literature from the fourteenth century or earlier[2] – to sustain the argument for a date around the time of Solomon.

---

[1] The Hebrew tradition preserved in the *Mishnah*, *Baba Bathra* 15a, that 'Hezekiah and his company ... wrote the Song of Songs' is probably to be understood in terms of editorial work on an already existing collection of material. See Pr. 25:1, and *cf.* D. Kidner, *Proverbs* (IVP, 1964), pp. 22–27; Young, p. 350; and R. K. Harrison, *Introduction to the Old Testament* (IVP, 1970), pp. 1049–1052.

[2] There is an extensive bibliography on this question. See particularly W. F. Albright, 'Archaic Survivals in the Text of Canticles', *Hebrew and Semitic Studies Presented to Geoffrey Rolles Driver*, ed. D. W. Thomas and W. D. McHardy (OUP, 1963), pp. 1–7; Rabin, pp. 205–219. Albright argues for a final editing in the fifth or fourth centuries BC, but notes the presence of much more ancient elements in the Song. See also H. L. Ginsberg, 'Introduction to the Song of Songs', *Jewish Publication Society Version: The Five Megilloth and*

It is commonly argued that the content demands a late date; but, as will be shown below (pp. 37–44), there is evidence of common themes and vocabulary from a wide variety of geographical areas and chronological periods, from which no firm conclusion can be drawn. Similarly, the so-called 'Aramaisms' in the language do not necessarily indicate a late date. Aramaic became the common language of the Jews after their return from Babylon in the sixth century, but the Aramaic language itself was in use at least as early as the ninth century BC, and probably goes back to the nineteenth century.[1]

III. SOLOMON

The traditional title 'The Song of Solomon' reflects the idea that the famous Hebrew king Solomon, the son of David and Bathsheba (2 Sa. 12:24f.; 1 Ch. 23:1), was the author of the Song (see commentary on 1:1). It was during his reign (971–931 BC) that the Kingdom of Israel reached the zenith of its glory and wealth. Solomon, the wise, wealthy ruler, became the patron of the arts (1 Ki. 4:32f.), architecture (2 Ch. 3 – 4), and international trade (1 Ki. 9:26–28; 10:11–22).

That a love song like this one should be attributed or dedicated to Solomon is not surprising. His vast harem and many wives were a byword in Israel. 1 Kings 11:1–3 remarks on 700 wives and 300 concubines, and probably does not include other liaisons such as that which Ethiopian tradition ascribes to Solomon and the Queen of Sheba (1 Ki. 10:1–13).[2] Among Solomon's wives was the daughter of the Pharaoh of Egypt.[3] That union is thought by some to be the specific occasion celebrated in the Song of Solomon. Be that as it may, Solomon

---

Jonah (Jewish Publication Society, 1966), pp. 3f. and Lys, pp. 170–178, for a different evaluation of the same material and a later dating.

[1] See K. A. Kitchen, 'Aram', *IBD*, pp. 88–92, and W. J. Martin and K. A. Kitchen, 'Language of the Old Testament', *IBD*, pp. 874–878.

[2] Ethiopian tradition identifies this liaison as beginning the line from which the present Ethiopian royal family is descended. Modern scholarship, however, places 'Sheba' in Southern Arabia rather than Ethiopia.

[3] The identity of the woman is not known. Possibly she was the daughter of one of the last members of the Twenty-first Dynasty, perhaps Pharaoh Siamun. See D. H. Lance, 'Gezer in the Land and History', *BA* 30, 1967, pp. 41f. *Cf.* 1 Ki. 9:16, 24.

does appear several times in the Song, and, in addition to the commentary on the specific verses (1:1, 5; 3:7, 9, 11; 8:11, 12), a general statement is necessary.

Many scholars consider only 1:5; 8:11–12 to be authentic, the others being editorial additions. These three (if in fact 1:5 is to be read 'Solomon') can be understood best as general or generic statements that have no precise reference to Solomon as a real person involved in the action of the poem. The king, with all his wealth and splendour, is introduced here only as a symbol of the class of society for which the desire is the same as possession. Money is no object – what they want, they get.

The reference in the title is rejected as only a late editorial addition by those who hold to a late date and who therefore reject the Solomonic authorship of the Song.

The other three references, it will be noted, all appear within a short section of ch. 3, and it is these that pose the most difficult problem. The options are simple: the choice among them is not.

1. For those who consider the Song (or at least 3:6–11) to be a composition to celebrate a royal wedding, Solomon's name is very much in order here, since he is the protagonist of the story. Gordis, for example, argues that it is '*a song composed on the occasion of one of Solomon's marriages to a foreign princess*, probably an Egyptian'.[1]

2. Solomon's name is introduced here in what has been called a 'literary fiction': if the Song is simply love poetry, the 'great lover' in Israel would naturally appear in the poem whether or not he really had anything to do with it. Similarly, Don Juan would conjure up the same picture in later love poetry.

3. If an allegorical or typical interpretation is followed, Solomon symbolizes either the LORD (*vis-à-vis* Israel the bride/wife) or Christ (*vis-à-vis* the church/bride). Although a case can be made for interpreting the great Messianic prophecy of 2 Samuel 7:11–17 in terms of both Solomon and Jesus, there is scant evidence in the New Testament for taking Solomon as a type foreshadowing Jesus.

4. Many scholars simply delete the Solomonic references in

[1] Gordis, p. 20. (italics in original). Delitzsch, on the other hand, pp. 4–6, argues cogently that the girl in the Song *cannot* be a foreign princess, but is the 'daughter of a humble family in a remote part of Galilee'.

20

ch. 3 as editorial additions. Such a solution is effective in removing the problem, but there is no evidence, either in the MSS or VSS, or internally, that gives serious support to this option.

It is obvious, then, that no simple solution can be assumed. The question of Solomon is inextricably linked with the way the Song is interpreted. To this topic we now must turn.

IV. THE INTERPRETATION OF THE SONG

The major problem a commentator must face with this book is deciding what sort of literature this is and what basic approach to take in interpreting it. Historically there have been four major ways of dealing with the question, with many variations within these broader categories. The complexities of the issue are demonstrated by noting that Pope devotes 140 pages to the problem of interpretation, remarking in passing that this is just a 'brief sketch based on previous surveys with some attention to more recent developments'.[1]

a. Allegory

Our English word allegory comes to us via a combination of two Greek words, *allos* 'other' and *agoreyō* 'speak' or 'proclaim'. It conveys the idea 'to say one thing but mean something else'. An allegory is, in its true sense, an extended metaphor, and if so used is a valid and helpful literary device.[2] However, *allegorizing* as a method of interpreting Scripture is something radically different.

Basic to the allegorical *method* is the idea that a given passage contains no factual or historically true record of any past event, but is merely a vehicle for some deeper spiritual truth. The grammatical-historical meaning of the text is ignored, so that what the original author *said* takes second place to what the interpreter wants to say.

While the allegorical method found a friendly home in Hebrew and Christian circles as early as Philo (20 BC – AD 54) and Origen (AD 185–254), it is originally a pagan Greek method of interpretation. Theogenes of Rhegium (*c.* 520 BC) was in the vanguard of the philosophical schools which were

---

[1] Pope, p. 89. For a good summary treatment of the issues, see Rowley, pp. 337–363.

[2] *Cf.* A. B. Mickelsen, *Interpreting the Bible* (Eerdmans, 1963), pp. 230–235.

attempting to re-interpret the ancient works of Homer and Hesiod to make them more acceptable to the enlightened citizens of the Greek city-states. Since the gods of Homer and Hesiod's writings were immoral, unjust, unpredictable, capricious, vindictive, and generally rather unlovely characters who nevertheless were intimately bound up with the life and popular feelings of the people, the philosophers felt it necessary to try to impose their own more advanced beliefs on the structure of the older popular literature. This they accomplished by allegorizing. They denied the historical reality and obvious teachings of the older writers, yet at the same time used their widespread acceptance among the common people as a base. The stories of the gods were not meant to be taken literally, they argued, but were only vehicles to convey the real hidden or secret meanings which the commentators knew. During the centuries before Christ, this method was developed and refined among the Greeks, eventually finding its way to the intellectual centres of Alexandria in Egypt, where first the Jew Aristobulus (*c.* 160 BC) and then Philo and Origen introduced the method into the study of the biblical materials.[1]

Applied to the biblical texts, the allegorical method proceeded in the same way. The literal or historical situation described in the text is ignored, either because it never happened, or because the events described are, for theological or aesthetic reasons, considered incapable of yielding any suitable sense or teaching. Those commentators who allegorize the Song ignore the male/female relationship so vividly described in the poem, and interpret the whole book in terms of God's dealing with Israel or Christ's relationship with his Church.[2] Underlying most of this sort of handling of the text

[1] For an examination and evaluation of Philo, see H. A. Wolfson, *Philo*, 2 vols. (Harvard U.P., 1948) or S. Sandmel, *Philo of Alexandria* (OUP, 1979). The contribution of Origen to the field is examined in detail by J. Daniélou, *Origen* (Sheed & Ward, 1955), pp. 139–174, and in briefer fashion in *The Pelican Guide to Modern Theology* 2: *Historical Theology* (Penguin, 1969), pp. 53–63; and G. L. Prestige, *Fathers and Heretics* (SPCK, 1940), pp. 43–66.

[2] *E.g.* P. P. Parente, 'The Canticle of Canticles in Mystical Theology', *CBQ* 6, 1944, p. 150, remarks 'The only sense of the canticle *intended by God* is the spiritual or allegorical sense. Those who stop at the literal sense of the text and perceive nothing of the spiritual meaning read something that refers to natural love only and find anything but edification. A carnal man should not read this book. It is the book of perfect souls' (my italics).

is an implicit acceptance of the Platonic or Gnostic belief that physical things, particularly those related to sexuality, are intrinsically evil, and are to be shunned by those who are seeking the spiritual life.

Allegorical writing usually gives hints that it is allegory. The places are fabulous – Doubting Castle, The Slough of Despond, Puritania, Orgiastica; the names are obviously symbolic – Mr Worldly Wiseman, Giant Despair, Mr Reason, the Clevers; and the story-line moves through obvious stages to climax and resolution. None of these elements is present in the Song of Songs. The places are real places – En-gedi (1:14), Sharon (2:1), Lebanon (3:9), Tirzah (6:4), *etc.* The people are real people – Solomon (but see above, pp. 19–21), the shepherd, the watchmen, the city-girls, and the lover and his beloved, even though no names are attached to them. Nor does the book reveal any progressive story-line; there are various episodes that set up a situation and then resolve it (*e.g.* 3:1–5), but the overall impression in the poem is one of the ebb and flow of the relationship and a kind of cyclic repetition of themes and ideas. (See below, pp. 44–49, on the Structure of the Song.)

The assumption that the Song is purely allegorical has been widespread amongst English-speaking evangelicals for many generations. Their devotional writing on the Song has sometimes been of a high order, but that does not, of course, settle the question whether their basic approach is true to the text itself. The recently published comment of the renowned Reformed theologian, the late Professor John Murray, provides an admirable summary of the general difficulties raised by this approach: 'I cannot now endorse the allegorical interpretation of the Song of Solomon. I think the vagaries of interpretation given in terms of the allegorical principle indicate that there are no well-defined hermeneutical canons to guide us in determining the precise meaning and application if we adopt the allegorical view. However, I also think that in terms of the biblical analogy the Song could be used to *illustrate* the relation of Christ to His church. The marriage bond is used in Scripture as a pattern of Christ and the church. If the Song portrays marital love and relationship on the highest levels of exercise and devotion, then surely it may be used to exemplify what is transcendently true in the bond that exists between Christ and the church. One would have to avoid a great deal of the arbitrary and indeed fanciful interpretations to which the allegorical view leads and which it would demand.'[1]

b. Typology

The second approach is that known as typology. Many writers and interpreters make no distinction between this method and allegory, but there is a clear difference which needs to be recognized.[2] Whereas allegory denies or ignores the historicity or factualness of the Old Testament account and imposes a deeper, hidden or spiritual meaning on the text, typology recognizes the validity of the Old Testament account in its own right, but then finds in that account a clear, parallel link with some event or teaching in the New Testament which the Old Testament account foreshadows.

Our English word *type*, in the sense that it is used here, comes from the Greek word *typos*, meaning either a pattern, or the thing produced from the pattern (*e.g.* a coin struck from a die, or the impression in the die itself). The related word *antitypos* 'antitype' means 'corresponding to something that has gone before'. Thus the New Testament fulfilment, or 'antitype', corresponds to the material presented in the Old Testament original, the 'type'. The typical interpretation does not provide a 'different' meaning that replaces the one the text appears to present, but gives *an added dimension* to the sense already present in the text. This is similar to the so-called 'dual fulfilment' of the Messianic prophecies of the Old Testament.

The key to understanding the nature of typology is the doctrine of the unity of Scripture. The New Testament is the fulfilment and culmination of the Old. The coming of our Lord Jesus is presented there as a fulfilment of all the law and

---

[1] Quoted in *The Monthly Record of the Free Church of Scotland*, March 1983, p. 52.

[2] The classic and still very valuable treatment is P. Fairbairn, *The Typology of Scripture*, 2 vols. (1886, reprinted Evangelical Press, 1975). More recent treatments, on a smaller scale, can be found in B. Ramm, *Protestant Biblical Interpretation* (Baker, ³1970), especially pp. 23–45 on allegory and pp. 215–240 on typology, and A. B. Mickelsen, *Interpreting the Bible*, pp. 23–38, 230–235 on allegory and pp. 236–264 on typology. Both have extensive bibliographies. Dorothy L. Sayers' essay, 'The Writing and Reading of Allegory', first published in *The Poetry of Search and the Poetry of Statement* (Gollancz, 1963), reprinted in *The Whimsical Christian* (Macmillan, 1978), pp. 205–234, discusses the method in its broader application to literature generally.

the promises. 'In these last days he [God] has spoken to us by his Son' (Heb. 1:2, NIV). Romans 5:14 is a clear example of typology: Adam, the head of the human race, is 'a type [Gk. *typos*] of the one who was to come', Christ, the head of a redeemed humanity. Luke 24:27 records that Jesus, in the afternoon of the resurrection, joined Cleopas and his companion on the road to Emmaus, and as they walked, 'beginning with Moses and all the prophets, he interpreted to them in all the scriptures the things concerning himself'.

In this light, many commentators have argued that typology is the correct approach to the Song of Songs. Most would reject the anti-historical perspective of the pure allegorist, and would recognize the Song to be describing real, though not necessarily 'historical', relationships among the characters of the book; but most would also go at least part way with Parente[1] in understanding the Song to be speaking of more than human love.

Historically, the preponderance of interpretative material on the Song has been of this typical character. For the Jewish interpreters the account was understood in terms of the LORD's relationship with Israel. As the prophet Hosea (chs. 1–3) used his own unhappy marital situation to illustrate the spiritual fornication (idolatry) that Israel committed by turning to worship the Canaanite god Baal, so it was an easy step from there to reading the Song of Solomon in a similar fashion: the beloved is Israel, the lover is the LORD, and the Song recounts the loving relationship which ideally exists between the nation and her God.

Some rabbinic writers constructed very elaborate typologies which used the Song to trace the whole history of Israel from its beginnings as a nation through all kinds of suffering and persecution. Even in the face of these tokens of rejection, Israel is the trusting bride whose faithful lover, the LORD, will support, encourage and preserve her as his Chosen beloved.[2]

---

[1] P. P. Parente, *art. cit.*

[2] Probably the most familiar of these is the *Commentary on the Song of Songs by Rabbi Abraham ben Isaac ha-Levi TaMaKH* (tr. Leon A. Feldman: Van Gorcum & Co., 1970), a celebrated Provençal poet and writer who died in Gerona in 1393. His commentary is typology rather than allegory, for he recognized two levels of meaning. '. . . I do not know of anyone who has ever written a commentary, containing both the plain meaning and the occult interpretation, which harmonizes the language with the context. I have humbly set myself the task of establishing the plain meaning in conformity

There are, of course, many variations on this basic theme. Some identify the beloved with Wisdom who is sought by the lover, the dedicated believer (*e.g.* Pr. 8 – 9). Others read the Song in terms of another prophetic theme, the LORD's, or Messiah's, loving preservation of the faithful Remnant who rejected the paganism of the bulk of the population and followed God in obedience.

Within the Christian community the Song is often understood to describe the loving concern Christ, the lover/bridegroom, has for his church, the beloved/bride, and for the individual believer. Each verse is then read through Christological eyes for what it can reveal about that relationship. Many popular commentaries still follow this approach to the Song, with typological application to Christ and the church being found in every phrase. A common medieval interpretation, still found among Roman Catholic commentators, identified the beloved with the Virgin Mary whom (they say) the true believer worships. Song 4:7, 'You are all fair, my love; there is no flaw in you', is used to support the doctrine of the Immaculate Conception of Mary (*cf.* JB notes). For others, the beloved is the established church which is sought by all true pilgrims and which will meet their spiritual needs. *E.g.* Song 7:2, 'Your navel is a rounded bowl that never lacks mixed wine', refers to the baptismal font and the efficacious sacrament.

One reason for the tenacity of this perspective on the Song is that there is an Old Testament 'Love Song', Psalm 45, which is quoted Christologically in the New Testament. The argument is frequently made that if an adequate case for a non-typical or non-allegorical interpretation of the Song is to be made, careful analysis of the two, noting the significant differences between them which call for different interpretative approaches, is essential. This argument needs to be faced directly.[1]

Psalm 45 is a 'love song' (NIV 'wedding song'; Heb. *šîr*

---

with phraseology and context and of reconciling, to the best of my ability, the occult interpretation with the figures of speech' (Introduction, pp. 50f., lines 12–15). This is essentially the position in the Targumic tradition, but more extensively developed.

[1] Exhaustive treatment of this point is too extensive for detailed treatment here. I have discussed the issue in more depth in 'The Old Testament Love Songs and Their Use in the New Testament', *JETS* 24, 1981, pp. 97–105. See below, pp. 41–44, on Vocabulary.

yᵉdîdôt, 'a song of loves'), in honour of a royal wedding. While there is nothing in the Psalm itself to identify the king to whom it was dedicated, or for which royal wedding it was written, the crux of the problem is the quotation of vv. 6f. in Hebrews 1:8f., where the author applies the Old Testament text to Jesus. The argument there concerns the superiority of the Son over all the angels. Apart from the quotation and the attribution 'but of the Son he says', there is no development of the Old Testament text, nor is there any other use of this Psalm either in Hebrews or elsewhere in the New Testament.

Admittedly, the whole question of the use of the Old Testament in the New is a vexed one, on which there is considerable difference of opinion;[1] nevertheless, some general observations can be made:

1. Direct quotation of, or obvious reference to, Old Testament passages is very frequent in the New Testament.

2. Apart from those which are merely historical references (*e.g.* Acts 7), most of the quotations are introduced either to support the argument for some doctrinal position, or are directly related to the person and ministry of Jesus.

3. The selection of Old Testament passages seems, at this distance, to be rather haphazard, with verses taken out of their Old Testament contexts and applied almost in a proof-texting fashion.

From these observations, certain operating principles can be identified:

1. When the New Testament writers, under the guidance of the Holy Spirit, selected certain Old Testament texts and applied them to Jesus, *etc.*, their application and interpretation are correct.

2. It is not legitimate, however, to say therefore that all the Old Testament or even other specific texts *must* also be interpreted in the same way. Where the New Testament does not make these connections we are not required to either.

---

[1] For some representative views see C. H. Dodd, *According to the Scriptures: The Sub-structure of New Testament Theology* (Nisbet, 1952); F. F. Bruce, *New Testament Development of Old Testament Themes* (Paternoster, 1968); B. Lindars, *New Testament Apologetic* (Westminster Press, 1961); E. E. Ellis, *Paul's Use of the Old Testament* (Eerdmans, 1957); and A. A. van Ruler, *The Christian Church and the Old Testament* (Eerdmans, 1971). For a summary treatment see G. W. Grogan, 'The New Testament Interpretation of the Old Testament: A Comparative Study', *TB* 18, 1967, pp. 54–76, and John Goldingay, *Approaches to Old Testament Interpretation* (IVP, 1981), pp. 97–122.

THE SONG OF SOLOMON

3. This does not mean that the rest of the Old Testament *may* not speak of Christ; it means only that it does not *necessarily* speak of Christ, even though there is a long tradition of such exegesis in the church.

4. Careful attention needs to be given to vocabulary, meaning, grammar and context before one can legitimately argue that any given text or passage be interpreted Christologically.

All this comes to bear on the Song and Psalm 45 in the following way. One feature that distinguishes Psalm 45 from the Song is the vocabulary. The Psalm is relatively short (seventeen verses plus a title), containing 160 words. Allowing for repetitions there are 120 different words in the Psalm. Of these, 51 are also used in the Song of Solomon, 69 are not, although most are used elsewhere in the Old Testament. What is of particular interest is that many of the 69 which are absent from the Song are cultic or 'theological' terms.

Some of the more important of these are: v. 2: *yāṣaq*, anoint, pour; *ḥēn*, grace; *ᵃlohîm*, God; *bāraḵ*, bless; v. 3: *hôḏ*, glory; *hāḏār*, majesty; v. 4: *'emet*, truth; *ᶜanāwâ* humility (but *cf.* the commentaries on alternate readings here); *ṣeḏeq*, righteousness; *yārē'*, fear; v. 6: *kisē'*, throne; *šēḇeṭ*, sceptre; *mîšôr*, equity; *malḵût*, kingdom; v. 7: *reša'*, wickedness; *māšaḥ*, anoint ('Messiah'); *śāśôn*, joy; v. 8: *beḡeḏ*, garment; *hêḵāl*, palace/temple; v. 9: *yāqār*, noble, honourable; *šēḡal*, queen (see below, p. 29); v. 10: *šāḵaḥ*, forget; *'aḇ*, father; v. 11: *'āwāh*, desire (in the form used here, always in a bad sense, see below, p. 29); *ᵃḏôn*, Lord, master; *yᵒp̄î*, beauty; *šāḥah*, bow down, worship; v. 12: *minḥâ*, offering, sacrifice (in Lv. *'meat offering'* AV, 'cereal offering' RSV; the probable meaning is something like 'free-gift' offering); v. 13: *kᵉḇûḏâ*, glorious; v. 14: *lᵉḇûš*, garment (occasionally 'sackcloth', but usually 'royal robe'); *yāḇal*, bring as a gift or sacrifice to someone, lead to; *bᵉtûlâ*, virgin (used in the Ugaritic texts as one of the epithets of the goddess Anat); v. 16: *śar*, prince;[1] v.

---

[1] In several of the Egyptian Love Songs, a 'Prince Mehy' appears. Some scholars argue that this may be a quasi-fictional character used to conceal the identity of the real person involved; others take him to be a real royal person, although no firm identification of the man or even of his dynasty can be made. He appears to be the legendary lover – a Don Juan type by reputation. For a brief discussion of the identity of Mehy, see P. C. Smither, 'Prince Mehy of the Love Songs', *JEA* 34, 1948, p. 116. For the text of the Love Songs, see Simpson, especially pp. 305, 317; and S. Schott, *Altägyptische Liebeslieder* (Artemisverlage, 1950), pp. 68f.

17: *dōr*, generations; *yādāh*, praise; *'ōlām*, forever (vs. 'death' in the Song of Solomon).[1]

In the two verses quoted in the letter to the Hebrews, there is a clear suggestion of the theological basis of the Davidic kingship; yet of the sixteen words in these verses, most of them common to the Old Testament, only four, 'love', 'therefore', 'oil' and 'fellows', are used at all in the Song of Solomon, and even these four are used in different senses in the Song. Other words in the Psalm are also used of Christ in the New Testament. For example, 'grace' (*ḥēn*, v. 2) and 'truth' (*'emet*, v. 4) are attributed to Jesus in John 1:14, 17; 'blessed' (*bārak*) may be reflected in Romans 9:5b, and 'humility' (*'anāwâh*, v. 4) is used, in a different form, in Zechariah 9:9 and the New Testament quotation of that text in Matthew 21:5.

In the Psalm, however, the subject shifts from the king/Messiah to his consort at verse 10, and an examination of some of the terms used in this section precludes the possibility of taking this passage as referring to the church as the bride of Christ. For example, the verb *'desire'* (*'āwāh* in the form used in v. 11) is to be understood in the bad sense of 'lust', not just a general attitude, but the actual individual impulse towards illicit sexual activity. Similarly, 'beauty' (*yᵒpî*) in the same verse has a pagan cultic connotation in the Ugaritic texts, where it is used of the offerings presented to the gods. Even the 'queen' (*šēḡal*) in v. 9 is not 'bride', but rather the 'harem favourite'. The verb from which this noun is derived was considered obscene by the rabbinic writers, and was everywhere replaced in the reading of the Scriptures by the more acceptable verb *šāḵab*, 'to sleep'.

Of the vocabulary which the Psalm shares with the Song, there are two distinct categories: those common words which are part of everyday speech and are frequent in all parts of the Old Testament – (*e.g.* good, strong, people, son, daughter, see, hear, *etc.*); and those that would naturally be expected in any poem or prose that deals with intimate relationships between male and female (*e.g.* body words, such as heart, tongue, lips, thighs, *etc.*; terms of endearment such as beloved, beautiful, love, friend, companion, *etc.*; or words such as perfumes, myrrh, aloes, gold, *etc.*). However, it must be understood that these words, and many others of the same type, are frequent in love poetry from all over the ancient Near East; the most that can legitimately be said is that they reflect a common way of expressing human emotional involvement with a loved one.

In addition to the problem of vocabulary, there are other items which need attention. Both Psalm 45 and the Song are 'songs' and probably both are 'wedding songs'. That is, both are lyrical compositions celebrating joyous experiences, rather than being overtly didactic.[1] Both are concerned with the sexual relationship between a man and a woman, specifically in a marriage context.[2] Both give prominent roles to friends (Ps. 45:9, 14; Song 1:7b; 5:1, *etc.*), to the perfumer (Ps. 45:8; Song 4:10–14, *etc.*); both note the excitement of the protagonists (Ps. 45:11, 15; Song 1:13–16, *etc.*), and both describe them in loving terms.

But there are important differences also. There is nothing in the Psalm that mirrors the Song's awareness of the threats and dangers that hinder love (Song 3:1–3; 5:7f.), or of the power of love and death (8:6f.). In Psalm 45:4, the 'right hand' is the one that 'teaches dread deeds', while in Song 2:6 and 8:3 it is the arm of tender embrace. Verses 14f. of the Psalm reflect the traditional wedding procession of the bride to the husband's home, but Song 3:4 reverses this with the girl bringing her lover to her mother's room. In Psalm 45 the palace is the place of the celebration of love; in the Song it is the garden where love is consummated.[3]

Further, in the Song there is no reference to the presence or authority of the girl's father. Mother (1:6; 3:4; 8:1f.), brothers (1:6; 8:1) and sister (8:8) are all present, but not the father. Yet in the ancient Near East the permission of the father was an essential element in the arranged mar-

---

[1] See, however, the argument in Seerveld, pp. 68–83 and Young, p. 336. See below, pp. 50–52, and commentary on 3:8.

[2] Some commentators identify a coronation ritual in these poems (*i.e.* Ps. 45:1–9 and Song 3:6–11) followed by a wedding celebration (Ps. 45:10–17 and Song 4:8–15). However, this parallel seems to me to be forced. There is nothing in the Psalm to suggest a coronation ritual, and in spite of numerous attempts to find a yearly enthronement festival in Israel, no convincing case has yet been made. For a concise summary of the issue and the problems involved, see E. Yamauchi, 'Cultic Clues in Canticles', *Bulletin of the Evangelical Theological Society* 4, 1961, pp. 80–88, and below, pp. 49–50.

[3] See below, Subject Study: The Garden Motif, pp. 55–60.

riages.[1] Psalm 45:10 recognizes this aspect of the m̲a
'Forget your people and your father's house'. In the ̲ ̲ ̲
the bride is to 'reverence' (*šāhah*) her 'lord' (*ᵃdôn*); in the Song
there is mutual sharing and delight in the other, with no hint
of subjugation.

Finally, the procreation of children is a primary reason
for marriage in the ancient Near East.[2] This concept is the
background of Psalm 45:16–17, where the Psalmist anticipates
a long and fruitful line as a result of this royal wedding. The
Song, on the other hand, ignores this aspect of the man/woman
relationship.

Given these similarities and differences between these two
'love songs', it appears that the question of different interpretative approaches can be answered legitimately. One may
argue that interpreting the Song as a commentary on the
nature of true love, regardless of any direct historical link with
Solomon and one of his wives, inevitably involves comments
on the greater love expressed in the relationship of God to the
world or of Christ to his church. In a sense that is true. But
that says little more than that everything good in creation
speaks of the relationship of God to his people. Such an
approach is too broad to be of much help in interpreting any
given text. One may use the Song to *illustrate* this relationship
(*cf.* the remarks of Professor John Murray quoted above, p.
23), but it must be observed that the text of the Song gives
no indication that it is intended as typology. The Song is
presented simply as an account of the relationship between
the lover and his beloved.[3] Nor is there any indication in the
New Testament that the Song has a Christological interpretation or application.[4]

---

[1] *Cf.* Gn. 21:21; 34:4–8; 38:6; Jdg. 14:2; Ru. 3:1–2. Of course, if the father
was dead, a different situation, where the brothers have responsibility, would
prevail. However, this would be unusual and may suggest that the Song was,
in fact, written for a specific wedding.

[2] *E.g.*, Gn. 15:1; 16:1; 19:30–32; 25:21; 30:1–2; 38:1–11; Dt. 25:5–10; 1 Sa.
1:1–20. See also the material discussed below on the Sacred Marriage Rite
in ancient Mesopotamia, pp. 49f.

[3] See below, pp. 52–54.

[4] In fact, the Song is one of only four Old Testament books not quoted in
the New Testament. J. S. Sibinga's effort in 'Une citation du Cantique dans
La Secunda Petri', *RB* 73, 1966, pp. 107–118, to demonstrate that 2 Pet. 1:19
was influenced by certain Old Latin versions of Song 2:17 and 4:6 is not
convincing.

While there is a modicum of truth in the typical interpretation as a method, there are ever-present dangers and serious difficulties in its application, not only to the Song, but to the Scriptures as a whole. Certain parts of certain Old Testament books and chapters are specifically interpreted in the New Testament with a Christological application. Other parts of the same book and chapter may be used to illustrate certain New Testament teachings without specific quotation by New Testament authors. But the burden of proof of the validity of this method in any given case lies on the side of those who see types and allegories in much of the Old Testament. Of course, none of this demands a non-Christological application of any or all of the Song (or Ps. 45, apart from vv. 6f.), or for that matter, any other Old Testament text; but it does suggest caution before arguing that, because one part of a particular passage of the Old Testament is used in the New in a specifically allegorical or typological way, any other verse or verses can legitimately be interpreted in the same way.

c. Drama

The third approach to the interpretation of the Song is also one that has long been a part of the church tradition. As early as about AD 250, Origen declared that the Song was 'a marriage-song which Solomon wrote in the form of a drama'.[1] This idea was largely ignored until the last century, when Delitzsch re-introduced it in his commentary. Since that time, a number of other writers have proposed this idea as the key to understanding the Song. These proposals range from an expansion of the 'enthronement festival' theme,[2] through the identification of an expurgated remnant of a cultic ritual celebrating the sacred marriage of a goddess with the king,[3] to the imaginative oratorio treatment of Seerveld.[4] In spite of the differences in these approaches, the common theme that ties them together is the perspective that the Song is a dramatic 'script' that was originally intended to be acted and/or sung.

In this context, however, it is essential to distinguish *drama*

---

[1] Origen, *The Song of Songs: Commentary and Homilies* (Newman Press, 1957), p. 21.
[2] See above, p. 30, n. 2.
[3] Kramer, pp. 85–106, and M. Pope, *passim*.
[4] See above, p. 30, n. 1.

from the similar but different genres of *liturgy*, *ritual* and *pageant*, particularly as these are applied to ancient cultic texts.

Liturgy, which originally meant the rendering of service to the nation or community at one's own expense, by the time of the New Testament came to mean service to God through ordered ceremony, in which the congregation as well as the leaders (priests) had specific, closely defined roles to play. This distinguishes liturgy from drama in that in drama the audience (congregation) is involved as observer, not participant.

Ritual, in its technical sense, is the recording and preserving of the precise words and actions used in liturgy.

Pageant, a word derived from the Middle English *pagyn* or *padgin*, is used to denote a procession with a series of open-air presentations. The episodic character of this form is manifested in the kind of patchwork assembly of individual scenes or tableaux linked rather loosely in chronological or geographic sequence. This term is not normally used in discussing ancient Near Eastern religious ceremonies, but in fact it is a much more accurate description of the form than is 'drama'.

Drama is distinguished from all of these by its narrow focus and essential unity. Aristotle's statement, that to be drama a piece has to have a beginning, a middle and an end,[1] correctly assumes that a drama has to be a self-contained and self-consistent unit. Beyond this, an effective drama must show elements of progression in the story, development of theme and character, and some sort of conflict and resolution. In the technical realm, dramatic works must also clearly indicate speakers, individual speeches and stage directions, and generally be written in dialogue form.

Many or most of these elements can be found in ancient ritual texts,[2] but it is only by the most radical emendation of the text that the Song of Solomon can be made to fit the criteria for drama outlined above. There are elements of conflict and resolution (*e.g.* 3:1–4; 5:2–7), but scarcely any development or progression in the story line. There is nothing in the way of stage directions, and little agreement on the assigning of speeches to various characters. Nor is there any clear agreement on the division of the books into 'acts' or

[1] *Poetics*, vii. 1450b–1451a.
[2] For fuller treatment of this relationship see G. L. Carr, 'Is the Song of Songs a "Sacred Marriage Drama"?', *JETS* 22, 1979, pp. 103–114.

'scenes'. There are almost as many suggestions on these as there are writers proposing them.[1]

Considerable experience in theatrical production and direction has persuaded me that the Song, as it now stands, is unactable. It would be virtually impossible to stage effectively without major rewriting, and it lacks the dramatic impact to hold an audience. One could, perhaps, choreograph a dance routine around 6:13 – 7:11 or a street fight around 5:6–8; or, if one followed Seerveld's woodcuts for wardrobe, one would probably attract an audience, but the spectacle would still fail as drama. The long speeches, the lack of character development and of a plot developing to dramatic climax and resolution, all militate against the Song being considered 'drama'.

d. Natural

The fourth approach, which is adopted in this commentary, is best described as the *natural* or *literal* interpretation.[2] This approach interprets the Song as what it appears naturally to be – a series of poems which speak clearly and explicitly of the feelings, desires, concerns, hopes and fears of two young lovers – without any need to allegorize or typologize or dramatize to escape the clear erotic elements present in the text.

It is often argued that such themes are unworthy of being treated in Scripture, since the focus of the biblical material is on the redemption from sin, and by definition, 'sexuality is sinful'.[3] However, even a casual reading of the Old Testament should reveal that this equation was never made by the biblical writers. It is illicit sexuality that is condemned, not sexuality *per se*. From the creation story in Genesis 1 – 2 to the marriage of the Lamb in Revelation 21, human sexuality is presented as a specific gift from God to his creation and serves as a suitable metaphor to illustrate the relationship between God and his people. The Old Testament is as replete with references to Israel as the wife of the LORD as the New Testament is with references to the church as the bride of Christ.

The creation of mankind in the image of God, yet created male and female (*i.e.*, as sexual beings) for the purpose of

[1] See below, pp. 44–49, on Structure, and pp. 41–44, Vocabulary.

[2] Of the two terms, 'natural' is preferred. 'Literal', literally understood, leaves no room for figures of speech, *etc.* in the writing.

[3] See above, p. 22, n. 2.

procreation (Gn. 1:28), fellowship, mutual support and dependence (Gn. 2:18), and physical as well as spiritual unity (Gn. 2:22–24), should be clear evidence that God's action of creating us as sexual beings was no accident or compromise. It was the divine intention from the beginning, and is, in fact, 'good' (Gn. 1:31).

In one sense, the Song is an extended commentary on the creation story – an expansion of the first recorded love-song in history. 'Then the man said, "This at last is bone of my bones and flesh of my flesh; she shall be called Woman, because she was taken out of Man" ' (Gn. 2:23). The author of Genesis draws the obvious conclusions from this: 'Therefore a man leaves his father and his mother and cleaves to his wife, and they become one flesh. And the man and his wife were both naked, and were not ashamed' (Gn. 2:24f.). The fulfilment of the creative act is unity, support, and an openness before each other and God.[1]

A frequent Old Testament term for the sexual union of man and woman is the verb 'know' (*e.g.*, Gn. 4:1, *etc.*). It is worthy of note that the most intimate knowledge of another person is not on the basis of intellectual exchange and the discussion of theological ideas, but in the intimate sexual union of male and female.[2] In this light it should not be considered obscene that at least one book of the Bible be dedicated to the celebration of one of the central realities of our creaturehood. 'The Song does celebrate the dignity and purity of human love. This is a fact that has not always been sufficiently stressed. The Song, therefore, is didactic and moral in its purpose. It comes to us in this world of sin, where lust and passion are on every hand, where fierce temptations assail us and try to turn us aside from the God-given standard of marriage. And it reminds us, in particularly beautiful fashion, how pure and noble true love

---

[1] *Cf.* D. Kidner, *Genesis* (IVP, 1967), pp. 35f., 52, 65f.
[2] 'This is piquant irony: here we are with all our high notions of ourselves as intellectual and spiritual beings, and the most profound form of knowledge for us is the plain business of skin on skin. It is humiliating. When two members of this godlike, cerebral species approach the heights of communion between themselves, what do they do? Think? Speculate? Meditate? No, they take off their clothes. Do they want to get their *brains* together? No. It is the most appalling of ironies: their search for union takes them quite literally in a direction away from where their brains are.' T. Howard, *Hallowed be This House* (Harold Shaw, 1979), pp. 115f.

is.'[1] There are many other passages where the relationships the LORD/Israel, Christ/church are clearly defined. It is not essential to those doctrines that the Song be so interpreted; but if the Song is understood primarily in those terms, we miss the Bible's clear teaching that will help us deal effectively with our own created natures.

V. THE SONG AS POETRY

Like many other parts of the Old Testament, the Song is poetical in form. Psalms, Proverbs, most of Job (3:2 – 42:6), most of Isaiah, extensive sections of Jeremiah, most of the minor prophets except Jonah, Haggai and Malachi, and frequent individual chapters or units in the other books are poetry. Extensive work has been done in this field, beginning with the publication in 1753 in Latin (English translation 1829) of Robert Lowth's *Lectures on the Sacred Poetry of the Hebrews* and continuing with many other contributions up to the present.[2] While there are many different treatments in this literature and a variety of opinions on many details, there is general agreement that the basic nature of Hebrew, and ancient Near Eastern poetry generally, is what is termed *parallelism* and that the main distinguishing feature of this poetry is some fairly regular pattern of accented syllables in any given pair of lines.[3]

Parallelism can be considered as 'thought rhyme' rather than 'word rhyme'. This thought rhyme may involve the repetition of an idea (*e.g.* Song 2:8b, 'leaping upon the

[1] Young, p. 354.

[2] A full bibliography would run to many pages. For a start, see the articles and bibliographies in *IBD*, pp. 1244f.; R. K. Harrison, *Introduction to the Old Testament* (IVP, 1970), pp. 965–975, Kidner, pp. 1–3, and F. I. Andersen, *Job* (IVP, 1976), pp. 32–41. For more recent material on poetic interpretation see D. K. Stuart, *Studies in Early Hebrew Meter* (Scholars Press, 1976), and M. O'Connor, *Hebrew Verse Structure* (Eisenbrauns, 1980).

[3] Stuart, pp. 10–17, argues that the precise number of syllables in any given line is not critical, but that the *relative* length of the lines is the more important factor. Lines of eight or more syllables are relatively long (*colum longum* or 'l'), and those of three to five syllables are relatively short (*colum breve* or 'b'), and those of six or seven syllables are considered 'l' lines if they occur in context with 'l' lines and 'b' if they occur in context with 'b' lines. The pairs (or triplets) of lines or colons (see on Song 1:2, p. 72, n. 1) show either regular balanced (*i.e.* l:l or b:b) or unbalanced (Heb. *qînâ*) metre (*i.e.* b:l or l:b).

mountains,/bounding over the hills'); the reversal or antithesis of an idea in a consecutive line (*e.g.* Song 1:6c, 'they made me keeper of the vineyards;/but, my own vineyard I have not kept!'); or the addition of a derived idea in the second part (*e.g.* Song 2:6, 'O that his left hand were under my head,/and that his right hand embraced me!'). There are many variations on these basic patterns, but the essential elements are present throughout.

One important consequence of this poetic form is that it permits the translation of the poetic ideas and structure into various languages. The translator is not forced to elaborate usually irrelevant exercises of juggling words and ideas in order to reproduce a rhyme or assonance in an unrelated, uncooperative language.

VI. THE SONG AS LOVE POETRY

The Song of Solomon is an example of a universal type of poem – the love poem. The world of the Old Testament provides numerous examples of the genre.[1] These are of widely differing styles and from widely scattered places, but they share certain common elements or *topoi*.[2]

---

[1] One serious problem that needs careful attention is that the extant Canaanite and Mesopotamian 'Love Poetry' is almost completely associated with the fertility-cult rituals of Baal/Anath or Dumuzi/Inanna, so that the separation of the 'love' elements from the 'cultic' elements is next to impossible. However, on the positive side, this linkage suggests that the *pattern* of love-making and the expressions of love used in a non-cultic situation would not differ from this 'approved' approach.

The Egyptian love poetry is of a very different, non-cultic type. The key, however, to this love-poetry problem is found in the fact that identical *topoi*, themes, and vocabulary appear in all these collections, including the Song of Solomon. For further discussion see J. B. White, *A Study of the Language of Love in the Song of Songs and Ancient Egyptian Poetry* (Scholars Press, 1978), Lambert, pp. 98–135, and above, p. 26, n. 1; p. 33, n. 2, and below, pp. 41–44, on Vocabulary. See also my article 'Ancient Near Eastern Love Poetry' (see above, p. 17, n. 2).

[2] A *topos* (pl. *topoi*) is an idea, stock phrase, epithet, or expression that is common currency in a literary tradition. The term is Greek for 'place'. This usage denotes a specific 'place' from which a particular view or panorama can be seen. In literary studies, it implies a rich literary tradition that does not need to be expressed verbally, but which colours the understanding of the phrase. Such expressions are general rhetorical patterns which may be used as building blocks for new literary structures. They are not usually intended to be understood literally, but as a conventional idiom: *e.g.* Homer's 'wine-dark sea', 'Rome, the Eternal City', 'Jerusalem the Golden', 'The

These common elements include at least the following:

1. When a third party is addressed or present, the third person form is used, but the bulk of the material is in the 'I-Thou' formulation (*e.g.* Song 8:1–2). With the almost universal adoption of the 'you' form for either individuals or groups, this distinction is not always evident in modern English; but it is clear where this convention is still used, as the French *vous* is more formal (as well as plural), while the singular *tu* is reserved for family or close friends.

2. The most common theme, expressed in a variety of ways, is the joy and excitement the lovers find in each other's presence (3:4; 7:6–12). These encounters are often hindered by some other person – mother, family, brothers, friends, authorities, *etc.* (1:6; 5:7), or by outside situation – distance, weather, accident, *etc.* But these events serve only as a foil to underscore the joy of reunion. The 'seek-find' theme (3:1–5) or the 'danger to be overcome' motif (1:5–8), are common examples of this form of development.

3. Elaborate descriptions of the beloved's physical beauty, often couched in highly erotic terms, are familiar elements. Associated with these are various combinations of bird and animal imagery, floral parallels, clothing, perfumes, jewellery, *etc.* The simple exclamation of Genesis 2:23, and the extended metaphors of Song 4:1–15 and 5:10–16 are good examples of the various possibilities on this theme.

4. Since physical intimacy is the goal, the bed-chamber (8:2) or some secluded area in the thickets or grottoes is frequently mentioned (*e.g.* 7:12).[1]

5. Specific descriptions of the joys of seeing (4:9), hearing the voice of the beloved (2:8), touching (2:6), kissing (1:2), smelling (7:8), fondling (2:6), *etc.*, ultimately leading to sexual consummation (7:12), are common to this literature as well.

6. Family terms such as 'sister' (5:1) or 'brother' (8:1), and

---

Holocaust', expressions which convey far more than the words themselves connote. They are 'codes' for something greater. A *topos*, of course, is not static. It changes and grows as it is used in the literature, each author and society adding its own unique elements to the whole *topos*. For basic work in this area see W. J. Ong, *Ramus: Method and the Decay of Dialogue* (Harvard, 1958), pp. 60f., 63–65, 84–91, and 127f. *Cf.* C. S. Lewis, *Studies in Words* (CUP, ²1967), O. Barfield, *History in English Words* (Eerdmans, ²1967), and T. H. Gaster, p. 108f.

[1] See below, pp. 41–44, on Vocabulary, and Subject Study: The Garden Motif, pp. 55–60.

royal designations such as 'king', 'queen', 'prince' or 'princess', are frequent epithets in the love poetry, although the Song uses only sister and king directly of the protagonists.[1] Many commentators take these words in their literal sense in these poems, but it is obvious from the literature generally that this sort of vocabulary is merely a convention for expressing the high regard the lovers have for each other.

Frankness, openness, tenderness, coupled with ardent longing, explicitly erotic descriptions and intent towards the lover and the beloved, mark the love poetry from all over the ancient Near East. The Song of Solomon is no exception.

There are, however, a number of motifs common in the ancient Near Eastern love poetry that are missing from the Song.

1. In the Canaanite and Mesopotamian love poetry, the focal point is the cultic celebration, and the 'love-poem' elements are essentially secondary. In the Egyptian love poetry, while there are some religious or cultic hints (*e.g.* the sacred gardens and canals), and frequent references to the various gods and goddesses (*e.g.* Hathor, Osiris, *etc.*), these appear not primarily to be worshipped, but to be invoked on behalf of the lover. Most Old Testament poetry uses the various names for God with great frequency,[2] but the Song omits all such references. God is not even mentioned in the Song (but *cf.* the Commentary on 8:6).

2. Hunting for sport and/or ritual slaughter of wild animals is a common motif in the love poetry, with the protagonists sometimes as the hunted, sometimes as the hunter. In the Chester Beatty Collection of Egyptian Love Songs, Poem G 2:1–5, the lover is pictured as

> ... a gazelle
> running in the desert
> its feet are wounded
> its limbs are exhausted
> fear penetrates its body
> the hunters are after it
> the hounds are with them

---

[1] 'Queen' is used twice in 6:8f., but in these verses the beloved is being praised by the queens. She is not one of them.

[2] See J. Muilenburg, 'A Study in Hebrew Rhetoric: Repetition and Style', *SVT* 1, *Congress Volume*, 1953, pp. 97–111.

> Before you have kissed your hand four times
> you shall have reached her hideaway
> as you chase the lady love.
> For it is the Golden Goddess[1]
> who has set her aside for you, friend.

Among the Israelites, even from the earliest times, hunting for food or killing animals in self-protection was acceptable, but sport-hunting never seems to have had a place. For the Hebrew, all life, even animal life, was God's and could not be taken lightly.

3. While there is a great deal of 'nature vocabulary' and 'nature imagery' in the Song, the Old Testament writers never go to the point of personifying nature as the other peoples of the ancient Near East did. For the Hebrew, the natural world is a reality that manifests God's creative power, and is the backdrop against which all human activity is carried out.[2] But it is never more than that. The world, God's creation, is simply there.

4. The use of wine (and beer, outside of Israel), frequently leading to drunkenness and seduction, is a common theme in much of the ancient Near Eastern love poetry. Even in the Old Testament these events occur, as the episode of Lot and his daughters illustrates.[3] However, although the use of wine appears several times in the Song, this aspect is never developed, with the possible exception of 5:1.[4] This is hardly surprising, for the emphasis here is on the mutual desire of the lovers. This is no seduction of a naïve or unwilling girl; love is freely given and freely received.

5. One final element that is frequent in the love poetry but missing from the Song is that of faithlessness and jealousy. Although some interpreters identify two men in the Song, lecherous King Solomon and the girl's simple shepherd lover, their position is not clearly evident in the text.[5] Love triangles

[1] *I.e.* Hathor, patroness of women and goddess of love, *cf.* Simpson, pp. 322f.

[2] Rabin, p. 210, notes that this attitude, unique to Israel in the pre-Christian era, did not even appear in the West until the 18th century. See below, p. 42.

[3] This motif survived into the intertestamental period in the apocryphal story of Judith and Holofernes (Judith 12:10 – 13:2).

[4] See Commentary, and Subject Study: Wine, pp. 66f.

[5] See below, pp. 44–49, Structure.

must have existed in Israel, but the Song is not concerned with that aspect of the human relationship.

As one would expect, the 'Love Poem Genre' and the various motifs and *topoi* which appear there are found in every culture and in every age. Its theme is one of the central human concerns, and the widespread distribution of the form makes it next to impossible to date the various pieces simply on the basis of vocabulary or content. What is evident is that, while these various poems share common ideas, these are always expressed in terms of local or regional experiences. The poets do not go far afield to find material to convey their ideas. They draw on the concerns, values and setting of their own society.

VII. THE VOCABULARY OF THE SONG

Although the Song is a relatively short book of only 117 verses, it has an unusually large number of uncommon words. Of the approximately 470 different Hebrew words it contains – a very high number for such a small book – 47 occur only in the Song (some only once) and nowhere else in the Old Testament. Of the words which do appear in other parts of the Old Testament, 51 occur five times or less, 45 occur between six and ten times, and an additional 27 between eleven and twenty times, leaving about 300 common words in the Song.

There is widespread distribution of these less common words. All but eighteen verses[1] scattered through the Song have at least one of these unusual words; several have six or seven such words. Fifty verses contain at least one word not used outside the Song, and an additional twelve verses contain words which occur not more than three times in the whole Old Testament. In other words, more than one third of the words in the Song occur so infrequently that there is little context from which accurate meanings can be deduced, and two thirds of the verses of the Song have uncommon words. Hence, many of the proposals made in the various translations and commentaries are, at best, educated guesses; particularly in the case of those words which are unique to the Song, they may well be incorrect.

[1] These are Song 1:1, 2, 4; 3:1, 3, 4, 7, 8; 4:10; 5:8, 9; 6:1, 12; 7:9; 8:7, 8, 10.

Since details on usage are found at the appropriate places in the Commentary, it will not be necessary to list all these words here; but it is in order to note some of the interesting patterns and important factors about the vocabulary of the Song. As noted above, pp. 29f., the love poetry generally uses many of the common words found in everyday speech, and particularly words that describe the body in an intimate and loving way. The Song follows this pattern.

Beyond these there are other standard groups of words which could be found in any collection of ancient Near Eastern love poetry. The lovers rendezvous in gardens or parks, bedrooms, fields, orchards, vineyards, or secluded valleys. They use imagery from nature, particularly plants or animals, to describe each other, or to set a mood for their love, *e.g.*, figs, apples, lilies, pomegranates, raisins, wheat, brambles, nuts, cedar, vines, palm trees, raven, mare, foxes, gazelle, goats, lions, fawns, doves, leopards, ewes and sheep.

Jewellery, precious stones, spices and perfumes appear regularly in all of this literature: gold, alabaster, ornaments, necklaces, ivory, sapphire, silver, oils, saffron, aloes, frankincense, cinnamon, nard, honey and myrrh. Various places such as Damascus, Tirzah and Zion, and beauty spots such as Engedi, Sharon, Carmel and Gilead are mentioned.

What is of particular importance about this sort of reference is not that the various collections of love poetry from the ancient Near East show similar groupings, but the particular items that appear in them are peculiar to the locale from which the poems come. The Egyptian poems speak of the Nile, of crocodiles, of Egyptian cities, places, plants and animals, and mention birds which can be identified from the various reliefs and paintings preserved on the monuments, *etc*. Similarly, the Mesopotamian poetry uses imagery drawn from items native to that region or which would be known from the traders passing through.

Certainly many of these items are common to all the region, but there are also items which are either unique to an area or are missing from it. And the love poetry reflects this situation. Lovers do not need to go to exotic places or invent fabulous creatures to define their love — they are quite capable of making do with what is at hand!

But of considerably more interest in the Song is the omission of certain common words and ideas. As noted above (pp. 39f.), there is a strong religious element in the love poetry from Egypt and Mesopotamia, with the gods and goddesses, their priests and priestesses, playing major roles in much of the literature, while the Song of Solomon does not even mention God. The only other Old Testament book not to refer to God is another of the Five Scrolls, Esther, which explains the origin of the feast of Purim and celebrates national deliverance, not by divine intervention (although the author seems to assume God's providence towards his covenant people, but through 'political intrigue and human intellectual acumen'.[1] Similarly, the Song, while recognizing that love has its origin in God (*cf.* 8:6), is more concerned with the value of 'mere' human emotion and simply takes for granted the whole theological structure of the Old Testament people and God's love for them.

Even more striking is the omission from the Song of *all* the major religious words in the Old Testament vocabulary. Incredible as it seems, none of the following appears in the Song: the divine names LORD (either Yahweh or Adonai; but *cf.* 8:6), Baal (except in the place-name Baal–hamon, 8:11), El, Elohim or their compounds, Glory, Sea (*yam*, one of the major gods in the Canaanite cult); words associated with the worship celebration in Israel: ark (of the covenant), high place, throne, mercy-seat, temple, sanctuary, tabernacle, or congregation; cult words: ram, ox, bull, altar, offering, sacrifice, lift-up, blood, to sacrifice, anoint, pour, priest, cover, atone, make atonement, use divination, celebrate a feast, bury or burial place (these last two words are very important cult words in the Tammuz literature in the Mesopotamian cult celebrations); basic theological terms which are frequent elsewhere in the Old Testament but omitted from the Song: evil, faithful, truth, covenant, bless, honour, sin, wisdom, grace, loving-kindness (mercy), law, statute, be clean, be unclean (ritually), fear (of the LORD), deliver, glory, commandment, justice, prophet or prophecy, to vow, save, do wrong, iniquity, do miracles, image, trespass, visit (frequent in the Old Testament of God 'visiting' man), righteousness (and its related words), holy (a frequent epithet for the goddess Inanna in the Mesopotamian literature), spirit, evil, wickedness, sabbath,

---

[1] R. K. Harrison, *Introduction to the Old Testament* (IVP, 1970), p. 1098.

covenant, blessing, bless, worship, heaven, judge, judgment, or law (Torah).

The total absence of any of the key theological and cultic words in the Hebrew Old Testament from the Song is the most cogent reason for rejecting the typical or cultic interpretation of this book. There is not a single hint of such a meaning anywhere in the text itself. Any theory of an 'expurgated sacred marriage drama', or a Mesopotamian cult ritual, or any serious typology founders on this simple fact.

VIII. THE STRUCTURE OF THE SONG

Almost without exception, contemporary commentators reject the idea that the Song of Songs is a single composition. Rather, they believe it is a collection of various longer or shorter individual love poems gathered together into a 'book' because they share the common themes of the 'Love Poetry' genre.[1] Not all writers, however, consider the book to be simply an anthology. Many opt for a literary unity in the Song. It may well be that much of the material in the Song is 'traditional', *i.e.* common coinage in the Hebrew society, and that the author made extensive use of already existing material; but even so the Song gives evidence of careful compilation and integration of the various ideas expressed. It does not possess the formal structure required of drama, as we noted above, nor does it show any sort of plot development as one would expect in a story; but there is an inner cohesiveness around its central theme of the lovers' mutual longing and surrender.[2]

---

[1] *Cf., e.g.,* O. Eissfeldt, *The Old Testament, an Introduction* (Harper & Row, ³1965), pp. 489f., who remarks 'the right assumption is that there are about 25. . . . A principle of arrangement is only observable here and there.' Pope, pp. 40–54, discusses the various options in some detail. *Cf.* above, pp. 17–21, on Authorship and Date.

[2] Among the older writers, Delitzsch makes the fullest case for the unity of the Song. The most detailed recent treatment is J. C. Exum, 'A Literary and Structural Analysis of the Song of Songs', *ZAW* 85, 1973, pp. 47–79. Her work is a careful examination of the elements in the Song by which the various segments have been integrated into a cohesive unity. See further W. H. Shea, 'The chiastic structure of the Song of Songs', *ZAW* 92, 1980, pp. 378–396. Rowley, p. 212, remarks: 'The repetitions that occur leave the impression of a single hand, and there is greater unity of theme and style than would be expected in a collection of poems from several hands and from widely separated sources.'

Whether or not there were separate poems or units used as sources, the book as we now have it lends itself to being treated as a unit — as done by the rabbis and Christian commentators for over 2,000 years. The issue is nonetheless complicated and no easy answer is evident. Two related questions require attention: How is the book constructed, *i.e.* does it show any literary structure that can be clearly identified? Who are the characters involved in the story?

There is no clear consensus among the translators or commentators as to the precise divisions of the text. AV, RV, ASV and RSV simply indicate paragraph or strophe divisions. NEB, JB and NIV both indicate the strophes and assign speakers to them. Some broad general agreement is evident in these, but there is no unanimity over the details. This commentary divides the poem into five main sections:

1:2 – 2:7	Anticipation
2:8 – 3:5	Found, and Lost – and Found
3:6 – 5:1	Consummation
5:2 – 8:4	Lost – and Found
8:5–14	Affirmation

Although any division is somewhat arbitrary, this outline is based on the following observations.

1. The clause 'Do not arouse or awaken love until it so desires' (NIV) occurs in 2:7, 3:5 and 8:4 as a kind of refrain that concludes three of the five sections. The other two conclude with a common theme of consummation: 5:1b 'Eat, O friends, and drink; drink your fill, O lovers' and 8:14 'Come away, my lover, and be like a gazelle or like a young stag on the spice-laden mountains' (both NIV).

2. Each of the sections begins with one or both of the ideas of arousal (2:10; 5:2; 8:5) or the arrival of one of the lovers and the invitation of the other (1:2, 4; 2:8, 10; 3:6; 5:2; 8:5f.). The repeating cycle of invitation, exhilaration and warning lends structure to the whole poem.

Among those who see a basic unity in the Song, there are two opinions as to the structure. Several commentators consider the poem to be the description of the wooing, betrothal, marriage, emergence of problems in the marriage, and ultimate reconciliation of the wedded couple. The Song then becomes an *apologia* for pure monogamous love,[1] or a description of the stages in the lovers' relationship.[2] Attractive as these options are, they run into difficulty with the overt sexuality in the first three chapters. Gollwitzer, although somewhat overstating, puts it this way: 'Interpreters, in an effort to keep the Song from being considered immoral, regarded it as the dialogue of a married couple, an extolling of married love. But there is nothing in the text to suggest that the two lovers are husband and wife. On the contrary, it is because they are *not* married that they long for a place where they can sleep together without being disturbed (7:12 – 8:2).' Setting aside the reference to 'bride' in 4:8 – 5:1 as being 'only a term of endearment equivalent to "sweetheart" ', he concludes: 'There is no way around it. These two people are simply in love with one another, and are planning to sleep together without anyone else's permission, without benefit of marriage license or church ceremony. And *that* is in the Bible!'[3]

While one would not want to accept all the implications of Gollwitzer's position, his argument is essentially correct. The Song is an affirmation of human sexuality *per se*. And even if, as I believe, there is a marriage celebration described prior to 4:16 – 5:1, it is impossible to ignore the explicit hopes, descriptions and participation in sexual activities by the lovers in chs. 1 – 4. The language in the early chapters is clearly describing sexual encounter, but it is not necessary to assume that this is outside marriage.

This impasse can be broken if one recognizes that the Song is not to be taken as a series of sequential events. Rather, it is constructed in chiastic form with the individual units arranged symmetrically around a central pivot. This literary form, most easily diagrammed A:B:C:C:B:A, is found in many passages in the Old Testament prophets and in the Psalms, sometimes in short units such as Psalm 51:1, but also frequently in longer sections, with intricate interlocking patterns.[4]

Many commentators argue for a series of dream-sequences

---

[1] See below, pp. 51f.
[2] See, most recently, J. C. Dillow, *Solomon on Sex* (Nelson, 1977).
[3] H. Gollwitzer, *Song of Love: A Biblical Understanding of Sex* (Fortress Press, 1979), p. 29.
[4] See, *e.g.*, G. J. Wenham, 'The Coherence of the Flood Narrative', *VT* 23, 1978, pp. 336–348, for a treatment of the chiastic structure of Gn. 6:10 – 9:19. For two detailed analyses of the Song, compare that of J. C. Exum with the more recent one of W. H. Shea (*art. cit.*).

(3:1–5 and 5:2–8) and reminiscences (2:3–7 and 8:5, or 2:16f. and 7:11), in which the protagonists recall the days of their early married life together. This approach seems to be the best response to Gollwitzer's statements noted above, but it must be admitted that the text of the Song does not give very good support for such an interpretation.

In the matter of the assigning of speakers, some are obvious, based on the gender and number of the Hebrew pronouns in the various sections, reinforced with information derived from verbal forms and other vocabulary items. But this approach does nothing towards *identifying* the speakers beyond the simple male/female, singular/plural categories. Who the various individuals are is next to impossible to decide on internal evidence. The copier of one of the oldest extant MSS of the Greek Old Testament (Codex Sinaiticus, fourth century AD) made marginal notes assigning the units to individual speakers, but there has been no agreement on either the divisions or the assignments in subsequent writers.[1]

The 'daughters of Jerusalem' are variously identified as the women of Solomon's harem, the companions of the girl, or the onlookers from the general population. (See Commentary on 1:3, 5.) The girl is usually identified as a country girl from Shunem, a small agricultural village in Lower Galilee ('Return, O Shulammite' 6:13), who is the beloved bride(-to-be?) of the 'lover'. Some commentators suggest she is one of Solomon's many wives, perhaps even the Egyptian princess described in 1 Kings 3:1; 7:8.[2]

---

[1] RSV has 36 stanza divisions with no speakers named; NEB has 38 divided among the bride, the bridegroom and the companions; NIV has 32 divisions assigned to the lover, the beloved, and the friends; JB has 26 including a prologue and four appendices supplementing the speeches of the bride, bridegroom and chorus. Second, in the standard French Protestant version, makes 12 divisions; the Vulgate indicates 44 as the correct number; the rabbinic division provides 21 segments, with no apparent concern for speakers. Exum makes 29 units in a series of parallel poems and *inclusios*, with the two lovers as the principal characters, supported by the daughters of Jerusalem. Gordis identifies 28 'songs and fragments' classified under nine different motifs and patterns. Delitzsch suggests a six-act, twelve-scene 'melodrama'. Seerveld divides the material into 62 separate speeches or songs with Solomon, Shulammite and lover as the lead characters, and lines given to a number of different harem women and Shulammite's eldest brother.

[2] Delitzsch, pp. 4f., presents the best refutation of the 'royal princess' identification for the Shulammite in favour of a country girl being brought into the royal harem.

THE SONG OF SOLOMON

It is with the male character(s) that the greatest divergence of opinion occurs. One common view is that there are two men here: King Solomon, his lechery not satisfied by his huge harem (1 Ki. 11:3), who attempts to add yet one more, the Shulammite, to that number; and the girl's shepherd-lover from Galilee, to whom she remains faithful against all the blandishments of Solomon, and with whom she is ultimately reunited. Other interpreters see Solomon as the sole male in the poem and treat the Song as a nuptial poem celebrating a royal wedding. Still others identify only the shepherd-lover in the poem and understand the Song as a celebration of the love he shared with his beloved. This is the reading followed in this Commentary.

The first view founders on the difficulty of separating the male speakers on the basis of the text itself; some other criteria must be assumed. Seerveld's version is based on the principle that masculine verb forms require male speakers, feminine forms require female speakers, and plural forms indicate groups speaking. The immediate context of a given speech determines who is being addressed, *e.g.* 'The King' in 1:4 or the 'lover' in 2:10. But the subjectivity of this approach is betrayed by Seerveld's own admission, 'The identification of voices and [interpretive] phrases . . . are admittedly careful precisions [*sic*] and imaginative extrapolations'.[1]

To decide between the other two views, however, is more difficult. Solomon's name appears in the text, and he may well be the protagonist; but the identification of Solomon with the lover is not made in the text itself.[2] Hints of some royal influence are present, but these are difficult to integrate with the obviously non-royal elements in 1:7f.; 2:16; 3:3f.; 5:6; 7:11; 8:12, *etc.*, if the king is the central character. On the other hand, the presence of 'royal names' applied to the lover in the Egyptian Songs[3] and this *topos* in the wedding songs[4] suggest the more probable view that the Song has nothing to do directly with a royal (Solomonic) wedding but is much more

[1] Seerveld, pp. 10f. He also overlooks the fact that masculine and feminine forms can be used interchangeably in certain situations in Heb. *Cf.* GK, pp. 462–468.
[2] See above, pp. 19–21 and commentary on 1:1, 4f., 12; 3:7, 9, 11; 7:5; 8:11f.
[3] See above, p. 28, n. 1.   [4] See below, pp. 52f., on the *waṣf*.

universal in its application. The lover and the beloved are just ordinary people.

All the lines of inquiry examined thus far come to a focus in these final questions: What was the intention of the author/compiler of the Song in writing it in present canonical form? And, derivatively, what purpose is it intended to serve in the whole process of scriptural revelation? The answer to this double question will to a large degree shape one's handling of the difficult and complex questions of interpreting this most difficult book. Three categories of answers are usually put forward. The Song is cultic, didactic, or celebratory, or some combination of these.

a. The Song as cultic ritual

One widely held opinion is that the Song is the Hebrew version, edited and expurgated, of some sort of pagan Canaanite or Mesopotamian religious ceremony.

Some relate the Song to the fertility rituals associated with the Dummuzi (Tammuz)/Inanna (Ishtar) cult in Babylon or the Baal/Anath cult in Canaan. The central item in these is the celebration of the sacred marriage of the goddess in the person of the priestess with the king, or of an enthronement festival celebrating the victory of the god/king over death and drought. The cult rituals associated with these are explicitly sexual. That there were elements of these cults in Israel is evident by the account in Ezekiel 8:14 where the women of Jerusalem are portrayed as 'weeping for Tammuz', and the frequent Old Testament references to the Baal cult with its sacred prostitution and worship on the 'high places' and in the 'sacred groves' (*e.g.* 2 Ki. 21:1–9; Ho. 4:12–14; *etc.*).[1]

Pope[2] picks up the cultic theme but with a different twist growing out of some of Kramer's suggestions. He argues at some length that the Song is really a funeral-feast song rather than a sacred marriage or enthronement festival. Taking 8:6b as the key to the Song and using material from ancient Near

[1] The most readily available example of this point of view is T. J. Meek, 'Introduction to the Song of Solomon', *The Interpreter's Bible* Vol. 5 (Abingdon, 1956). For a more complete treatment, see Kramer, and, above, p. 33, n. 2.
[2] Pope, pp. 210–229.

Eastern records of festival banquets associated with burial ceremonies, Pope suggests that this is the proper original context for the Song. The purpose is to teach the community that love and life are as strong as death.[1] Yet this emphasis is almost like whistling in the dark. Ultimately, every person will himself face death. There is no *permanent* hope here. The question of Hosea 13:14 finds no answer in the celebration of love but only in the victory of 1 Corinthians 15:51–56.

In spite of the apparently impressive array of evidence presented by those who hold to the pagan cultic origin of the Song, the fact remains that to make the book fit the theory requires a major juggling of the text and an importing into the book of a vast number of elements of which the text gives no hint.[2]

b. *The Song as a vehicle of instruction*

A much better case can be made for understanding the Song as a didactic poem. Since all Scripture is 'profitable for teaching . . . and for training in righteousness' (2 Tim. 3:16), there is a sense in which this must be its purpose. But saying that does not explain *what* the Song is supposed to teach.

The traditional allegorical and typical approaches assume that the Song is intended to teach something of the relationship between God and his people. Whether that be couched in terms of the history of Israel (the Song read at Passover to celebrate God's great love for Israel demonstrated by the deliverance from Egypt), or in Christian terms of Christ and the church, the soul and Mary, or the believer and wisdom, the Song becomes an instrument to provide access into some deeper spiritual truth, not a means of exploring relationships

---

[1] '. . . certain features of the Song of Songs may be understood in the light of the considerable and growing evidences that funeral feasts in the ancient Near East were love-feasts celebrated with wine, women and song. . . . This approach seems capable of explaining the Canticles better than any other and is able to subsume other modes of interpretation as enfolding elements of truth. The connection of the Canticle with the funeral feast as expressive of the deepest and most constant concern for Life and Love in the ever present face of Death adds new insight and appreciation of our pagan predecessors who responded to Death with affirmation and even gross demonstrations of the power and persistence of Life and Love: . . . For Love is as strong as Death.' Pope, pp. 228f.

[2] See above, p. 30, n. 2; p. 33, n. 2.

on a more personal, human level.[1] Implicitly or explicitly, this approach denigrates the very physical beings we are by virtue of our creation.

Those who see two male protagonists in the Song usually argue that the purpose of the material is to teach the value of true, pure, monogamous love in contrast to the gross polygamy and degradation associated with the Solomonic court. Simplicity, faithfulness, purity and virginity are approved: scheming, wantonness, ostentation and licentiousness are scorned.

Taking this one step further, the Song is sometimes seen as a critique of the whole Solomonic kingdom, not just of Solomon's personal life-style and attitudes. The record in 1 Kings 11 is that Solomon's foreign wives were the vehicle by which the pagan cults were introduced into official Israelite circles. The common people had long followed the fertility cults, but now with Solomon the approval of the royal court is given to this aberration. Seerveld remarks, 'The Song, with Solomon as a miserable case in point, not as a villain, was given to teach the sex-saturated populace who had forgotten the Way [= Law, = Wisdom] of the Lord the meaning of faithfulness again and to capture the hearts of frustrated men and women by the telling beauty, joy, and freshness of human love that honored the Law of the Lord. When the fear of the Lord ruled their man-woman love relationships again, the fact that Javeh was the jealous lover of Israel would not be so foreign to their consciousness.'[2] Only in commitment to the LORD can sexuality be harnessed and glorified, but in such a commitment that is precisely the result.

One needs to ask, however, if this understanding grows out of a reading of the Song or is really carried into the Song by

[1] Young remarks, 'The Song does celebrate the dignity and purity of human love . . . The Song, therefore, is didactic and moral in its purpose . . . it reminds us, in particularly beautiful fashion, how pure and noble true love is. This, however, does not exhaust the purpose of the book. Not only does it speak of the purity of human love; but . . . by its very presence in the canon (for, in the last analysis, it is God who has put these books in the canon, not man), it reminds us that God, who has placed love in the human heart, is himself pure. . . . We are not warranted in saying that the book is a type of Christ. That does not appear to be exegetically tenable. But the book does turn one's eyes to Christ. . . . The eye of faith, as it beholds this picture of exalted human love, will be reminded of the one Love that is above all earthly and human affections – even the love of the Son of God for lost humanity' (pp. 354f.).
[2] Seerveld, p. 76.

the interpreter. The Song may allow this interpretation but the text itself does not *say* these things.

c. The Song as celebration

If the Song was not primarily a cultic ritual text nor a teaching tool, can it be argued any more convincingly that the author's aim was (merely) celebratory? To do so means setting aside the combined opinion of most rabbinic and Christian interpreters. Yet some are willing to do so.

Rabbi Aqiba's dictum, 'He who trills his voice in chanting the Song of Songs in the banquet house and treats it as a sort of song [Heb. *zāmir*, nor *šir* as in Song 1:1] has no part in the world to come', makes it obvious that the Song was used that way in his day, even though the good rabbi disagreed.[1] 'Banquet house', 'tavern', and 'wedding celebration' are variant translations of the Aramaic word used in this rebuke. The one chosen here is the most neutral of the three, but the idea of celebration is present in any one of them.

Theodore of Mopsuestia (late fourth century AD) adopted this view, but in 553 was condemned by the Second Council of Constantinople for it, just as a thousand years later Sebastian Castellio (Châteillon) was forced to leave Geneva after he argued, against Calvin, that the Song ought not to remain in the canon. Both Theodore and Castellio questioned the canonicity of the Song because they believed it spoke explicitly of human sexual love and therefore had no place in Scripture. Both read the Song in a literal way as an erotic song.[2] A number of other scholars since have come to similar conclusions.

In 1873, the German consul to Syria, J. G. Wetzstein, published an article on marriage customs among the village people of the area. He described several practices which had some similarity with the Song: the 'crowning' of the bride and groom as 'king' and 'queen' (1:4), war-songs as part of the festivities (3:6–8), a sword-dance performed by the bride (6:13), and descriptive poems called *waṣfs* (7:1–5), sung in

---

[1] Tosefta, Sanhedrin 12:10. *Cf.* Bab. Talmud, Sanhedrin 101a. *Cf.* Gordis, p. 6, n. 30 and Rowley, p. 198, n. 2.

[2] Rowley, p. 216, quotes Calvin, *Ioannis Calvini Opera quae supersunt omnia* (*Corpus Reformatorum* xxxix, 1873), col. 675. 'He [*i.e.* Castellio] considers that it is a lascivious and obscene poem, in which Solomon has described his shameless love affairs.'

their honour. All these characterized the week-long marriage celebration. Of course there is no evidence that there is any link between the nineteenth-century Arab festivities and the ancient Hebrew life, but it may suggest some sort of celebration sequence which the Song mirrors.[1]

The Song obviously has been associated with nuptial celebrations – not always with the approval of the religious establishment, but certainly in the mind of the common people. And this is to be expected. The Song is explicitly erotic in much of its imagery, and makes no apology for such an emphasis. But it does not give any hint of being a fertility ritual. Reproduction of crops and animals and the birth of children to parents were items of highest priority in the ancient Near East and formed an integral part of the cultic life of its peoples, but such items are missing entirely from the Song. The wedding blessing included the wish for many sons (*cf.* Ps. 127:3–5) and to be barren was to be cursed (*e.g.* Rachel, Gn. 29:31; 30:1f., and Hannah, 1 Sa. 1:1–8). The Song says nothing at all of these hopes or fears.

For the ancient Hebrew, sexuality was one of the facts of life to be enjoyed (*cf.* Pr. 5:15–21), but approved only within the confines of an established marital relationship.[2] The Song does not, except in 3:6–11, make explicit reference to a wedding, but the appearance of the 'bride' figure for the girl in the central part of the book (the term occurs only in 4:8, 9, 10, 11, 12; 5:1 of the Song) suggests this point is important in the presentation.[3] The theme of sexual enjoyment and consummation runs through the book, and the theme of commitment is central to that whole relationship. This is no passing encounter: this is total dedication and permanent obligation. The Hebrew marriage ceremony is called *Kiddushin* 'The Consecration' and the couple 'consecrate' themselves to each other in a celebration of mutual sharing.

[1] J. G. Wetzstein, 'Die syrische Dreschtafel', *Zeitschrift für Ethnographie* 5, 1873, pp. 270–302. A summary of the relevant section can be found in Delitzsch, pp. 162–176.

[2] For a very helpful examination of this question and the implications for our own time, see M. Harris, 'Pre-Marital Sexual Experience: A Covenantal Critique,' *Judaism* 19, 1970, pp. 134–144.

[3] The ten verses 4:8 to 5:1 are almost the exact centre of the book. There are 52 verses (97 lines in the Hebrew text) between 1:1 and 4:7, and 55 verses (111 lines) from 5:2 to 8:14. There are 20 lines in the Heb. of 4:8 to 5:1. *Cf.* commentary on 4:16 – 5:1 for further refinement.

THE SONG OF SOLOMON

In the Song the woman is not reticent about taking the initiative. Nearly twice as many verses are from her lips than from his. She is not ashamed to express her longing for love and her willingness to give freely to her beloved. But she is careful to keep herself exclusively for him. She is his 'sister', his 'bride' and as such remains steadfast even in the face of death. The exhortation of Hebrews 13:4 'Let marriage be held in honour among all, and let the marriage bed be undefiled', and Paul's word to the wayward Corinthians (1 Cor. 7:2–5) find their source in this ancient love song.

The Song is a celebration of the nature of humanity – male and female created in God's image for mutual support and enjoyment. There is nothing here of the aggressive male and the reluctant or victimized female. They are one in their desires because their desires are God-given. It is only a community which is uncomfortable with such a concept that excommunicates those who understand the Song in its natural sense, or those who, having understood it correctly, refuse to allow 'such a book' to be part of God's revealed word.

SUBJECT STUDIES

THE GARDEN MOTIF

IN addition to the extensive use of plant, tree and flower names in the ancient Near Eastern love poetry discussed in the Introduction, one of the common themes which runs through this literature is that of the (walled) vineyard, orchard, or garden. On the surface it is a plain enough subject, yet close investigation reveals a highly erotic *double entendre* in the treatment of the theme. Both of these elements need examination if the Song of Solomon is to be understood in its literary genre. Setting aside for the moment the use of these terms in the Song, and focusing on the other Old Testament books, the following patterns emerge:

a. *The garden as garden*

As one would expect, the majority of scriptural references to vineyards and gardens are simply to places where food products are grown. On at least some occasions they were enclosed or walled, and of course, needed a nearby water-supply.[1]

Geographic place-names sometimes reflect the agricultural nature of the territory. Abel-keramim (AV '*the* plain of the vineyards', Jdg. 11:33), an otherwise unknown site, is apparently a good grape-growing area in the Ammonite district. Beth-haccerim ('the house of the vineyards', Ne. 3:14; Je. 6:1) is probably to be identified with Ramat Rahel, a beautiful site two and a half miles south of Jerusalem, where, from the ninth century BC, a Judean administrative and government centre was established. Similarly, the modern city of Janin at the northern end of the Dothan Valley, where it joins the plains of Esdraelon, still bears witness to the accuracy of that site's

---

[1] Nu. 22:24; 2 Ki. 25:4; Ne. 3:15.

ancient name Beth-haggan, 'Garden City' ('the garden house', 2 Ki. 9:27, AV).

b. The garden of God

A second common motif is that of the garden as the place where God's presence and blessing are found. From the very beginning, God met with the man and the woman he had created in the garden where he had placed them. That garden was a place of beauty, peace, fruitfulness and contentment. The very name Eden means delight, luxury, joy, or rapture, and for the original Pair, that delight centred in their Creator.

The Eden theme runs through much of Scripture. The ultimate praise that could be bestowed upon a place was to describe it as 'like Eden, . . . like the garden of the LORD' (Is. 51:3; *cf.* Gn. 13:10; Ezk. 28:13; 31:8f.). The strong eschatological note that runs through the Old Testament picks up this theme, for the great promises of God to redeem and restore his people are often presented in terms of the Edenic paradise, where gardens and vineyards become symbols of peace and security.[1] This is, of course, God's doing, just as the original creation was his work. The garden is his possession, as the identification of Israel as God's vineyard reflects his concern and care for his chosen ones.[2] And, ultimately, in Revelation 21 – 22, the heavenly City – New Jerusalem – the place of fulfilment and ultimate delight, the place of the ultimate encounter with God (22:4), takes into itself the great river and the tree of life. This is not Eden restored; it is Eden fulfilled and transcended.

c. The garden as royal retreat

The Naboth/Ahab story in 1 Kings 21 suggests the kingly penchant for gardens and parks near the palace. These apparently were not public parks, but were rather royal preserves, walled off from common eyes where trees and fountains (Ne. 3:15) provided a beautiful setting for royal banquets (Est. 1:5), or a retreat where the king's anger could be subdued (Est. 7:7f.). Solomon, if he indeed wrote Ecclesiastes, notes that one of his accomplishments was to plant vineyards and

---

[1] *E.g.*, Nu. 24:6; Is. 58:11; 65:21; Je. 31:12f.; Ezk. 36:35; Am. 9:14; *etc.*
[2] Is. 5:1–10; 27:2; Je. 12:10. *Cf.* above, pp. 26–32, on the relationship of the Song to Ps. 45.

make gardens and parks with all kinds of fruit trees, fountains to water them, and to appoint servants to care for them.[1]

One further note of interest here is the comment in Jeremiah 39:4 (*cf.* 2 Ki. 25:4; Je. 52:7) that, during the Babylonian invasion and capture of Jerusalem, some of the inhabitants escaped 'by way of the king's garden through the gate between the two walls'. This hint of extensive grounds and labyrinthine passages suggests something of the royal interest in elaborate garden areas.

d. The garden as cultic centre

Closely linked with the royal garden is the use of the garden as a cultic centre. Admittedly, in orthodox Old Testament religion, such an idea is unthinkable, but it must be remembered that the majority of the Hebrew kings, both north and south, were unorthodox in their religious commitments, and that, according to both the prophets and the historical books, the common people were more frequently worshippers of Baal than of the LORD.

As early as the period of the judges, gardens and vineyards were marked as places of pagan celebration. Gaal and his kinsmen 'went out into the field, and gathered the grapes from their vineyards and trod them, and held festival, and went into the house of their god, and ate and drank' (Jdg. 9:27). Another festive occasion, recorded in Judges 21:19–21, is described as 'the yearly feast of the LORD at Shiloh'; this provided an opportunity for the men of Benjamin to 'lie in wait in the vineyards, and watch; if the daughters of Shiloh come out to dance in the dances, then come out of the vineyards and seize each man his wife from the daughters of Shiloh'.

By the time of Isaiah, about 700 BC, the 'gardens' have become centres of degraded pagan rites. Israel is 'a rebellious people, who walk in a way that is not good, following their own devices; a people who provoke me to my face continually, sacrificing in gardens and burning incense upon bricks; who sit in tombs, and spend the night in secret places; who eat swine's flesh, and broth of abominable things is in their vessels' (Is. 65:2–4).[2] These strange practices are further

---

[1] Ec. 2:4–7; *cf.* 1 Ch. 27:27 and David's appointed vineyard keepers.
[2] The 'abominable things' were probably snails and lizards made into a sort of stew or soup. *Cf.* Lv. 7:21; 11:11, 29. An interesting juxtaposition of

described in Isaiah 66:17: 'Those who sanctify and purify themselves to go into the gardens, following one in the midst, eating swine's flesh and the abomination and mice, shall come to an end together, says the LORD.' There is some textual variation on the gender of the Hebrew word translated 'one' in this text. The 'one' appears to be the cultic leader, but whether a priest or a priestess is unclear. The pagan elements in the cult, however, are obvious, and Isaiah's opening words to Israel, that they will 'blush for the gardens which [they] have chosen' (Is. 1:29), take on fuller meaning in the light of this closing accusation.

Much more specific information is recorded concerning Manasseh (*c*. 687–632 BC) in 2 Kings 21. By far the worst of the Davidic kings, he is indicted for all manner of idolatrous and pagan practices: restoring the high places and sacred groves; rebuilding the altars of Baal and Asherah and thus re-instituting the sexually-oriented fertility cult of the Canaanites;[1] worshipping 'the host of heaven', the deities of the Assyrian/Babylonian cultures; practising child sacrifice (possibly to Molech, the god of the Ammonites); consulting mediums and practising witchcraft; and even placing an idol of Asherah, the female fertility deity, in the temple of the LORD. But of crucial importance for our topic here is the comment that Manasseh 'was buried in the garden of his house, in the garden of Uzza' (2 Ki. 21:18); whether the choice of burial place was his own or someone else's, it is significant that he was not buried in the royal tombs. Similarly Amon, Manasseh's son, who followed his father's idolatry, was also buried 'in the garden of Uzza' (2 Ki. 21:26). Manasseh's burial was not necessarily a 'cultic' practice, but such an interpretation is certainly in keeping with everything else we know about his religious perspective. Even the Chronicler's account of his conversion (2 Ch. 33:12–20) concludes with his burial 'in his house', rather than in the royal tombs.

---

the cult of the dead (the 'sitting in tombs') and the cultic garden is found in the Egyptian love poems preserved in the Papyrus Harris 500. The Song of the Harper, preserved in numerous funerary inscriptions from the tombs of Egypt, is found in the Harris collection inserted between songs 16 and 17. No satisfactory explanation has been offered for its being found here. See further the material in the Introduction on the vocabulary of the love songs. Simpson, pp. 297–309, has translations of these.

[1] For an extensive treatment of the nature of the Baal cult see John Gray, *The Legacy of Canaan* (E. J. Brill, [2]1965).

There is a very early tradition which identifies Uzza with Venus, the goddess of love and sex.[1] The tendency of the ancient peoples to identify the various gods and goddesses by different names in different geographic areas but recognizing common attributes in spite of the different names seems to support the contention that the 'garden of Uzza' was a familiar site for the practice of the fertility rituals with the temple prostitutes in Judah.

That this was, in fact, a common practice is seen by the similar situations in other parts of the ancient Near East. Several of the Egyptian love songs discussed in the Introduction (above, pp. 37–41) suggest that enclosed gardens overlooking the Nile river near the sacred city were centres of erotic experience in worship. One of the Ugaritic deities is identified as 'Reshep of the Garden'; while little is known of the precise nature of his cult, it was probably similar to the extreme sexually oriented worship of the other gods in the Ugaritic pantheon.[2] Finally, a number of sacred-marriage ritual texts from Mesopotamia identify the 'garden' as the place of sexual fulfilment and erotic pleasure. Fruitfulness for the land and cattle is the central aim of the sacred marriage, and the ritual re-enactment of the marriage and its consummation between the goddess/priestess and the king is the focus of the celebration.

e. The garden as erotic symbol

The ritual texts are quite explicit with the goddess's invitation to the king to 'plough me', and in this literature as well as in the later Greek writings it is only a short step to the well-attested use of the term 'garden' as a euphemism for the female genitalia specifically and of her sexual charm generally.

One of the Egyptian Love Songs begins:

---

[1] Much of the detailed evidence for this identification comes from the pre-Islamic Arabic religion, where a strong cult of Uzza flourished. The origins of the cult are lost in antiquity, as are many of the specific practices of the cult. What is known, however, is that *Al Uzza* was the 'strong one', the mightiest of the goddesses, whose area of influence was in all facets of the love relationship. Sacred prostitution was part of the ritual. One account records that *Al Uzza* was the name of a *house* (temple) honoured by certain tribes out of which, when it was destroyed, a naked Abyssinian woman (the goddess herself?) tried to depart.

[2] See W. J. Fulco, *The Canaanite God REŠEP* (American Oriental Society, 1976), especially pp. 11, 28–33, and 56–62. *Cf.* below, on 2:7.

> Distracting is the foliage of my pasture:
> [The mouth] of my girl is a lotus bud,
> her breasts are mandrake apples . . .

and proceeds to describe her charms in similar figures of speech.[1]

In the 'Songs of Entertainment', which have clear sexual overtones, the girl declares:

> I am your best girl:
> I belong to you like an acre of land
> which I have planted
> with flowers and every sweet-smelling grass.[2]

It would be going too far to argue that the 'garden' references in the Song are all cultic,[3] but it is evident that the Song uses similar imagery. Vines, vineyards, garden and orchard ('paradise', Song 4:13 only) are mentioned some twenty times in the Song.[4] While detailed discussion of these texts will be reserved for the appropriate place in our Commentary, it needs to be noted that there are numerous cases of *double-entendres* and metaphorical uses of garden terminology in the Song. Note specifically the descriptions in the marriage/consummation section (4:12 – 5:1) and the seek/find section (6:2f.).

LOVE

It has become commonplace in contemporary Christian writing to draw rigid distinctions among the several Greek words translated 'love': *storgē*, *philia*, *erōs*, and *agapē*. The first, *storgē*, is common in the classical and Hellenistic periods, and usually means love in the sense of affection, especially of parents and children. Occasionally in the Hellenistic period

[1] Simpson, p. 299, no. 3. Mandrake apples are a renowned aphrodisiac and both the lotus and the 'mouth' are universally recognized euphemisms for the vulva.

[2] Simpson, pp. 308–309, nos. 17–19, especially no. 18, lines 3–6.

[3] See above, pp. 32–34.

[4] 'Vine' appears in Song 2:13 (twice); 6:11; 7:8, 12. 'Vineyard' is in Song 1:6 (twice), 14; 2:15 (twice); 7:12; 8:11 (twice), 12. 'Garden' appears in Song 4:12, 15, 16; 5:1; 6:2, 11; 8:13.

it was used of sexual love. It is not used in the LXX or the New Testament.

The verb *phileō* and the related nouns *philia*, *philos* and *philē* are normally understood as expressing friendship or 'brotherly love'. 'Friend' or 'companion' catches the personal element of the words. In Song of Solomon 1:2, and 8:1, *phileō* is used in the LXX for *nāšaq* 'kiss'. Interestingly, the LXX uses *phileō* to translate *'hb* only when the 'love' was directed towards things or conditions (Gn. 27:9, food; Pr. 8:17; 29:3, wisdom; Is. 56:10, sleep). The only New Testament quotations from the Old Testament where *phileō* is used for *'hb* are Revelation 3:19, 'those whom I love, I reprove', which may be quoted from Proverbs 3:12, and James 2:23 which is paralleled by 2 Chronicles 20:7 and Isaiah 41:8, 'Abraham . . . was called the friend of God'. In all three of these passages, the LXX uses *agapaō*.

Eros (with either a long or short *o*) is also frequent in the literature from all periods from Homer until after the New Testament era. It is not found in the New Testament itself, although the early Christian apologist, Ignatius (martyred *c.* AD 115), appears to use it in his Epistle to the Romans 7:2 (although the text for this epistle is in a poor state of preservation): 'I write to you in the midst of life, yet lusting after death. My lust hath been crucified, and there is no fire of material longing in me' (Lightfoot's translation).

Used as a proper name, *Eros* was the name of the god of love, traditionally identified with sexual passion. The word occurs only twice in the LXX, at Proverbs 7:18 and 24:51 (Heb. and English 30:16). In both verses the classic idea of sexual intoxication is at the heart of the meaning. The first records the invitation of the harlot to share 'lovemaking [*dōdîm*; LXX, *philias*] until the morning . . . and delight . . . in loves [*bā'ʰābîm*; LXX *erōti*].' The second is a little more difficult. The passage lists four insatiable things: 'Sheol [the grave], the barren womb, the earth ever thirsty for water, and the fire which never says, "Enough." ' The Hebrew for 'barren womb', *'ōṣer rāḥam*, is rendered by the LXX as *erōs gynaikos*, the 'passionate woman'. The parallelism between *dōdîm* and *'ʰābîm* in the Hebrew and *phileō* and *erōs* in the LXX is of interest in light of the next stage, for the crux of the issue for us is the relationship between *erōs* and *agapē*.

There are three words in the *agapē* word-group that need notice: the verb *agapaō*, the noun *agapē*, and the verbal adjective *agapētos*, 'beloved'. The latter is used about 60 times in the New Testament, and the other two about 150 times each. In the LXX *agapē* is used 16 times, *agapētos* 17 times, but the verb is very frequent, occurring nearly 120 times.

The common idea that *agapē* denotes a particular kind of bodiless, non-sensual, emotion (if that word can be used in this context), that expresses the love of God for man, or of redeemed man for God, needs examination. Nygren's distinction that *erōs* is love that strives for its own fulfilment, 'acquisitive desire, appetite, which, as such strives to obtain advantages' (p. 212), while *agapē* is pure, self-giving love, has merit, particularly in later theological expression; but an examination of the Old Testament and the LXX reveals clearly that this distinction between these two words was not part of the Hebrew mind up to and including the early centuries of the Christian era.

It is important at this point to note that the LXX uses the *agapē* word-group as the common translation of the Hebrew *'hb* group. This verbal root and its derived nouns and adjectives cover the various elements which are distinguished in the classical Greek uses of *philia*, *storgē* and *erōs*. *Agapē* is not common in pre-LXX Greek, although some instances of its occurrence have been found. It appears as if the LXX translators deliberately adopted the rather colourless *agapē* group simply because they could infuse it with the multifaceted concepts of the Hebrew *'hb*. None of the other Greek words lent themselves to the variety of meanings that the Hebrew contained.

In the Old Testament, *'hb* is used of the passionate, sexual love between man and woman, and is the common word used to describe marital relations, *e.g.* Isaac and Rebekah (Gn. 24:67, *cf.* Gn. 26:8), Samson and Delilah (Jdg. 16:4, 15) and particularly the Absalom/Tamar story (2 Sa. 13:1–22) and the Hosea/Gomer union (Ho. 3:1). The same word-group is used to express loyalty and friendship to members of the same sex (*e.g.* father/son, Gn. 25:28; in-laws, Ru. 4:15; or David/Jonathan, 1 Sa. 18:1–3; 2 Sa. 1:26). The relationship between the LORD and his godly people is described in identical words (Dt. 10:12, 15; Jos. 22:5; Am. 5:15; Ho. 11:4). There is here the element of exclusive selection and loyalty to the chosen one and it is this element that is present in the later uses of *agapē*. By New Testament times, the meaning of the word has been filled and shaped, via the LXX, by a rich range of Hebrew connotations.

Concomitant with this is the element of loyalty and service which is present in the *'hb* words. The basic motivation to *'hb/agapē* is a compelling inner disposition that makes itself manifest in outward actions on behalf of the one loved. Jonathan's love for David resulted in his helping David to escape Saul's murderous intentions (1 Sa. 20:17–42). Jacob's love for Rachel involved him in fourteen years' service to her father (Gn. 29:30). There are important non-biblical texts that reveal this same attitude. A text of 1375 BC from King Nikmadu to the Egyptian Pharaoh reads, 'The king of Shechem does not love me any longer. He now loves the king of Damascus. But I love you, O Pharaoh.' Love in the international political realm means alliance and loyalty. Love is something you *do*. It is not feeling, but activity. Jesus' words capsulize the case: 'If you love me, you will keep my commandments' (Jn. 14:15).[1]

In summary, *agapē*, at least in the Old Testament, is not to be limited to self-giving, non-sensual 'love'. It is a word filled with all the Hebrew concepts of passion, sexual attraction, friendship, obedience, loyalty, duty, and commitment to the other person. *Agapē*-love is not just for bloodless 'saints'; it is the expression of our full humanity and wholeness.[2]

---

[1] I am indebted to my colleague, Dr Douglas Stuart, for bringing the Nikmadu text to my attention. For further examples see W. L. Moran, 'The Ancient Near Eastern Background of the Love of God in Deuteronomy', *CBQ* 35, 1963, pp. 77–87.

[2] For further reading on this topic, there are standard presentations which argue for a clear distinction between *erōs* and *agapē*. C. S. Lewis, *The Four Loves* (Bles, 1960), is a popular treatment, while his *The Allegory of Love* (OUP, 1936) deals with the issue from a more academic, scholarly perspective. D. de Rougemont, *Love in the Western World* (Harcourt, Brace & Co., 1940, rev. ed., 1956), and A. Nygren, *Agape and Eros* (SPCK, ²1953), are both classic treatments which have done much to influence the thinking of the Christian church in the last generation. On the other side of the question see the following major articles: G. Wallis *et al.* ' *'āhabh*', *TDOT* 1:98–118; G. Quell and E. Stauffer, *'agapē, etc.'*, *TDNT* 1:21–55; G. Stahlin, *'phileō, etc.'*, *TDNT* 9:113–172. Wolff has an important section on love, pp. 166–184. B. B. Warfield, 'The Terminology of Love in the New Testament', *PTR* 16, 1918, pp. 1–45, 153–203 gives a thorough treatment of the issue, reinforced by the considerable material which has since come to light. A more popular recent treatment is W. E. Phipps, 'The Sensuousness of Agape', *Theology Today* 29, 1973, pp. 370–379. *Cf.* L. L. Walker, 'Love in the Old Testament' in *Current Issues in Biblical and Patristic Theology* (Eerdmans, 1975), pp. 277–288.

LOVER (BELOVED)

The most frequently used epithet for the man in the Song is 'my beloved' (Heb. *dôḍî*). Some 27 times in the Song[1] the girl addresses the man this way. Another five times[2] the women of Jerusalem pick up the title and use it of the man, 'your beloved'. Four additional uses seem to demand the translation 'love-making'.[3]

Outside the Song, *dôḍî* occurs an additional twenty-one times. In seventeen of these cases the term is translated 'uncle'. This concept is attested in both the biblical and extra-biblical literature, sometimes specifically of the brother of a parent, and sometimes more generally of any relative or kinsman (*e.g.* Nu. 36:11; 2 Ki. 24:17; Am. 6:10). The early literature from the ancient Near East, however, is clear that the word originally meant a 'beloved partner'. The word was used in an erotic sense in love poetry and the fertility rituals, occasionally occurring as a euphemism for the genitals, or as an epithet for some deity. The use of *dôḍî* in Isaiah 5:1 may be an example of this latter idea. The other three occurrences of *dôḍî* in Proverbs 7:18; Ezekiel 16:8; 23:17 demand the idea 'love-making' in its specific physical, sexual union. This parallels the use of the word in Song 1:2, *etc.* The Song preserves the ancient meaning of *dôḍî*, 'beloved (sexual) partner', in its application to the man.

A similar idea is expressed by the use of the Heb. *ra'yâ* 'my love' in Song 1:9, 15; 2:2, 10, 13; 4:1, 7; 5:2; 6:4, all addressed to the girl. In 5:16, the masculine form addressed to the man is used in parallel with *dôḍî*. BDB, p. 945, derives the noun from a verbal root *r'h* which has a probable meaning 'associate with', and gives the connotation 'friendship' or 'companion' to the noun form. Delitzsch[4] argues that the noun is from the more common meaning of the root *r'h* 'to pasture', 'shepherd', and the noun means 'to delight in something (or someone)'. The general sense seems to be one in whom one takes delight, *i.e.* a special companion or lover. In Judges 11:37, Jephthah's daughter takes her female companions with her to 'bewail

---

[1] Song 1:13, 14, 16; 2:3, 8, 9, 10, 16, 17; 4:16; 5:1, 2, 4, 5, 6 (twice), 8, 10, 16; 6:2, 3 (twice); 7:9, 10, 11, 13 (Heb. vv. 10, 11, 12, 14); 8:14.
[2] Song 5:9 (twice); 6:1 (twice); 8:5.
[3] See the Commentary on 1:2, and the references there.
[4] Delitzsch, p. 32.

[her] virginity', while in Lamentations 1:2, none of Israel's 'lovers' is there to comfort her in the disaster of exile and the destruction of the city. In the Song, this expression includes both the ideas of companionship and sexual partner.

As is so frequent in this book, the meaning of the words is clear. The problem lies in the interpretation of their significance. The juxtaposition of 'king' in 1:12 and 'my beloved' in 1:13f. serves to point up the problem. Three items need attention.

The first is the relationship between these two titles. Those who see two male protagonists in the book point to the contrast between these two – the (lecherous) *king* Solomon, and the rustic *lover* who retains the girl's love. As noted in the Introduction, this is a widely held interpretation. Others, who hold to the royal lover interpretation, see only one male figure, King Solomon himself the lover. It is worth noting here that the name David (Heb. *dawid*) is derived from the same Hebrew root as *dôdî*, and in the old consonantal text the two words would be written in identical form *dwd*. Might it be worth suggesting here that, if the Song is to be understood as a royal wedding song, the king in question ought to be David rather than Solomon? King David, *mlk dwd*, would be the 'beloved king', and the lover of the Song.

The second option is to allegorize the whole Song and take the 'beloved' as either the LORD (for the Jew), or as Christ (for the Christian). There is some evidence that *dôd* was used in the ancient Near East as a divine name, or at least as a descriptive adjective modifying some god-name, and this may suggest that the application of 'the beloved' to God (or Christ) is valid. Numerous other ancient Near Eastern epithets were so transferred.

The third choice is to recognize the word in its simple sense of 'beloved' without any royal or divine connotations. This pet name emphasizes the human relationship between the man and the woman.[1]

[1] See above, Introduction, pp. 21–36, on the whole question of interpretation. For more detailed treatment of the term *dôdî*, *cf.* J. Sanmartin-Ascaso, '*dôdh*', *TDOT* 3:143–156, and the extensive bibliography there.

WINE

There are a number of words in the Hebrew and Aramaic of the Old Testament for 'wine'. Although there is no consistent and clear-cut distinction among them, there are several different categories apparently represented. Apart from relatively infrequent words such as *ḥᵃmar*, 'red wine'; *sōḇe'*, 'drink'; and *'ēnâḇ*, 'the blood of grapes', there are two words which need some attention here. By far the most common is *yayin*, used of the fermented juice of grapes (and occasionally of other fruits), which was the common beverage of the ancient Near East. The other word is *šēkār*, usually translated 'strong drink', and frequently occurring in conjunction with *yayin*.

Neither of these words refers to the distilled 'hard liquors' we today identify as 'strong drink' or 'spirits'. While the distillation process was known in very early times, and was in fact common in the Far East, there is no evidence of extensive use of these drinks in the Egypt/Palestine/Mesopotamian region. The common drinks there were these fermented beers and wines. Beer, however, was apparently not brewed in Israel; perhaps the relative scarcity of grain was one reason for this. In the rabbinic literature it is noted that wine is normally diluted with two parts of water to one part of wine, and that for Passover the wine is to be diluted three to one. Either of these dilutions is called *yayin*. If the ratio is one to one, the resultant mixture is called *šēkār*, 'strong wine'. According to one record, drinking undiluted wine was 'barbarian'.[1]

The Old Testament recognizes what was common all through the ancient Near East, that wine played a significant role in various types of celebrations: weddings, reunions, banquets, religious ceremonies, *etc.* But it always recognizes the dangers of over-indulgence. Nor is the use of wine always reserved for public celebrations. Frequent reference is made to the place of wine in the male/female encounter. The picture in Proverbs 9:2, 5, gives a positive emphasis to this relationship. Significantly, the 'foolish woman' of Proverbs 9:13–18 does not use the wine motif in her plea of seduction. The links between wine and sex are well attested, and frequently fire is

---

[1] For further details see R. Stein, 'Wine-drinking in New Testament Times', *CT* 19 (20 June, 1975), pp. 9–11.

also introduced as a third element in the encounter.[1] The several references to wine in the Song of Solomon reflect these ideas of excitement and joy associated with it. An interesting comment on this is found in the 'Cairo Love Songs' from the New Kingdom period in Egypt (1300–1100 BC). Number twenty-three of the collection reads:

> I embrace her,
> and her arms open wide,
> I am like a man in Punt,
> like someone overwhelmed with drugs.
> I kiss her,
> her lips open,
> and I am drunk
> without a beer.[2]

[1] H. Cohen, *The Drunkenness of Noah* (Univ. of Alabama Press, 1974), pp. 1–30, draws a number of episodes from Greek, Egyptian and Hebrew literature to illustrate the relationship of fire, wine and sex in the ancient Near East. He argues that wine functions as an aphrodisiac to stimulate the 'seminal fire' necessary for the continuation of the race through procreation. *Cf.* Gn. 9:7, 19–24; 19:30–38.

[2] This quotation is from Simpson, whose translation of these songs is readily available and reads easily; the love songs are found on pp. 296–325. *ANET*, pp. 467–469, has selections from this material.

ANALYSIS

IV. LOST — AND FOUND (5:2 – 8:4)
    a. The break (5:2–8)
    b. A leading question (5:9)
    c. A joyous response (5:10–16)
    d. A second question (6:1)
    e. A curious response (6:2–3)
    f. The lover overwhelmed (6:4–10)
    g. The beloved's excited anticipation (6:11–12)
    h. A request, a question, and a reply (6:13 – 7:5)
    i. The lover's praise (7:6–9a)
    j. Consummation – again (7:9b – 8:4)

V. AFFIRMATION (8:5–14)
    a. Arousal (8:5)
    b. Commitment (8:6–7)
    c. Contentment (8:8–10)
    d. Communion (8:11–14)

COMMENTARY

TITLE AND ATTRIBUTION (1:1)

The book takes its title, in English as in Hebrew, from the opening words *šîr haššîrîm*. The repetitive construction of the first two words is a Hebrew idiom that expresses the superlative. 'Of all the songs, this is *the* song', *i.e.* the best, or most beautiful one. More familiar uses of this same idiom are the common *holy of holies*, *i.e.* the most holy place (Ex. 26:33f.), the innermost part of the tabernacle and temple containing the ark of the covenant and the mercy seat, or the phrases *King of kings*, *Lord of lords*. The common abbreviation 'Ct.' comes from the Vulgate title, *Canticum Canticorum*.

There are numerous Hebrew words for the various types of songs. This one, *šîr*, is a general word for any sort of happy song, and is most frequently used of the music at celebrations (*e.g.* Is. 24:9; 30:29). Simple, unaccompanied vocal music would be so identified (Ec. 12:4), although there is usually mention of some sort of musical accompaniment (tambourines and harps, Gn. 31:27; Am. 6:5; Is. 24:8). The frequent use of this word to describe the music associated with various cultic celebrations may lend support to the ritual interpretation discussed above.[1]

Whether or not the title is original, it conveys something of the beauty and depth of meaning in the Song. Rabbi Aqiba (d. AD 135) summed it up: 'In the entire world there is nothing equal to the day on which the Song of Solomon was given to Israel. All the Writings are holy, but the Song of Songs is most holy.'[2]

The relative pronoun *ʾašer* occurs only here in the Song.[3]

---

[1] See Introduction, pp. 32–34, 49f.   [2] *Mishnah*, 'Yadayim' 3:5.
[3] See Introduction: Vocabulary, pp. 41–44, and Date, pp. 17–19.

NEB emends to read *'āšîrâh*, *I will sing*, but there is no manu-script support for the change, nor does the content of the Song clearly suggest Solomon is the object of the Song. Delitzsch (p. 17) notes that the relative clause does not mean that this is 'the Song' from all the Songs of Solomon, but rather that it qualifies the whole first expression 'The Song of Songs' which is Solomon's.

The possessive is indicated by the preposition *lᵉ* which is used in a variety of ways in Hebrew and in the other ancient Near Eastern languages.[1] The most common, popular under-standing is that of authorship (*e.g.* Psalm 3 'of' = 'from' David)[2] so that this Song would be from the pen of Solomon himself. Another suggestion is that the person named is the collector of the material rather than the author. *The Song of Songs which is Solomon's* could be, then, the Song which Solomon wrote, or which was dedicated to him, or one which was edited or published by Solomon. Other possibilities, however, are attested for the form *lᵉ*. There are songs preserved in the Ugaritic materials which are *lᵉ* one of the gods (Baal, *etc.*), and this motif is also represented in, *e.g.*, Psalms 72 and 127, 'to' or 'for' the choirmaster. Psalm 4 uses the word twice in the title: '*lᵉ* the music director . . . *lᵉ* David'. The suggestion here is that of material produced for the individual specified (*i.e.* the music director), and either 'dedicated to' or 'referring to' the one named. This may indicate that Solomon is the object of the Song (*i.e.* the male protagonist), but see pp. 19–21.

I. ANTICIPATION (1:2 – 2:7)

The overall structure of the Song displays a series of mono-logues, dialogues and reminiscences of the protagonists that revolve around the central pivot of 4:16 – 5:1. In this first major section the happy, excited couple exchange expressions of desire, self-doubt, encouragement and expectation in their

---

[1] Dahood identifies four different uses of the form *lᵉ*; 1. as a preposition with meanings 'to, for, against, from, in than' (III, pp. 394f., 437); 2. as an emphatic particle suggesting 'even, truly, indeed, completely' (III, pp. 406f.); 3. as a vocative 'O (God, *etc.*)' (III, p. 407); and 4. as a negative 'not' (II, p. xvi).

[2] *Cf.* Kidner, p. 33.

love-play. Whether the lovers are looking back on their first encounter as young marrieds or are actually still unmarried but anticipating wedlock is a moot point (see above, pp. 45f.), but the general progress towards fulfilment is unquestioned.

a. The beloved's first request (1:2–4)

The first words we hear are the girl's urgent pleadings to her lover as she links her happiness and surprise with her desire to share her love with him.

2. The RSV *O that you would kiss me with the kisses of your mouth! For your love* . . . has brought artificial consistency to the pronouns in this verse. The AV and NIV (*Let him kiss me with the kisses of his mouth – for your love*) are more accurate here. Some commentators have argued that the first colon,[1] which is in 3rd person forms, is a statement of the beloved to her friends (4b), and the second colon, in 2nd person masculine forms, is the response of those friends to the lover. This necessitates a shift of speakers again in v. 3 when the beloved addresses her lover directly. Such a series of shifts is possible, but very awkward, and with no compelling need. The shift from *kiss me* to *his mouth* to *your love* appears awkward to us, but such a sequence of shifting pronouns is a common phenomenon in biblical poetry (*e.g.* Am. 4:1; Mi. 7:19; *cf.* Song 4:2; 6:6), and is also known in Phoenician and Ugaritic. Similar shifts are evident in some of the Sumerian Sacred Marriage texts. The sense of this passage is correctly rendered by the RSV. Delitzsch takes the preposition as a partitive, 'from his kisses', *i.e.* the speaker in this verse is only one of the recipients of the lover's kisses, but there is ample evidence for the common translation 'with'.

The NEB *smother me with kisses* takes this as an intensive construction, and accurately reflects the sense of the Hebrew. *Your love*, in the second colon, is a plural form (AV mg.) that has caused considerable discussion in the commentaries. The

[1] Scholars disagree on the names to apply to the parallel sections of Hebrew and other ancient Near Eastern poetry. Many continental scholars use 'stich' (or 'stichos'), 'distich', and 'hemistich' for the line, double-line and half-line respectively. Others use 'couplet' for the two-line unit, but that leaves the problem of calling one line a half-couplet or something similar, and a three-line unit a triplet. In this commentary I shall use W. F. Albright's terminology: a single line is a colon, the two-line unit is a bicolon, and a three-line unit a tricolon.

LXX and Vg. read 'your breasts' here, as well as in 1:4; 4:10; and 7:12. In addition, the LXX adds the same clause in 6:11. The basis for this rendering is somewhat obscure, but both the Hebrew word 'loves' (*dôdîm*) and the Hebrew word 'breasts' (*dadayîm*) would be written simply as *ddm* in the old consonantal text.[1] The plural form is found only in Numbers 36:11; Proverbs 7:18; Ezekiel 16:8; 23:17; and Song of Solomon 1:2, 4; 4:10; 5:1; and 7:12.[2] It is obvious from the context of the Proverbs and Ezekiel passages that the term means 'love-making' with physically erotic connotations, rather than 'love' in some abstract idea. The translation 'love-making' or 'caresses' fits best in the Song passages listed.

For, or 'because', is perfectly acceptable to introduce the second colon, but the particle can also be translated 'truly' or 'how much'. Coupled with the adjective the construction can be read 'How much better than . . .'[3]

Better is a straightforward rendering of the Hebrew, but the NIV *more delightful* fits better with the 'love-making'. NEB *more fragrant* suits 'wine', but is unsatisfactory with 'love-making'.

Wine. Although the Hebrew community was aware of the dangers of indiscriminate use of wine and other 'strong drink' (Pr. 20:1; 23:31; 31:4, 6), they played a significant role in times of celebration. The close relationship between wine and sex is well attested (see Subject Study: Wine, pp. 66f.).

3. The use of olive oil as a base for various perfumed lotions was common in the ancient Near East.

The preposition *lᵉ* which begins this verse causes trouble for all the translators. Possibly it should be taken in parallel with the last clause of v. 2, the *ki* doing double duty, so that the thought expressed there continues here '. . . better than the fragrance of your perfumes'. On the other hand, the force may be intensive: 'Truly, the scent of your oils is delightful.' Delitzsch suggests 'to the smell thy ointments are sweet', taking the noun *rêḥa* to mean 'sense of smell', but such a meaning for *rêḥa* is not attested in biblical Hebrew or the cognates.

The RSV *your name is oil poured out* follows the LXX and Vg.,

[1] See Pope, pp. 298f. for further discussion.

[2] See Subject Study: Lover (Beloved) above, pp. 64f., for an examination of the singular form, and the Nu. 36:11 use of the plural.

[3] The same pairing appears in Pss. 63:4; 84:11; and 147:1, with the same meaning. For discussion, see Dahood I, p. 197, on Ps. 32:10.

taking the middle word of the unit as a verb form with the meaning 'poured out' or 'clarified' (by pouring from container to container to remove the dregs, *cf.* Je. 48:11). However, the meaning of the Hebrew word is uncertain. Pope suggests, on the basis of Ugaritic parallels, the term describes a kind of expensive and scarce cosmetic oil.[1]

Name occurs only this once in the Song, and in this context is used in the broader sense for the true being of the person.

The attractiveness of the whole personality of the lover is such that others beside the beloved are drawn to him. *Maidens* (AV, ASV *virgins*) are unmarried young women of marriageable age. The word itself does not necessarily mean 'virgin' (*i.e.* sexually inexperienced), but the common Old Testament position on pre-marital sexual purity is clear (*cf.* Dt. 22:13–29). Every 'maiden' (*'almāh*) is assumed to be virgin and virtuous until she is proven not to be.[2] In 6:8, the only other use of this word in the Song, the 'maidens' are distinguished as a separate group from the 'queens and concubines'.

Love. The object of the passionate emotional feeling is a person rather than a thing (see Subject Study: Love, pp. 60–63).

4. The opening colon resumes the urgent plea that opened the Song. Twice elsewhere in the Old Testament (Je. 31:3; Ho. 11:4) this verb is used to describe the power of love to draw the beloved to the lover. Now, though, the plea shifts to the cohortative, *let us hurry* (NIV).

The king has brought me into his chambers. The vocative of the NEB, *bring me into your chamber, O king*, follows the Syriac and the Greek translation of Symmachus. The MT and the other versions are declarative with 3rd person pronouns.

Chambers (note the plural here) usually refers to private rooms. In 3:4 the context demands 'bedroom' for this word, but that is not necessarily always the meaning (*cf.* 2 Sa. 13:10; Joel 2:16). The sense of privacy is an important element here – being away from the eyes of those who would look on the most sacred things.

We will exult and rejoice (NIV *We rejoice and delight*). Frequently

---

[1] Pope, p. 300, on *U.T.* 145:20.
[2] For further discussion see R. D. Wilson, 'The Meaning of *'almah* (A.V. "virgin") in Is. vii. 14', *PTR* 24, 1926, p. 316; C. Gordon, "*'almah* in Isaiah 7:14', *JBR* 21, 1953, p. 106; and J. A. Motyer, 'Context and Content in the Interpretation of Isaiah 7:14', *TB* 21, 1970, pp. 118–125.

the Old Testament writers link these two words in exclamations of praise to the LORD, for his deliverance either promised or actual. They are also attested individually and together in the cultic texts from Ugarit. They are used in situations where good news has been received and appropriate celebration is called for.[1] Here in the Song the lover is the object of the rejoicing.

In you (masculine singular, referring to the lover) may be translated 'with you', *i.e.* his joy is also theirs (*cf.* Rom. 12:15).

This section is a key one in the various dramatic theories of interpretation of the Song (see Introduction, pp. 32–34, 49f.). It is one of five places in the Song where the word *king* is used (1:4, 12; 3:9, 11; 7:5). Those who see three main characters in the Song, the beloved, the lover and King Solomon, understand this section to be a plea for the lover to hurry to save her from the king who has already taken her (against her will) into his bedroom. If there are only two characters in the poem (Solomon and his new bride), this is her acknowledgment that the consummation of the marriage is at hand. Such a view, however, has difficulty with the shift to the third person here from the cohortative in the first colon. The words can legitimately be translated 'Even if the king were to bring me into his chambers . . .' (so Ibn Ezra (1084?–1164), followed by Delitzsch and Gordis). This rendering requires that the speaker conclude the conditional sense thus introduced 'still I would rejoice and be glad in thee' (Ibn Ezra). The forms, however, of this next bicolon are plural: *We will exult.* Delitzsch solves the problem by assigning the whole first section to the women of Jerusalem who are praising Solomon. In this case, the beloved's words begin with v. 5. NIV ends the beloved's speech with the *chambers* phrase, and attributes *We rejoice* to the friends. No solution is entirely satisfactory, although, as noted above on v. 2, similar apparently incongruous pronoun shifts are relatively common in ancient Near Eastern poetry.[2] Perhaps the best explanation is to hear these words from the mouth of the girl. If she is expressing her own deep feelings for the lover, they two (*we*) will find their happiness not in the king, but *in you* (masculine singular), the lover.

We will extol (NIV *praise*; AV *remember*). AV reflects the root

---

[1] *E.g.* Pss. 16:9; 48:11; 96:11.

[2] See Kramer, pp. 92, 99 for examples of the bride using plural pronouns of herself.

meaning of the verb. The sense here is 'commemorate'. The rabbinic scholar Ibn Janah (*c.* AD 1025?), followed by Gordis and Pope, interprets the verb 'inhale' (*e.g.* the smoke of the sacrifice, Lv. 24:7; Ps. 20:3), so that the sense of the phrase is something like 'we will accept your lovemaking as better than wine'.

Your love. Cf. v. 2. LXX reads *breasts* here also.

Wine. Cf. v. 2 and Subject Study: Wine, pp. 66f.

Rightly. The differences in the ancient versions and English translations indicate a problem. AV *the upright* follows the LXX. The MT (*mêšārîm*) term, which is used elsewhere in the Song only at 7:9, means level or straight. (The same word is used in Is. 40:4 'make straight in the wilderness'; Mt. 3:3 and Lk. 3:4 follow LXX.) NEB *more than any song* emends the text to read *miššîrîm* 'from songs' (*cf.* 1:1). There is no manuscript support for this change, but it does make an attractive parallel reading with the preceding colon. Several rabbinic writers suggest sexual potency as the underlying meaning, with a translation 'for thy manliness do they love thee'.[1] Overall, the RSV and NIV catch the meaning well.

They love you. See Subject Study: Love, pp. 60–63.

b. The girl's shy uncertainty (1:5–7)

The difficulties of v. 4 make it impossible to be completely certain of the identity of the speakers there, but with v. 5 the doubt disappears. The beloved speaks first to her female companions (vv. 5f.), expresses self-doubt about her desirability and then turns her words to her lover (v. 7) as she expresses her fear at being taken for a wandering prostitute by the shepherds on the hills. Such conflicting emotions are the experience of many people.

5. Several times in the Song (1:5, 6; 2:1, 5; 5:2, 5, 6, 8; 6:3; 7:10; 8:10) the separate, emphatic pronoun 'I' (or 'I am') is used rather than the more common verbal ending. In every instance it is the girl who uses it. NIV catches the lilt of the original: *Dark am I.*

RSV *very dark* (JB, AV, ASV more correctly *black*. Lehrman, *swarthy*. Heb. *šāḥôr*). This particular form is used only six times

---

[1] Gordis, p. 79. For fuller discussion of the options, see Pope, pp. 304–307; Gordis, pp. 78f.; Delitzsch, pp. 23f.

in the Old Testament (Lv. 13:31, 37; Zc. 6:2, 6; and Song 1:5; 5:11). In this context the word is hyperbolic: sun-tan makes one 'swarthy' but not 'black', although the simile at Song 5:11 indicates that the meaning of the word is 'shiny black'. Some scholars have suggested that the word is to be revocalized to *šaḥar*, a more common word in the Old Testament, which means 'dawn' (*cf.* Song 6:10; Is. 14:12).[1] This reading, along with the suggested re-vocalization of *Solomon* at the end of v. 5, has led Dahood to propose that the author may have been making a veiled reference to the Canaanite myth from Ugarit concerning *The Birth of the Gods Dawn and Dusk*. At least the roots for the names are the same as those found here.

But comely, RSV, AV, ASV (*lovely*, JB, NIV). The conjunction is variously rendered 'and', 'but', 'yet', or 'that', so that various implications are drawn from the juxtaposition. The context seems to require a contrast, *yet* or *but* being the most suitable. The context (v. 6) makes it clear that the girl is not of negroid stock, but has simply been tanned very dark. In complexion she is darker than her companions, but her beauty shines through.[2]

Daughters of Jerusalem. This group of maidens ('virgins'(?), *cf.* v. 3) appear again at 2:7; 3:5, 10f.; 5:8, 16; and 8:4. They are addressed only by the girl (unless 6:9 also refers to this group), usually with some sort of exhortation or request. Most interpreters assign all the plural speeches in the Song to these women. Those who follow a cultic or dramatic interpretation of the Song see them as a sort of Greek chorus who appear as a foil to the beloved and serve to advance the action by posing rhetorical questions or making interpretative comments on the action between the principals. A similar role is played by the chorus in the Egyptian *Myth of Horus* play (see above, p. 33, n. 2) and in some of the Egyptian love songs (*e.g.* the 'Songs of the Orchard' from the Turin Collection, Simpson, nos. 28–30, pp. 312–314). Other interpreters see them as the female members of the wedding party or the women of the king's harem. The text itself gives no indication of their iden-

---

[1] *E.g.* Delitzsch, p. 24; Dahood I, p. 55.
[2] For an extended summary of this theme, including a number of quotations and treatment of the many 'Black Madonnas', see Pope, pp. 307–318. For a critique of Pope's arguments here, see J. M. Sasson, 'On M. M. Pope's *Song of Songs*', *Maarav* 1, 1979, pp. 177–196. C. J. Exum, 'Assertive *'al* in Canticles 1:6?', *Bib.* 62, 1981, pp. 416–419, argues that there is no negative in v. 6.

tity except their association with the city of Jerusalem. Frequently in the Old Testament the term 'son' or 'daughter' is not to be understood in a relational sense, but rather as indicating character (*e.g.* 1 Sa. 14:52, 'a son of might' = a strong man). If this is the idiom here, the women would be those who display the characteristics of the city girls.

Tents of Kedar. NIV adds *dark* here in order to tie the colon to the first in v. 5 more clearly. In a strict geographical sense, *Kedar* refers to the territory south-east of Damascus and then to the nomadic tribes which inhabited that region. Generally, however, the name was applied to any of the Bedouin tribes whose tents, made from the hair of the black goats so common among them, are a frequent sight on the fringes of the deserts.

Curtains, RSV, AV (*pavilions*, JB; *tent-curtains*, NIV, NEB). Forty-one of the forty-eight uses of this word in the Old Testament are in connection with the tabernacle which Israel constructed in the wilderness. In Exodus 26 and 36, Moses was directed to make a series of 'curtains', some from fine linen and some from animal hair, and from them build a structure to serve as the centre of worship and sacrifice for Israel. These 'curtains' were a specific size and designed to be hung from the portable framework of the tabernacle. While it is not obvious from these pentateuchal passages, it becomes clear on the basis of a number of poetic parallelisms that the term is really synonymous with *tent* (*cf.* Is. 54:2; Je. 4:20; 10:20; 49:29; and especially Hab. 3:7). Many commentators note that the beautiful hangings of the Solomonic court were in mind here as a contrast with the rustic nomadic tents. If this is valid, there is an interesting parallel with the first part of the verse: dark/Kedar; lovely/Solomonic hangings.

Solomon. See above, pp. 19–21. The NEB *Shalmah* and JB *Salmah* read this word as the name of a southern desert tribe which lived in the vicinity of Petra sometime prior to the fifth century BC. A number of commentators follow this suggestion, although there is no firm evidence for the identification.

6. *Do not gaze* (*stare*, NIV). The construction here (followed by LXX) can also be translated 'stop staring'. There is no suggestion in the verb of either revulsion or envy – just interest. *Swarthy* (Heb. *šeḥarḥōr*) occurs only here in the Old Testament. Most authorities identify it as a diminutive of *šāḥor* in 1:5. The reason for her dark colour is her exposure to the intense sun because of her outdoor activities. It is apparent that the girl's lack of self-confidence and her self-abnegation hinted at here is unfounded. The frequent descriptions of her obvious beauty are a main element in the Song.

Mention of the role of her brothers (*mother's sons*), and the omission of any reference to father anywhere in the Song, suggest that the father was dead, and that the brothers were fulfilling the role of leadership in the family (*cf.* Song 8:8f.; Gn. 34:25–31). Such a situation may indicate that the Song was originally composed in connection with a specific wedding, and is not for some general cultic celebration. No reason is given in the text why the brothers are *angry*. There is a play on words here, as the root meaning of the verb is 'become hot, burn'. The similarity between the heat of the sun and the heat of the brothers is evident. Ordered into the vineyard by them, she is forced to care for and guard the vines. The contrast here between the *vineyards* she was ordered to care for and *my own vineyard* (emphatic construction, *cf.* 8:12) which has been neglected poses some interpretative problems. A straightforward literalism would indicate that she had spent her days caring for the family vineyards to the neglect of her own. But even assuming she was in her own right a land-holder, would not her possessions be part of the family hold-ings? It appears that there is another word-play going on in this colon. *My own vineyard* is, apparently, a metaphor for her own person which has been neglected as she performed her other enforced duties. Fuerst suggests this is a kind of Cinder-ella story.[1]

7. The shift from the maidens to the lover is paralleled by the shift from tending vineyards to watching sheep. Her request, directed to the lover, *whom my soul loves*, is to expedite her finding him without a lengthy search among all his companions. The idiom 'my soul' includes the whole of the life and person of the individual. It involves the strong desire of a lover for the beloved (*cf.* Gn. 34:2–4), of man for a favourite food (Mi. 7:1) or possession (Dt. 14:26), *etc.*, but always with the clear emphasis on one's own choice (*cf.* Dt. 21:14; Je. 34:16).[2]

The question is completed by the two parallel clauses. Both are introduced by *'ēkâh*, the interrogative particle here

[1] Fuerst, p. 171. See further, Subject Study: The Garden Motif, pp. 59f.
[2] See Wolff, pp. 10–25, for an extended discussion of *nep̄eš* as 'needy man'.

translated *where*, but which is commonly 'how' or 'what' (*cf.* La. 1:1; 2:1; 4:1f., *etc.*). See Song 5:2.

AV and ASV correctly indicate that *thy flock* and *it* are not in the Hebrew text except by implications. Since there is no expressed object in the MT for either verb, it may be that she is addressing the lover himself. The Heb. *rā'ah*, 'tend' (RSV *pasture*; NIV *graze*), is used of various types of domestic animals, but also is used figuratively of people, *i.e.* the rulers who have oversight of a nation, or a teacher in an academic or pastoral situation. An identical root and its derivatives means 'to associate with', or 'friends, companions'. The second root *rābaṣ*, 'cause to lie down', is much less frequent in the Old Testament, and is usually used of domestic animals resting lying down. But in Job 11:19; Isaiah 14:30; Ezekiel 34:14–15; Zephaniah 2:7; 3:13; and especially Psalm 23:2, the same form of the verb is used as here in the Song; all these verses use the verb of people rather than animals.

Noon. In the tropic and semi-tropic areas of the world – including ancient as well as modern Palestine – the oppressive heat of the middle of the day drives people and animals to rest in shady places. Note the contrast with the cool of the dawn and evening elsewhere in the Song (2:17; 4:6; 5:2; 7:12).

For why. NEB, JB, *That I may not*, follow LXX *mēpote*, 'lest'. The negative connotation fits better with the following clause, as the girl seeks to avoid the scandal of appearing as a wandering harlot among the shepherds.

Veiled woman, NIV (AV mg., ASV, Pope, Lehrman similar), follows MT *'tyh* and LXX *periballō*. This is the only use of this verb in the Song of Solomon, although it is used some sixteen times elsewhere in the Old Testament, always with the meaning to cover or veil (*e.g.* 1 Sa. 28:14; Lv. 13:45; Mi. 3:7). RSV, JB, AV follow Vg., Symmachus and Syriac, emending to read *ṭ'yh* (*i.e.* reversing the first two consonants) *one who wanders*. NEB takes the root *'āṭah* to mean 'pick up, grasp with the hand', and interprets to mean *pick lice from a garment* (*cf.* Is. 22:17; Je. 43:12), *i.e.* while away the siesta-time grooming herself.[1] Neither of these translations improves on the MT with its picture of the veiled cult-prostitute soliciting business among the shepherds (*cf.* Gn. 38:14–23, especially v. 15) – an implication the girl wants to avoid at all costs.

[1] For further discussion of this suggestion see G. R. Driver, 'Lice in the Old Testament', *PEQ* 106, 1974, pp. 159f.

c. The lover's gentle encouragement (1:8–11)

The lover's response to her expressed fears is to reassure her of her beauty and desirability. There is general agreement that vv. 9–10 are the words of the lover, but considerable disagreement as to whether vv. 8 and 11 are also his. Many commentators follow RSV and JB in attributing v. 8 to the friends. The Living Bible follows the ancient rabbinic pattern and assigns the verse to the girl. NEB assigns v. 11 to the friends.

8. NEB *If you yourself do not know* best reflects the sense of the Hebrew in the opening clause. The shift to the feminine forms here indicates a different speaker from v. 7, but as noted above, there is some confusion as to who the speaker is. The context seems to require the lover here (so LXX). *Know*, a very common verb in the Old Testament, occurs in the Song only here and at 6:12. Very frequently it is used as a euphemism for sexual intercourse (*e.g.* Gn. 4:1, *etc.*), but in both cases in the Song the ordinary meaning is present.

Most beautiful of women, NIV (AV, RSV, NEB *fairest*; JB correctly notes the vocative sense *O loveliest*). The lover's response to the girl's self-deprecation in vv. 5f. is the superlative praise *most beautiful*. In 5:9 and 6:1, the only other uses of this exact phrase in the Song, it is the women of Jerusalem who describe the girl's beauty. In that light, it may be that this verse is also from their lips, but it is more likely that in chs. 5 and 6 the women have picked up the lover's words here and are mocking her with them. Although this superlative is used only these three times in the Song, the girl's beauty is a constant theme of the lover. Beginning in 1:15, and then in 2:10, 13; 4:1, 7, 10; 5:9; 6:1, 4, 10(?); 7:1 (Heb. 7:2), 6 (Heb. 7), he praises her beauty. Only once in the Song (1:16) is the word applied to anyone but the girl, and there she echoes her lover's word, and turns the compliment back on him.

The rest of this verse is obscure. While the general idea is clear, the precise implication of the passage is not. The words are all common in the Old Testament, and the syntax is normal, but the sense is awkward. It appears, at first glance, that the lover is instructing her simply to follow the sheep-path until she finds him, and there graze her own flocks while the two of them enjoy one another's company. But the girl's expressed concern in v. 7 is that she not be subjected to that process, lest her mission be misunderstood. The issue is further complicated by the fact that the Hebrew word translated *tracks* (*footsteps*, AV) here, and *heel* or *hoof* elsewhere (*e.g.* Gn. 3:15; 49:17, *etc.*), is occasionally used as a euphemism for the genitals (*e.g.* Je. 13:22), and that the *young goat* or *kid* (AV) is an erotic emblem and the appropriate offering to present to a cult-prostitute (*cf.* Gn. 38:17), or to a king (*cf.* 1 Sa. 16:20).

The *tents of the shepherds* (NIV) likewise may have cultic or royal connotations. The word for *tent* is the one used for the tabernacle in Exodus and Leviticus; in fact, three-fifths of the Old Testament uses of the word are in that context. The theme of the king as shepherd of Israel is also common in the Old Testament (*e.g.* Zc. 10:1–3; 13:7; *cf.* Is. 40:11; Mt. 26:31), and so this passage is frequently seen in similar terms. Those who see some cultic ceremony or Solomonic connection in the Song find some support for those views here.[1] It would be unwise, however, to push these concepts too far in trying to understand this text.

9. Animal names are common expressions of endearment in many cultures. Here we find the first of several in the Song. The comparison naturally must be understood as complimentary, since her beauty is the central theme of the section. The emphasis of *compare* is always on the mental image conveyed. The term is never used in the Old Testament of physically making a thing look like something else.

This verse also marks the first use of the term *my love* (NIV *my darling*; NEB *my dearest*). It occurs nine times in the Song, always on the lips of the lover, and usually in conjunction with an explicit statement about her beauty.[2] The central meaning of the verbal root is to guard, care for, or tend, with an emphasis on the delight and pleasure which attends that responsibility. Again, as noted above,[3] action takes precedence over words, and the concepts of friendship and companionship are linked with the expressed concern for the protection of her well-being. Note the contrast here with the attitude of the brothers in v. 6.

The comparison with *a mare of Pharaoh's chariots* has

[1] *Cf.* Pope, pp. 333–336 for additional material, and above pp. 19–21, 49f.
[2] The six references where these two are combined are Song 1:15; 2:10, 13; 4:1, 7; 6:4. In addition, the word is used in 1:9; 2:2; and 5:2, and in these cases her beauty is described in simile.
[3] See Subject Study: Love, p. 63.

produced a plethora of translations and interpretations. In the ancient Near East, Egyptian horses were the most desirable strain, and of course the royal steeds would be the best of the best. But the meaning of this text is usually missed. As Pope correctly notes,[1] in ancient Egypt after the middle of the second millennium BC, mares were never used to draw chariots. Stallions, hitched in pairs, were the standard motive-power of both war-chariots and other royal vehicles. Yet the text here has the feminine singular *mare*. The preposition linked with *chariots* is better translated 'among' rather than as a possessive. These factors suggest that the comparison here underscores the girl's attractiveness. A mare loose among the royal stallions would create intense excitement. This is the ultimate in sex appeal! *Cf.* 3:10; 6:12.

10. The bridles of the chariot horses were elaborately decorated with jewels, precious metals, feathers and multi-coloured leathers and fabrics.[2] The lover transfers to his beloved the image of this decorated beauty. The beauty of her face (*cheeks*) is enhanced by the *ornaments* surrounding it. The precise nature of these decorations is unclear. NEB and ASV translate *plaited hair*, and the NIV reads *ear-rings*, while the others are more generally *jewels* or *ornaments*. The word so translated occurs only five times in the Old Testament – here and in the next verse, in 1 Chronicles 17:17, and in Esther 2:12, 15. The root meaning is *one's turn*, as in Esther, where *her turn* to go in to the king's presence marks the climax of her choice as queen to succeed Vashti. The Chronicles passage also suggests the 'turn of the future'. In the context here, the 'turnings' could be either the *braided* 'turned' hair that covered her cheeks, as the manes of the horses were sometimes twisted into fancy patterns,[3] or the elaborately fashioned jewellery that covered her face, much as the bridle covered the cheeks of the horse. So, too, is her neck decorated with strings of jewels.

11. The shift to the 1st person plural suggests to some that this verse is spoken by the women, but most translators and commentators include it with the lover's words (see above on 1:4). The word for *ornaments* is the one used above in v. 10, but these are designed especially for her, made of gold and

[1] Pope, pp. 338f.
[2] For illustrations, see Yadin 1, pp. 192–195, 200, 212–216.
[3] See Yadin, p. 195.

silver, and perhaps decorated with jewels or small globes of glass. The emphasis in these last two verses is not on the attractiveness of the ornaments, magnificent as they are, but on the way these enhance the girl's natural beauty.

d. The beloved's soliloquy (1:12–14)

In a rapturous soliloquy, the girl responds to her lover's praise with three erotic similes.

12. This is the second reference to the *king* in the Song.[1] Commentators who understand there to be two male protagonists differentiate between the king and the lover, but the structure of vv. 12–16, including the use of the personal pronouns, make it much more likely that the *king* in v. 12 and the *lover* in vv. 13–14 are the same person. This in no way requires the lover to be of royal blood, for, as noted above, the title can be used of any bridegroom. See Subject Study: Love, pp. 60–63.

The setting for this verse is usually understood to be a royal banquet, with the king *at his table* (AV, ASV, NIV). However, there is nothing in the text to suggest that anyone other than the king was present. The JB, *the king rests in his own room*, and the NEB (and RSV), *(reclines) on his couch*, reflect the LXX *anaklinō* and the Persian/Greek/Roman custom of reclining on couches at formal banquets. However, this practice does not seem to have been used in Israel in the pre-exilic period.[2] The Hebrew root used means 'surround' and is perhaps best understood here as 'among his own surroundings'. The broader context is a combination of bedroom motifs (1:4, 16f.) and banquet motifs (2:1–5), and this translation preserves the ambiguity of the original.[3]

The eroticism of her response is reinforced by her reference to three different perfumes. *Nard*, RSV, JB or *spikenard* (that is 'pure nard'), AV, ASV, NEB, or simply *perfume*, NIV, was a very expensive perfume/ointment derived from a plant native to the

---

[1] *Cf.* the note on 1:4, and the Introduction, pp. 19–21.

[2] See Delitzsch, p. 36. M. Dahood, 'Eblaite and Biblical Hebrew', *CBQ* 44, 1982, p. 12, suggests, on the basis of the Eblaite *ma-za-bu*, the meaning 'a round cushion made of wool' for the Heb. *mesab*, 'table' or 'couch'.

[3] Pope, pp. 347f., notes the passage in 2 Ki. 23:5–11 where this word is linked with the pagan shrines 'around' Jerusalem, where fertility rites and ritual prostitution were carried on. The sexual innuendo may be present in the Song.

Himalayan region of India. The scarcity, and hence the value, of this exotic fragrance made it much in demand as a love-potion.

13. *Myrrh* is a resinous gum gathered from a species of a South Arabian tree. It was in use as a perfume in Canaan at least as early as the Ugaritic period (17th – 14th centuries BC). Myrrh was a major ingredient in the holy oil used in the tabernacle (Ex. 30:23–33), and was also traditionally associated with death and the embalming process (*cf.* Mt. 2:11; Mk. 15:23; Jn. 19:39). In liquid form it would be carried in small bottles like nard, but it was also used in solid form. This way it could be carried in a small cloth pouch or sachet and worn next to the body. The Egyptian 'Song of the Harper' mentions placing myrrh on the head as a sign of rejoicing. The myrrh was mixed with fat, shaped into cones, and placed on the heads of the guests. As the fat melted from the body heat, the aroma of the myrrh and the anointing oil would fill the room.

The sense of the main verb is correctly rendered by the AV *shall lie all night* (*cf.* Song 7:11).

14. The *henna* plant (AV *camphire*, mg. *cypress*) is a common Palestinian shrub. The leaves, when crushed, produce a bright orange-red to yellow dye often used to colour hair or finger nails. Here, however, the girl refers to the fragrant blossoms from the plant. *Cf.* 7:11.

In all probability, she was not in actual possession of any of these items. Rather, they are similes that express her sweet feelings towards her lover.

The lush oasis *En-gedi*, 'the place of the wild goats' about half-way down the western shore of the Dead Sea, has for millennia been a traveller's delight. The *vineyards* include grapes, but are not limited to them. All sorts of tropical and semi-tropical plants grow there. Historically, the major crops of the area were exotic spices and plants that were manufactured into cosmetics and perfumes. Just as in Song 1:9, where Pharaoh's horses were the best, so here, the produce from En-gedi is the best of the best. The girl returns her lover's compliments in terms of the best she knows.

e. The lovers' banter (1:15 – 2:2)

These five verses are a series of rapid, bantering exchanges between the two that leads into the girl's monologue in 2:3–13.

15. The lover again compliments his lady's beauty, picking up from v. 9 the address *my darling* (NIV) and the animal comparison to emphasize it. RSV, NIV, JB translate literally, *your eyes are doves*. There are many similar direct comparisons in the Song (*e.g.* 5:13–15; 7:2f.). The exact point of the simile is obscure; most probably the comparison is to the deep, smoke-grey colour with flashes of iridescence. Beautiful eyes were a hallmark of perfection in a woman (*cf.* Rachel and Leah, Gn. 29:17). Rabbinic tradition identifies beautiful eyes with a beautiful personality. *Cf.* 2:12, 14.

16. Except for the change of gender, the opening words are an exact repetition of those of the previous verse. *How beautiful* (*handsome*, NIV). The word occurs fourteen times in the Song, but only this once in the masculine form directed toward the lover (*dôdî*).[1] The other four Hebrew words in this verse are found only here in the Song, although they occur elsewhere in the Old Testament.

RSV *truly lovely* captures the intensive force of the particle better than the other versions which simply take the particle as conjunctive. *Lovely*, RSV; *pleasant*, AV, ASV, NEB; *delightful*, JB; or *charming*, NIV are all possible translations. The word occurs only ten times in the Old Testament, mostly in Psalms and Proverbs, but also in 2 Samuel 1:23 and 23:1, in both cases in songs of David.

NEB places the last colon with v. 17 and assigns it to the lover, but there is no compelling reason for this except the shift to the plural form. It is just as plausible that she make the shift as he – unless girls are not supposed to think in those terms. *Couch* or *bed* equally renders the meaning. The word is one of several Hebrew words so translated. This one usually implies some sort of fancy or elaborate bed, probably canopied or screened, and decorated with carved panels, not just the simple peasant pallet.[2] This bed is described as *green* (*verdant*, NIV), but the word is not so much used of the colour proper, but of a tree that is alive and in leaf. The NEB *shaded with*

---

[1] *Cf.* v. 13 and Subject Study: Lover (Beloved), pp. 64f.
[2] *Cf.* Dt. 3:11. King Og's iron bedstead was an unusual item in Bronze-Age Canaan. Any iron items would have to be imported from the Hittites or other territory where the Iron Age was already established. Pr. 7:16 remarks on the expensive coverings, and Am. 6:4 mentions the ivory carvings inlaid on the beds.

branches is a good paraphrase – the canopy of their love-bed is the leafy branches of the trees of the garden.

17. The lover again picks up the cue from his beloved and continues her imagery. The word translated *rafters* occurs only here in the Old Testament, hence the meaning is uncertain. *Panels, wainscoting, gutters,* or *ceilings* have been suggested, but the parallelism with *beams* in the first colon seems to require something like *rafters*. Wood was scarce enough in ancient Canaan for it not to be used in wall-construction except in the most expensive temples or palaces. In 1 Kings 7:1–8, Solomon's panelled palace is identified as the House of the Forest of Lebanon.

The two trees mentioned here are not certainly identifiable. The *'erez* is traditionally the 'cedar of Lebanon', a beautiful tree with many convoluted trunks and branches. The second tree, the *bᵉrôt* (AV, ASV, NEB, NIV *fir*; JB *cypress*; RSV *pine*) is perhaps the Phoenician juniper.

If this text is describing the actual construction of a house it would be a relatively small one. But one point missed in all the translations is that the word *house* is in the plural form 'our houses'. Frequently in the Semitic languages, including Hebrew, the plural is used in a singular sense, and that may be the case here. But if the picture of the garden as the place of love is accurate, there is no reason to ignore the plural form. The couple is not restricted to secret chambers behind solid walls and closed doors for their lovemaking – they have the whole garden with its many-shaded bowers at their disposal.

2:1. The rapid interchange continues as the girl modestly compares herself to common wild flowers. The traditional translation *rose of Sharon* (*asphodel*, NEB) is not really satisfactory. Nor are the ancient versions much help, most of them simply using some broad generic term. Some species of wild rose probably grew in Palestine in Old Testament times, but the word so translated here is derived from a Hebrew verb, 'to form bulbs'. Certainly the rose bush produces bulbous fruit, the hips, but the general consensus is that the plant described here is one of the bulb family. Crocus, narcissus, iris, daffodil are the usual candidates.

Sharon, or more correctly *the Sharon*, is the low coastal plain stretching south from Mount Carmel. In ancient times it was a swampy area, due to the presence of impermeable kurkar ridges running parallel to the shore which trapped the run-off from the Samaritan hills. The combination of low sandy hills and swampy lowlands produced heavy vegetation. Various types of wild flowers were abundant in the area.

The *lily of the valleys* is not our common white, bell-shaped plant of that name. The word may be derived from the root for 'six', *i.e.* six-leaved or six-petaled flower; but more likely it is cognate with the Egyptian and Akkadian words for the lotus or water lily, and may refer to any similarly shaped flower that grew along the fertile, watered *valleys* (Hebrew plural). Some commentators, on the basis of Song 5:13, argue for a red or reddish-purple colour for the flower, but no identification is certain.

2. The lover again, in playful mockery, picks up the imagery she has proposed. She is a *lily* indeed, but her beauty far surpasses the thorny weeds all around her. An alternate understanding of this verse is suggested by the fact that the rabbinic tradition links the word *thorns* with an identical root meaning a crevice in the rock. In this case, the girl's beauty is compared to the beautiful wild flowers which grow in the most unpromising rocky outcroppings.

She is his *darling* (NIV), his friend and companion, the most beautiful among the women.

f. The beloved's second request (2:3–7)

The Song opened with the beloved's urgent pleading to her lover as she realized that she was to share her love with him. Now she calls for aphrodisiacs on the one hand and requests on the other that love be not awakened until all is ready. After the request for his kisses (1:2), her desires are given further expression. She continues the comparison with plants and animals, then quickly moves on to her own excited response to his presence.

One of the unusual features of the Song is the major place the words of the girl have in it. Of the 117 verses in the book, 55 are directly from her lips, and another 19 are probably assigned to her. In the Song, as in much of the other ancient Near Eastern love poetry, the woman is the one who takes the initiative, and who is the more outspoken.[1] Similarly, in

---

[1] *Cf.* the Egyptian Love Songs. In the Simpson list, 23 of the 47 are spoken by the girl.

the Mesopotamian Ritual Marriage materials, much is placed on the girl's lips. Our contemporary attitude, where the girl is on the defensive and the man is the initiator, is a direct contrast with the attitude in the ancient world.

The section which begins in 2:3 and continues through 3:5 is really all of a piece, and any divisions are somewhat arbitrary. 2:14–15 is usually assigned to the lover, but it may, in fact, be part of the girl's speech which begins in 2:10 where she is reporting his words to her. Fortunately, it makes no difference to the sense of the passage if a break is made there.

A more obvious division occurs with 2:7 where the adjuration not to 'stir up love' appears for the first time in the Song. It appears in identical form in 3:5, and in somewhat truncated form again in 8:4 as a sort of refrain which ties several ideas together.

3. The *apple tree* to which the lover is compared is not certainly identifiable. Most versions translate the Hebrew word as *apple* (NEB *apricot*). The term is found in the Song at 2:5; 7:8 (Heb. 9) and 8:5, and elsewhere in the Old Testament only at Proverbs 25:11 and Joel 1:12. The fruit is aromatic (7:8),[1] with a sweet taste. In Joel, it is one of the important agricultural trees associated with the vine, pomegranate and date-palm. Of the trees native to Palestine, the citron was the one identified by the Targumic writers who commented on this passage. The very acidic taste of that fruit, however, makes this identification improbable. The apricot, although not native to Palestine, was grown there from Old Testament times and may have been introduced early enough to be the fruit in question. Although there is no clear evidence that the apple was cultivated in the ancient Near East, and the Proverbs passage speaks of 'apples' of gold, any of the aromatic, sweet, globe-shaped fruits, including the apple (*Malus pumila* or *Pyrus malus*), may be what is described here.

The *wood* (*forest*, NIV) is an uncultivated wild place. The Hebrew root *ya'ar* means a rugged, mountainous place, and although the word is apparently used in Ecclesiastes 2:6f. of a cultivated *park*, the JB *orchard* seems to be going beyond the meaning of the word.[2] Note the parallel between her words and his in the previous verse.

[1] The Heb. root means 'breath' or 'scent'.
[2] The same word is used in Song 5:1 where it is translated 'honeycomb'. *Cf.* the discussion there. See above, Subject Study: Garden, p. 55.

The literal meaning of the next clause is *in his* [or, *its*] *shadow I delighted and I sat down*. Most versions approximate to the AV *I sat down with great delight*, rendering the first Hebrew verb as if it were a noun. The NIV, however, catches the force of the construction best with *I delight to sit*.[1]

His shadow (*shade*, NIV, JB) here suggests delight and comfort. The meaning *protection*, common elsewhere in the Old Testament for this word (*e.g.* Gn. 19:8; Jdg. 9:15; Pss. 17:8; 91:1), is out of place here.

Some commentators have suggested that *fruit* is to be taken as equivalent to *lovemaking*. While the *apple* is frequently an erotic symbol,[2] such an interpretation is unnecessary here.

Taste is more correctly *palate*, often including the lips, teeth, and the whole mouth. The Hebrew word for *discipline* or *training* (*ḥānak*) is derived from the same root. The first step in teaching a child is the anointing of his lips with honey so that learning is identified with sweetness.[3] If this idea has any application in this text, the girl may be expressing her delight in the ways of love in which he has instructed her.

4. The practice of setting this verse to music and using it as a chorus celebrating the believer's relationship with Christ is widespread in the contemporary church. It is no doubt well-intentioned and could be broadly defended on the grounds that the Song illustrates the relation of Christ to his church (see above, p. 23). But such an application runs into serious difficulty if the text is correctly understood. The crux in the interpretation is the meaning of *bêt hayyāyin* (*banqueting house*; *wine-garden*, NEB) and the meaning of the root *dgl* in the second colon. The *bêt hayyāyin* is literally 'the house of wine'. This combination is. found only here in the Old Testament, although the expression *bêt mišteh* (*hayyāyin*) 'the house of drinking (of wine)', and *mišteh hayyāyin* 'wine-feast' are more frequent.[4] Idiomatically, the 'house of wine' could be the place where wine is grown (*i.e.* a vineyard), manufactured, stored,

---

[1] The Piel stem usually indicates intensification of the basic root. Here, that would translate as 'desire passionately' or 'with great delight'. Less frequently the Piel stem is used to express the active accomplishment of the state described by the related noun or adjective. That is the case here.

[2] *Cf.* T. H. Gaster, *Myth, Legend, and Custom in the Old Testament* (Harper & Row, 1969), p. 811.

[3] *Cf.* Marvin R. Wilson, 'The Jewish Concept of Learning: An Appreciation', *Christian Scholar's Review* 5, 1976, pp. 350–363, and *cf.* Pr. 22:6.

[4] *Cf.* Est. 7:8 for the full expression, and Est. 5:6; 7:2 for the latter.

or consumed. The frequent use of the outdoor motifs in the Song, particularly of the garden as a place for the lover's rendezvous, suggests that the vineyard itself is what is intended here.

A more difficult issue is the meaning of *dḡl*. Altogether there are 18 occurrences of this root in the Old Testament, 14 of the noun form and four verbal uses. Eight times, all in Numbers,[1] the versions translate 'standard' (or 'banner') 'of the camp of Judah, Reuben, *etc.*'. Five other references in Numbers[2] add a pronoun, 'his' or 'their' standards. The context for these thirteen references seems to require some sort of symbol – perhaps a flag or banner – which would serve to identify the various tribal units and which could be picked out easily in the complexities of the Hebrew camp. The sole remaining noun form is here in Song 2:3, with the pronoun attached, 'his *dḡl*'.

Most versions read *his banner over me was love*. The flying of a banner indicates possession, which is appropriate enough, although the military overtones seem out of place. But an examination of the literature indicates that there is no consensus among the translators as to the meaning of this phrase in this context. Our task, therefore, is to seek to break through this impasse and make contextual sense out of this difficult text.

A better understanding of this text, as well as of the four where a verbal form of the root is used,[3] is possible with the simple lexical meaning 'look on' for *dḡl*. This meaning is attested in the Akkadian *dagâlu*, 'to look with astonishment or admiration'; and on this basis, Gordis translated this colon as 'his look upon me was in love' (*i.e.* 'loving').[4] This translation also illuminates the other uses of *dḡl*. A 'banner' is something to 'look at' to find your place. Pope takes this one step further with a note that the Akkadian root *diglu* is also used in the sense of 'wish', *i.e.* desire or intent.[5] Thus this colon correctly reads 'and his wish regarding me was love-making' or more simply 'his intentions were to make love'. On love (or 'love-making'), *cf.* Song 1:4 and Subject Study: Love, pp. 60–63.

[1] Nu. 2:3, 10, 18, 25; 10:14, 18, 22, 25. [2] Nu. 1:52; 2:2, 17, 31, 34.
[3] Ps. 20:5; Song 5:10; 6:4, 10 (*q.v.*).
[4] Gordis, p. 81. *Cf.* R. Gordis, 'The root *dgl* in the Song of Songs', *JBL* 88, 1969, pp. 203f.
[5] Pope, p. 376.

5. The verbs in the first two cola, both imperatives (vs. NEB, *He refreshed me*), are infrequent in the Old Testament, and hence difficult to translate. Although the forms are masculine plural, the appeal seems to be directed to the lover, unless there is in this verse an anticipation of v. 7 addressed to the daughters of Jerusalem. More likely, this is simply a general appeal to anyone who is within hearing.

Sustain me (*stay me*, AV, ASV; *strengthen me*, NIV; *feed me*, JB; Heb. *sammᵉkûnî*). The normal meaning for the root is 'to place the hand on' something (*e.g.* a sacrificial animal, Lv. 1:4; 3:2, *etc.*), or to lean on something (2 Ki. 18:21; Am. 5:12); but in poetic sections the frequent meaning is to *support* or *sustain* (*e.g.* Pss. 3:5; 51:12; Is. 26:3). The Piel form used here occurs only this once in the Old Testament, and probably is to be understood as an actualization of the poetic meaning (see note on 2:3, *delight to sit*).

Refresh me (*comfort me*, AV; *restore me*, JB; *he revived me*, NEB; Heb. *rappᵉdûnî*) occurs only three times in the Old Testament.[1] The meaning appears to be 'stretch out' or 'spread' (bedclothes) (Jb. 17:13; 41:30), and hence to prepare any kind of supporting couch or bed (*i.e.* a place of restoration from sickness, fatigue, *etc.*, as in the third colon).

Coupled with these two difficult verbal forms are two difficult nouns. AV *flagons* is corrected in all the later versions to *raisins* or *raisin-cakes* (JB). The word occurs only four times in the Old Testament.[2] From these contexts it is apparent that this is some sort of food associated with religious festivals (so 2 Sa. 6:19). The Isaiah and Hosea passages put these in the context of pagan cultic celebrations, and Jeremiah (7:18; 44:18f.) describes 'cakes' made to *portray* (ASV mg.) the 'Queen of Heaven'. As is well known, the worship of the 'Queen of Heaven' (Ishtar) was essentially a fertility cult centred around the extensive sexual rites. It is apparent that these 'cakes' were made either in the shape of a nude female with exaggerated sexual organs, or frequently in triangular shape representing the female genitalia. *Raisin-cakes* are therefore a highly erotic symbol.

Apples also are generally considered to have the powers of an aphrodisiac (*cf.* above on 2:3 and the bibliography there),

[1] A derived noun *rᵉpîdāh*, the *arm* or *back* of a palanquin, appears once in Song 3:10.
[2] 2 Sa. 6:19; Song 2:5; Is. 16:7; Ho. 3:1.

and combined with the *raisin-cakes*, will restore her strength for more lovemaking, because, she says, *I* (emphatic) *am sick* (*faint*, NIV) *with love. (Cf.* 1:3.)

6. *O that* assumes an exclamation here, but the text gives no justification for that (*cf.* NEB, NIV). The rest of the verse, repeated in 8:3, is straightforward. Only *embrace* needs comment. The word is not frequent in the Old Testament, and is used both of friendly greeting (Gn. 48:10) and of sexual union (Pr. 5:20). The position of the left hand *under* her head would suggest that the two are lying down and that with the right hand he is enfolding and caressing her.

7. This unit recurs at 3:5 in this exact form and in 8:4 slightly modified. NEB and JB attribute all three to the lover, others to the beloved. It is impossible to decide grammatically, but the context suggests a continuation of the girl's speech. It is possible that 2:7 and 3:5 serve as an *inclusio* to begin and end the second section, but it seems better to take 2:7 as the conclusion of the first section.

Adjure or *charge* (AV, NIV, JB, NEB) is a common Old Testament word, and in the Hiphil form used here has the meaning 'beg urgently' rather than the idea of taking an oath. According to Deuteronomy 6:13; 10:2-, oaths are to be taken only in the name of the LORD – anything else is idolatry and forbidden (*cf.* Mt. 5:33–37).

Daughters of Jerusalem: cf. 1:3.

By the gazelles [Heb. *ṣᵉḇā'ôt*] or *the hinds* [Heb. *'ayᵉlôt*] *of the field.* This unit is found in 3:5, but is omitted from 8:4. LXX reads 'in the powers [Gk. *dynamesin, cf.* Mk. 13:25; Acts 8:10; Rom. 8:38] and strengths [Gk. *ischysesin*]', taking *ṣᵉḇā'ôt* as 'hosts' or 'angelic powers' [*cf.* Yahweh Sabaoth, LORD of Hosts (angels)], and *'ayᵉlôt* from a root meaning 'strength' or 'help'. NEB renders this *by the spirits and goddesses of the field*, following the lead of the LXX. All of this is unnecessary, since the words are common enough as the names of wild animals. 'Gazelle' is more correct than the AV *roe*, as Acts 9:36 indicates.[1] This graceful member of the antelope family is still common in Israel, frequenting pasture lands as well as being able to survive in the near-desert areas of the Negev.

[1] Gk. *dorkas* 'gazelle', Aramaic *tabitha* is the direct equivalent of the Hebrew. In Ugarit and Egypt, the gazelle is often associated with the god Rešep, who like many others, is a god of both fertility and death (war). *Cf.* above, p. 19, n. 2, Subject Study: Garden, pp. 57–59, and commentary on 8:4.

Hinds (NIV *does*) are the females of the deer. Three species were known in biblical Palestine: the Red Deer, the Fallow Deer and the Roe Deer. The former two were a common source of meat (*cf.* Dt. 12:22), and were easy to take because they run in herds. The Roe Deer is considerably smaller, about 28 inches at the shoulder, a graceful little creature that is much more solitary in its habits. (*Cf.* Song 2:9, 17; 8:14.)

Fields: open country, occasionally cultivated areas, but not 'gardens' which were often walled.

To follow the LXX/NEB in this section tends too closely to polytheism to be correct, although these may be here simply an effort to soften the oath by the substitution of similar sounding words (of which there are many English equivalents, *e.g.* 'gosh', 'darn', *etc.*). To swear by animals seems equally senseless. Interpreters who accept the Inanna/Dumuzi sacred marriage source for the Song see this as a reference to two animals noted for their sexual potency. No explanation is entirely satisfactory, although the potency suggestion seems least problematical.

The two verbs in the third colon are different forms of a common root. The meaning is not *stir up*, *i.e.* a repetition of the same act, but is rather first the act of awakening or *summoning* something, and then doing what is necessary to *sustain* the activity already begun, *i.e.* being so fully awakened that sleep becomes impossible. *Cf.* 5:2.

Love, not *my love* (AV, JB, NEB), which could be misconstrued either as the girl's own feelings, or as her lover himself (*cf.* NEB). This is more general: love itself (*cf.* Commentary on 1:3f.).

Until it please. The verb form here is feminine singular; NEB *until she is ready* is possible if the speaker is the lover, but this seems unlikely, as *love* itself is a feminine noun in Hebrew. The verb, which is frequent in the Old Testament, conveys the idea of being willing, desirous, and enjoying something. It often has sexual overtones (Gn. 34:19; Dt. 21:14; Est. 2:14; 3:5), but it is also used simply of being ready for something or being agreeable to a suggestion. This request to let love take its natural course concludes both the first and second major sections of the Song.

The request here can be understood in one of two ways: either, as Delitzsch suggests, 'don't interrupt the sweet dream of love she is enjoying [so NIV, *disturb*], by calling her back to the reality of the present situation', or, as is more likely in the context, 'don't start the process of loving exchange until the opportunity and appropriate occasion is present'. If Delitzsch's suggestion is adopted, there would be no ground for the girl's excited reaction to her lover's approach in the next section. For her the reality of his coming is far better than any dream of love.

II. FOUND, AND LOST – AND FOUND (2:8 – 3:5)

The second major division begins with a response to the request of 2:7 and concludes with a reprise of the same plea. Although the lover is pictured as present and speaking to his beloved, his speeches are reported at second hand (see 2:10). A series of remembered, or perhaps imagined, exchanges that express their love are suddenly terminated as the beloved turns and finds that she is alone.

a. The lover's arrival (2:8–9)

The beloved's ruminations on her lover are interrupted by the sound of his approach.

8. *The voice* takes the most common meaning of the Hebrew. JB *I hear* assumes a form that is not present in the text. NIV *listen*, NEB *hark* suggest it is the sound either of his voice or his footsteps approaching. The context supports the latter, which makes a nice parallel with *look* in the second colon.

The parallelism is carried out in the second half of the verse, *mountains and hills* being a common combination in Hebrew poetry (*e.g.* Is. 40:4; Ezk. 6:13). There are often cultic connotations associated with these 'high places' (*e.g.* 1 Ki. 20:23; 2 Ki. 16:4), but that seems unnecessary here.

Leaping (Heb. *dālaḡ*, five times in the Old Testament) and *bounding* (Heb. *qāp̄aṣ*, seven times) are usually taken in parallel. The root meaning of *qāp̄aṣ* is to draw together, shut (*e.g.* Dt. 15:7; 'shut the hand'). The Piel form used here may mean 'jumping by contracting the body' or 'running doubled over' (so BDB, p. 891), but the root meaning may be present, as the lover 'closes the distance' between himself and the beloved by his rapid approach. Note the progression from the first sound of his coming until he stands at the wall (v. 9).

9. *My beloved* (see Subject Study: Lover (Beloved), pp. 64f.). Her analogy from the wild animals continues, picking up the imagery of v. 7. These are the same creatures, except that these are masculine forms and the deer is a *young* one. Now the gap is closed, and her lover has arrived.[1]

Wall (Heb. *kōtel*) is not just 'garden wall' but rather the wall of the house. This is the only occurrence of the Hebrew word in the Old Testament, although the Aramaic word is used of the wall of the rebuilt temple (Ezr. 5:8) and of the palace wall where Belshazzar saw his downfall written (Dn. 5:5).[2]

RSV *gazing* is more suitable than NEB *peeping* for the Hebrew *mašgîaḥ*. The word occurs only three times in the Old Testament, but the contexts of the other two demand the idea *gaze* or *survey*. In Psalm 33:14, the LORD enthroned 'looks forth on all the inhabitants of the earth', and in Isaiah 14:16, the fallen king of Babylon, Lucifer, is stared at in disgust.

RSV *looking* is preferred to NIV *peering* (Heb. *mēṣîṣ*). This is the only occurrence of this word in the Old Testament, although there is an identical root meaning 'sprout' or 'shoot' which occurs five times in the Psalms and three times elsewhere.[3] NEB *glancing* is also somewhat weak.

Windows and *lattices* are both plurals, perhaps suggesting the lover flitting from window to window to get a better view. *Lattice* (Heb. *ḥᵃrakkîm*) occurs only here, but a verbal form is found in Proverbs 12:27. Neither context is decisive, although the parallel with *window* suggests some sort of opening, perhaps a ventilation hole, in the wall.

The AV, reversing the picture with the lover looking *out* from the window and *shewing himself through the lattice*, strains the text.

b. His first request (2:10–13)

After the introductory colon, which is couched in standard idiom, these verses form a self-contained unit marked off by

[1] See Introduction, p. 40, n. 1, on Egyptian Love Poetry with gazelles and encounters.
[2] Pope, p. 391, identifies an Akkadian parallel *kutallu*, 'backside', or the Arabic *kawṭal*, 'stern of a ship', which may suggest the 'back wall' of the house, off the street, away from public view.
[3] Nu. 17:23; Pss. 72:16; 90:6; 92:7; 103:15; 132:18; Is. 27:6; Ezk. 7:10.

the *Arise, my love* sequence. The lover pleads for her to join him in a romp in the spring countryside.

10. The urgency of his request is emphasized by the Hebrew imperatives with the pronouns following: 'get you up' and 'come you away'. The call to 'get up' may refer back to the mood of vv. 5f. where her love has prostrated her. The second verb is the common 'walk'. The dual invitation is to a pleasant stroll away from the city simply to enjoy each other's company.

My darling (NIV); *cf.* 1:9; 2:2. *My beautiful one* (NIV); *cf.* 1:8.

11. The introductory conjunction *kî* and the demonstrative *hinnēh* tie this colon to the preceding by drawing her attention to the reason for the invitation. NEB *now* lacks sufficient emphasis to be satisfactory.

Winter (Heb. *seṭān*), a loan-word from Aramaic, occurs only this once in the Old Testament. It is used in the Targum on Genesis 8:22 as a comment on *ḥōrep*, 'winter, the time of sowing crops'. The parallel with *gešem*, 'heavy rain', in the last colon acknowledges that in Palestine winter is the rainy season. Snow is not common, except in the higher elevations. The three verbs almost personify the winter rains as a traveller who has passed through and has gone.

12. *The flowers*. This is probably a diminutive from a root meaning 'to shine' or 'sparkle' (so BDB), as do small spring wild flowers amid the green of the foliage.

Appear is the same verb that was used in 1:6, 'gaze', and which reappears in 2:14 with the same meaning.

Earth and *land* are different translations of the same Hebrew word *'ereṣ*. The two uses in this verse are the only ones in the Song, although it is common elsewhere in the Old Testament.[1]

The time (NIV *season*) *of singing has come.* AV reads *the singing of birds*, but there is no textual evidence for adding the birds; the Hebrew word *zāmir* is not normally used of bird-songs.[2] There are three separate and apparently unrelated Hebrew roots *zmr* from which the form *zāmir* could be derived. The most common (about 115 times) is 'to make music', 'hum',

---

[1] Appeal is frequently made to this passage to support a cultic interpretation of the Song (see above, pp. 32–34, 42–44, 57–59). The fertility rituals of the ancient Near East focused on the need for sympathetic magic to guarantee the fruitfulness of the land, but this element was never part of orthodox Old Testament religion. It is notably absent from the Song.

[2] *Cf.* Delitzsch, p. 51, n. 1.

'sing', and the derivatives include 'songs', 'instrumental tunes', 'melodies', *etc.*[1] Next, occurring about eighteen times, is the word for 'cut' or 'prune' vines or trees (and the derivative *mazmērâ*, 'pruning hook'), and finally a root used only rarely (*e.g.* Gn. 43:11; Dt. 14:5) of choice fruits or animals. BDB (p. 274) takes the 'prune' meaning for this passage. RV mg. follows this, as does Pope, p. 395. This is really the traditional understanding, going all the way back to the LXX which has *tomē* 'cut, prune, incise' here. Although the Gezer calendar (*c.* 925 BC, *ANET*, p. 320) puts two months between 'harvest' and 'vine-tending', Pope argues, on the basis of Isaiah 18:4–6, that the 'pruning time' coincided with the formation of the green grapes, and that pruning was carried out then. While that is possible, it seems from the context that it is more likely that the Isaiah passage is talking about *premature* pruning, *i.e.* the land will be desolate *before* the harvest.

Singing may apply here to some sort of ritual singing. The word is widely used in that context both in the titles of Akkadian ritual songs to Tammuz and in the biblical uses of *zᵉmîr* 'song'.[2] Gordis identifies the *zᵉmîr* of Isaiah 25:5 as a 'secular' song: 'the song of the ruthless is stilled'; but since this term (Heb. *ʿārîṣ*) is used of the oppressors of Israel (*e.g.* Assyria and Babylon) who will themselves be destroyed,[3] these may have pagan cultic meaning even here. The 'songs' of the 'ruthless' may well have been the songs sung to the gods of Assyria and Babylon by their victorious armies (*cf.* Is. 36:18–20). This same word was used by Rabbi Aqiba in his comment about making the Song of Solomon a 'secular' song by 'trilling' it in the banquet halls.[4]

As is frequently the case in the Song, none of these explanations is entirely satisfactory. 'Pruning' is easiest to defend linguistically, but breaks the parallelism and runs into

[1] The word *mizmôr* appears in 57 Psalm titles as 'A Psalm of . . .'.

[2] The best preserved, but still fragmentary, Babylonian ritual text relating to the Tammuz/Ishtar cult is that published in Lambert, pp. 98–135. According to the tablet (BM 41107 obv. I:6), the ritual takes place 'as in the month Tammuz' *i.e.* the fourth month (June/July). That was the time of the grape harvest (and later pruning). It is much too late for the spring season, which in Palestine begins in early February, with the dry season already beginning by late April or early May. Old Testament uses include 2 Sa. 23:1; Jb. 35:10; Pss. 95:2; 119:54.

[3] Is. 49:25; Je. 15:21. *Cf.* Gordis, p. 6, n. 30.

[4] See Introduction, p. 52.

difficulty agriculturally; songs from human voices are no more prevalent in spring than at other times; and the evidence for cultic ritual is so weak that this proposal is extremely unlikely. Although it cannot be argued conclusively, AV 'singing of birds' fits the context best.

Turtledove (AV *turtle*; Heb. *tôr*, LXX *trygōn*; *Streptopelia turtur*). This species is primarily a migratory spring/summer resident of Palestine (*cf.* Je. 8:7), whose distinctive cooing call is one of the signs of spring. The *dove* mentioned elsewhere in the Song (*e.g.* 1:5; 2:14, *etc.*) is the genus *Columba livia* (Heb. *yônâ*), the Rock Dove, which is a permanent resident in large numbers in Israel. The NIV use of *dove* to translate both *tôr* (v. 12) and *yônâ* (v. 14) is confusing.

13. *The fig tree*, next to the olive, was the most important tree in ancient Israel (*cf.* Jotham's parable, Jdg. 9:1–21), and, like the grapevine, was a symbol of peace and security (1 Ki. 4:25; Mi. 4:3f.; Zc. 3:10). The fig tree blossoms mid to late March, and the early fig (Heb. *pagâ*; LXX *olynthos* or *olonthos*) begins to form immediately. This sterile summer fig is the precursor of the true fig which is produced on new growth and matures in August or September. A tree which does not produce these early figs will not yield a crop of real figs either (*cf.* Mt. 21:18f.).

Put forth (NEB *ripen*; Heb. *ḥānaṭ*) occurs only this once in the Song, and only four other times in the Old Testament (Gn. 50:2 (twice), 3, 26), where it is translated 'embalm'. There seems to be no link between the two meanings, unless it has to do with the change of colour of the skin that is associated with the embalming process.

The fig was a common sexual symbol in the ancient Near East, but there seems to be little evidence that the early fig or the flowering tree had these associations

Vines is the general term for any clinging-type plant, but in the Old Testament is used almost exclusively for the grapevine.

Blossom (AV *tender grapes*; Heb. *sᵉmādar*) occurs in the Old Testament only here and at Song 2:15; 7:12. No suggestion as to derivation has won widespread acceptance. The rabbis identified the *sᵉmādar* as the stage of the tiny grapes after the blossoms disappear (so AV), but the expression 'give forth fragrance' would be meaningless at that stage of the development. Blossoms seems to fit the context better. Recent studies of material from Ebla suggest that the blossom (Heb. *sᵉmāḏar*) is really a place-name, 'Semadar', from which a specially good variety of grapevine was imported into Israel. This understanding of the term would make it possible to render the phrase 'the Semadar vines' in each of these references.[1]

The unit closes with a reprise of the *arise* invitation of 2:10. The slight difference between *lāḵ* in v. 10 and *lāḵᵉy* in v 13 may be due to a transcriptional error by a scribe in v. 13, as the Massoretes thought, or else, as Delitzsch suggests, to the preservation in v 13 of a northern Palestine dialectical variation (*cf.* Mt. 26:73) There is no difference in the meaning or translation.

c. The lover's intercession (2:14–15)

Whether both these verses are spoken by the lover is a moot point. Certainly v. 14 is his, after the self-contained song in vv. 10–13. One possibility is that v. 15 may be a separate stanza of that song, or another similar one called to mind by the 'vine' motif in v. 13.

14. *My dove.* This word, here a pet name for the beloved, appears for the second time (*cf.* 1:15), and will re-appear again in 4:1; 5:2, 12; 6:9. This is the common Rock Dove (*Columba livia*) not the turtledove (v. 12). Its nesting preference is sheltered ledges or caves in the cliffs of low mountains. Delitzsch identifies this as the Wood Pigeon (*Columba palumbus*), a slightly larger bird that is also a permanent resident. Its nesting preference, however, is for farmland or woods, rather than rocky cliffs. The dove is a common symbol of love (the 'lovebird'). It was associated with Inanna, the fertility goddess, in the Mesopotamian literature and with Aphrodite/Venus in the classical material.[2]

Clefts of the rock, or more properly 'the secure hiding-places in the crevices' (*cf.* Ob. 3 and Je. 49:16 where Edom's desert fortresses are described in these words), is parallel to the next colon.

Covert of the cliff (AV *secret places of the stairs*). Gordis (p. 83) suggests 'terraces' used for agricultural cultivation, and LXX reads 'fortification wall', but neither of these seems as satisfac-

[1] *Cf.* M. Dahood, 'Ebla, Ugarit, and the Bible', in G. Pettinato, *The Archives of Ebla* (Doubleday, 1981), p. 312.

[2] See above, pp. 49, 57–59.

tory a parallel to 'crevice' as the RSV or as NIV *hiding-places on the cliffs*. BDB identifies the term (Heb. *maḏrēḡâ*) as an Aramaic loan-word with a root meaning 'to go step by step' or 'to lift'. In Ugaritic a *mdrn* is a particular type of bladed weapon and the soldiers who used them were *mdrgl*. This may suggest a meaning 'cut' or 'pass' in a mountain, or, more generally, any crevice that provided shelter. The Hebrew word occurs only here and in Ezekiel 38:20.

Just as the doves take refuge in the cliffs (*cf.* Je. 48:28) and when frightened are reluctant to leave, so the girl shyly waits in the secluded protection of the house (v. 9). Her lover's entreaty continues with the seeing/hearing motif in a chiasmus that encourages her to come out of hiding.

Let me 'gaze upon' (as in 1:6) your *face*. The latter is too limited. The Heb. *mar'eh* is more properly *vision* or *appearance*. He wants to feast his eyes on the loveliness of her whole person, and fill his ears with the pleasing sweetness of her *voice*. This is the same word used in v. 12 of the voice of the turtledove, the soft, gentle cooing.

15. This verse is a problem. The verb form is imperative, masculine plural, but there is no indication whether the speaker is male or female. All that is clear is that 'for us' is plural, *i.e.* it is probably not the girl herself speaking. Delitzsch, who posits a hunting party here, has Solomon address his companions. Lehrman[1] understands this as the girl's response (in song) to her lover's plea of v. 14. Gordis takes it as 'patently symbolic'[2] of either a plea to save her chastity, or as an open invitation to promiscuity. This latter he rejects, rightly, as contrary to the whole tenor of the Song. Lys[3] sees a whole series of *double entendres* here that cover an overt plea for defloration – 'she is in blossom, there is no fruit'. The lover is, in the eyes of the bystanders, like a little fox who simply destroys the beautiful and makes a home in the deserted place (*cf.* La. 5:18; Ezk. 13:4). Some ground for this word-play is evident in the various meanings assigned to the words. *Foxes* (Heb. *šû'āl*) or *jackal* (NEB) is from a root *š'l* which also means 'hollow' or 'deep place', and the verbal root *ḥbl* can mean either 'ruin, destroy' (Jb. 17:1), or 'be pregnant, in travail' (Song 8:5), or 'pledge' (Ex. 22:26).

Vineyard. See on 1:6; 2:3, and Subject Study: Garden, p. 60.

---

[1] Lehrman, p. 9.   [2] Gordis, p. 83.   [3] Lys, p. 171.

If the erotic symbolism is indeed evident, the vineyard may again be an erotic metaphor.

Seerveld (p. 30) gives these lines to the girl, identifying it as 'a ditty they used to sing together'. Lehrman suggests vv. 14f. may be snatches of a folk-song associated with the harvest festival.

d. The beloved's response (2:16–17)

Delitzsch considers v. 16 to be connected with vv. 14 and 15 rather than beginning a new section, but as noted, v. 15 can hardly be spoken by the girl. Verse 16 is repeated at 6:3 (with the first words reversed), and at 7:10 in a modified form. The expression emphasizes the mutual devotion and exclusiveness of the lovers for each other. If the erotic imagery is in fact present in v. 15, this verse stands in strong contrast to the wanton rampage through the vineyard. Here her lover is not the spoiler, but the gentle, caring companion. See pp. 64f.

16. *He pastures his flock.* The Hebrew participle *harō'eh* occurs nearly one hundred times, and is the common term for feeding domestic animals (*cf.* 1:7f.), *i.e.* performing the function of a shepherd. Metaphorically, the king or leader of a people was a 'shepherd', *e.g.* Dummuzi (Tammuz) was 'shepherd' of the Akkadians, and David the 'shepherd' of Israel (2 Sa. 5:2). A few times the participle is used of the act of feeding (*e.g.* Jb. 1:14; Pr. 29:3; Song 4:5). The NIV *he browses* (AV *he feedeth*) follows this latter option which seems to fit the context better (*cf.* 7:10–12).

Lilies, cf. 2:1f. If 5:13 can be borrowed here, the 'feeding in the lilies' may be a circumlocution for sharing kisses or more intimate behaviour.[1]

17. Although the preposition can be translated 'while' (*cf.* 1:12), 'until' is more common and fits the context better here. Many of the older commentators took the opening colon to mean the approach of evening when the shadows get gradually longer until they are swallowed up by darkness (ASV *until the day be cool*). The expression is repeated at 4:6. The Hebrew verb *pûaḥ*, which occurs only fifteen times in the Old Testament, means to 'blow' or 'breathe out' (*cf.* Song 4:16),[2] and

[1] See Pope, pp. 405–407.
[2] Six of the seven uses in Proverbs (6:19; 12:17; 14:5, 25; 19:5, 9) refer to 'uttering [breathing out] lies', and the seventh (29:8) is rendered 'scoffers'.

here means the breaking of day when the breezes stir and the protecting shadows (*cf.* 2:3) of night slip away, and the lovers' tryst must end.[1]

The last bicolon picks up the imagery from 2:8f. (*cf.* 2:7).

Rugged mountains or *rugged hills* (NIV); *mountains of Bether* (AV, ASV). No known geographic site seems entirely suitable, although four are possible. In 2 Samuel 2:29, Abner's army marched 'through all Bithron' (AV) until 'they came to Mahanaim' (AV). The Hebrew is *bitrôn* and the NIV margin suggests 'ravine'. If the NIV (mg.) and the AV text are correct, the 'Bithron ravine' would be either the Jabbok River gorge or the Wadi Shuweib, assuming Mahanaim is to be identified with Tell er Reheil where the road to Bashan fords the Jabbok.[2] Kirbet el Yahudi, seven miles south-west of Jerusalem, a mile north of the Bethlehem-Gath highway, is another possible site for Bether (Beththter). A small town and fortress surmount a hill surrounded on all sides by deep canyons. It is included in the LXX list of cities in Judah's territory (Jos. 15:59a, omitted from Heb. text), and in AD 135 was the site of the final defeat of Simon bar Kokhba and his revolutionary followers. The other two sites, Bethar (et Tira) on the Sharon plain, twenty miles west of Nablus (Shechem), and Bether (Kirbet el Bitar), six miles west-south-west of Beersheba, do not have the appropriate geographic features to make these possibilities.

The word *beter* occurs only four times in the Old Testament: here, at Genesis 15:10, and at Jeremiah 34:18, 19. The verbal root occurs twice in Genesis 15:10, where the meaning obviously is to divide an animal in a sacrificial ritual. The JB

Pss. 10:5 and 12:5 are similar, describing the wicked; Ezk. 21:31 uses the word of the fire of God's wrath which will be 'blown' upon the Ammonites. The final use is in Hab. 2:3 where the vision 'hastens to the end – it will not lie'. The imagery of the certainty of dawn at the appointed time is clearly present.

[1] *Cf.* the Egyptian love poem (Harris Papyrus V: 6–8. Simpson, p. 304, no. 14). 'The voice of the turtledove speaks out. It says:/day breaks, which way are you going?/Lay off, little bird,/must you so scold me?/I found my lover on his bed,/and my heart was sweet to excess./We said:/I shall never be far away from you/while my hand is in your hand,/and I shall stroll with you/in every favorite place./He set me up as the first of the girls/and he does not break my heart./'

[2] For the two possible sites of Mahanaim, see the *Macmillan Bible Atlas* (Macmillan, ²1977), maps 10, 99, 101. *Cf.* commentary on Song 6:13. This text may give some support to this identification.

rendering *mountains of the covenant* is based on this passage which established a 'covenant' with Abraham through this 'division' of the sacrifice. But the 'mountain of the covenant' was Mount Zion, and long before David's time was a settled area that was hardly the place where wild gazelles and deer would be found.

The idea of *rugged* mountains is derived from the meaning 'divide', *i.e.* they are mountains of such a quality that they themselves are 'divided' (rank on rank of them), or that they 'divide' or separate the lovers. Lys (*cf.* 2:15) sees another erotic touch here, with the 'divisions' being the breasts of the beloved (*cf.* 4:5f.; 7:7).[1] NEB *hills where cinnamon grows* takes *beter* as a synonym for 'spices' (Heb. *beśāmîm*) from 8:14. There is no warrant for this. 'Cinnamon', which occurs in 4:14, is an entirely different word.

e. The beloved's search (3:1–5)

This unit is one of the few in the Song where the vocabulary and syntax are relatively straightforward. The only problem is with the interpretation. The story-line is clear: the beloved, in her bed at night, seeks intently[2] for her lover. Unable to find him there, she goes out into the street, encounters the watchmen, enquires of them, and immediately afterwards finds her lover and brings him back to her home and her mother's bedchamber. The unit closes with a repeat of the request found at 2:7.

Lys takes this as evidence of a pre-arranged rendezvous which for some unexplained reason the lover was late in keeping. Delitzsch and others, perhaps correctly, take this as a 'dream sequence' the girl is recounting. This approach evades the overt suggestion of regular sexual encounters having already taken place between the girl and her lover – a thing unthinkable, for Delitzsch, in such a modest one as the heroine of the Song. Pope avoids the problem with the idea that the girl, even in the privacy of her room, could not get her lover out of her thoughts. Those who see the Song as a cult ritual identify this section with the 'Search-Find' motif

---

[1] Lys, pp. 172–174.
[2] Piel, *cf.* above on 2:3, p. 90, n. 1.

known from the ancient Near Eastern liturgies.[1]

1. *My bed.* This is the common word for bed, distinct from the word for 'couch' in 1:16. In Ezekiel 23:17 the connotation is 'love bed',[2] and in Genesis 49:4 and Numbers 31:17ff. is used with overt sexual meaning. This is its only use in the Song.

By night. NIV *all night long* catches the force of the Hebrew plural 'nights' as well as NEB *night after night*.

Sought (Heb. *bāqaš*) is very common in the Old Testament, and is used both literally and figuratively. It is always a conscious act, frequently requiring a great deal of effort (*e.g.* 1 Sa. 10:14; Pr. 2:4) but with no guarantee of success. The repetition here strengthens the figure.

But did not find, NIV (Heb. *māṣā'*) can mean to find after a diligent search (*e.g.* Gn. 2:20; 1 Sa. 20:21, 36), or to stumble upon accidentally (2 Ki. 22:8).

My soul loves. NIV *heart* and NEB *true love* lack the broad meaning of the Hebrew *nepeš*, 'soul'. *Cf.* 1:7. The NEB and RSV add a fourth colon, *I called him, but he gave no answer,* to complete the parallel with 5:6. It is not found in the MT.

2. *I will arise* (NEB). *Cf.* 2:10, 13, as she now acts on the earlier invitation. *Go about, i.e.* 'go around' (Heb. *sābab*), traverse (*cf.* 2:17 'turn') the streets and squares of the city – *i.e.* the whole place. *The city,* perhaps Jerusalem (*cf.* 3:5), but any walled city as opposed to an unwalled town or village is possible. Gk. *polis* generally has political connotations, whereas the Heb. *'îr* means primarily a protected (*i.e.* walled) place. The second and third lines repeat v. 1, but with the change to the determinative 'I will'.

3. The impact of the poetry is lost in most of the translations. Verse 2 ends with the anguished cry 'And I found him not' (Heb. *welō' meṣā'tîw*) and v. 3 begins *They found me* (Heb. *meṣā'unî*) *the watchmen, as they went around the city.* The word order in the second colon also reverses the order of the same experience in v. 2. *He whom my soul loves, have you seen [him]?* It does not occur to her that the local constables would have no idea who it was she was seeking – she knows her lover, and therefore the whole world does too!

---

[1] See T. Jacobsen, 'Religious Drama in Ancient Mesopotamia', *Unity and Diversity*, pp. 67, 90, 93, and *cf.* the Anat-Baal Cycle, *ANET*, 140a–141a, especially col. ii, lines 27–30 and col. iv, lines 25–45.

[2] Heb. *miškāb dôdîm, cf.* Subject Study: Lover (Beloved), pp. 64f.

4. Immediately after leaving them she finds her lover. *Held* (NEB *seized*) is satisfactory (*cf.* 2:15 *catch the foxes*), but 'clutched and refused to slacken her embrace' catches the urgency and relief of the discovery better. Still clinging to him, she leads him gently but forcefully to her mother's house[1] and into the maternal bedroom (*cf.* 1:4, and 8:2).

5. This closing element of the second unit of the Song is an exact repetition of 2:7.

III. CONSUMMATION (3:6 – 5:1)

This unit is in many ways the heart of the Song, and verses 4:16 – 5:1 the central pivot around which the rest of the Song revolves. The broad progression in the relationship which has been traced thus far now develops into the actual wedding sequence and the consummation of their love. Her beauty surpasses the beauty of the king's chariots. Her person is more desirable to her lover than all the attractions of the city and the land. Her invitation (4:16) to him to 'take possession of his vineyard' leads to the nuptial embrace.

a. A wedding song for Solomon (3:6–11)

These six verses pose one of the most difficult questions in the interpretation of the Song: how does this unit fit with the rest of the book? At first glance it seems to have nothing to do with the context: 3:4 records the girl's determination to take her lover to her own home; 4:1–7 is a detailed description of the physical charms of the bride. This section is a description of a procession with soldiers and one or more palanquin/chariot/sedan-chair conveyances, and a wedding celebration for King Solomon. What is the connection, if any? The specific problems of the unit have to do with the naming of Solomon in vv. 7, 9, and 11; the presence of what have been identified as 'nationalistic' elements in the passage – the use of *Israel* (v. 7), *Zion* (v. 11); the appearance of the military motif (vv. 7f.); and the question of the identification of the protagonist in the section.

---

[1] *Cf.* 1:6 and Introduction, pp. 30f. *Chamber* (Heb. *ḥeḏer*) is the common word for a room. In modern Hebrew it is most frequently used of a school classroom (*cf.* 8:2), but the context here requires the translation 'bedroom'.

The simplest solution is to conclude that the unit has no contextual connection. If the Song is nothing more than a haphazard collection, there is no need to try to identify the reason for its presence here. But if the Song does have some inherent cohesiveness and unity, that solution is too facile.

Alternatively, the view that the Song is a nuptial celebration and that this section, like Psalm 45, celebrates that union, has many adherents.[1] Seerveld takes this poem as describing the return of Solomon to the palace and the harem to continue his seduction of the Shulammite (pp. 34f.); but as Delitzsch noted, with the joyful consent of the mother-in-law (v. 11), 'the seduction fable is shattered' (p. 69). Delitzsch interprets this as the bringing of the bride from her isolated Galilean home to her new 'home' in the royal city, and while the 'royal wedding' interpretation is probably inaccurate, the identification of the girl rather than Solomon as 'the one coming up' (v. 6) is probably correct. This provides the best clue to the link between this unit and the following section: the parallel and contrast of the girl's beauty with the beauty of the royal chariot (*Behold* 3:11/4:1); the wilderness/garden contrast (3:6/4:15); the use of myrrh and frankincense (3:6/4:6, 14); and the aromatic wood from Lebanon (3:9/4:11) serve to illustrate how the link is established.

6. *Who is this* (AV, ASV, NIV) or *what is this* (RSV, JB, NEB) (Heb. *mî zō't*). The problem is to decide whether *this* (*zō't*) refers to a person or a thing. The form is feminine singular, and could refer either to the girl or to the 'bed' (v. 7, AV) which is also a feminine noun. In either case it cannot be Solomon (or the 'king') who is described. To decide between the two options is a little more difficult, but the use of *mî* presumes a person rather than a thing (which would normally be introduced by *mâ*). The procession is still at a distance, but the panoply and wealth of the entourage make it obvious that this is a noble, if not a royal, wedding-train that has appeared. Pope observes correctly that if there is any contextual continuity, the answer to the question must be obvious –

---

[1] There are some superficial resemblances between this section and Ps. 45, *e.g.* the military motif, perfumes, the wedding motif itself, and some vocabulary similarities, but there are enough significant differences that one needs to be cautious in identifying these two poems. *Cf.* above, Introduction, pp. 26–32, and see R. Gordis, 'A Wedding Song for Solomon,' *JBL* 63, 1949, pp. 263–270.

that it is the bride herself.[1] This same idiom appears in Song 6:10, again with no answer in the text, and in 8:5 where the second half of the colon demands the answer 'the girl' (bride).

Coming up. Jerusalem, like all pre-Roman cities in the ancient Near East, was built on a hill, and any traveller literally 'came up' to the city.

Wilderness is better than *desert* (JB, NIV). The latter brings to mind vast expanses of sand like the Sahara, while the Hebrew word more properly means an area without permanent settlements, but which can serve as pastureland. The word is very common, occurring about 270 times in the Old Testament. The 'wilderness' was the home of the Israelites for the forty years between the exodus from Egypt and the conquest of the land under Joshua, and in Israelite thinking was remembered as the place where the refugees had been forged into the strong nation that could carry out God's command to possess the land. The allegorists have made much of this in the interpretation of the Song, but the context makes no such demand (*cf.* 8:5).

Pillars of smoke, AV, ASV, retains the plural of the Heb. *tîmᵃrôt.* This term occurs only here and in Joel 2:30. It is not the common word *'ammûd* used elsewhere for the pillar of cloud and fire that guided the Israelites in the wilderness.

Perfumed with (Heb. *mᶜqutteret,* passive form with force similar to Piel).[2] Although this form occurs only here, the word occurs elsewhere about 115 times with the meaning 'go up in smoke' or 'make (a sacrifice) go up in smoke'. NEB *from burning myrrh* preserves this idea that the column of smoke is the result of the elaborate ceremonial burning. This is the only distinctly cultic word used in the Song.[3]

Myrrh, see on 1:13.

Frankincense (Heb. *lᵊbōnâ,* 'white stuff'), an amber resin covered with whitish surface dust, that is exuded from the bark of the *Boswellia carterii* and related species of trees which were abundant in India, south-west Arabia, and along the north-east coast of Africa. Frankincense was one of the ingredients in the holy oil (Ex. 30:34), and was extensively used as an incense for burning. It was one of the gifts brought by the Magi to Jesus (Mt. 2:11). The word occurs in the Song only here and at 4:6, 14.

[1] Pope, pp. 423f. [2] *Cf.* above, p. 90, n. 1.
[3] *Cf.* above, Introduction VII, Vocabulary, pp. 42–44.

Fragrant powders (NIV *spices*, *cf.* NEB). This uncommon word (ten times in the Old Testament) is usually translated 'dust', or 'wrestle' *i.e.* 'get dusty' (Gn. 32:24f.). The context here seems to demand the idea of the RSV, but it may be simply 'the dust (of the procession) mingles with the clouds of incense'.

Merchants (or *traders*). According to 1 Kings 10:15, much of the wealth of Solomon's empire was derived from the taxes levied on the income of the traders. Ezekiel 27:22 lists the traders of 'Sheba and Raamah', two territories in south-west Arabia, bringing in 'the best of all kinds of spices'.

7. Most of the versions get the general sense here, but the AV most accurately reflects the Hebrew syntax of the first colon.

Bed, AV (ASV, RSV, NEB, JB *litter*; NIV *carriage*; Heb. *miṭṭâ*) is the common word for a place to sleep. It is used of a sick-bed (Gn. 47:31), or of the bier of one dead (2 Sa. 3:31), but does not normally have specific sexual implications. Frequently they were beautifully decorated ('beds of gold and silver', Est. 1:6; 'beds of ivory', Am. 6:4) but this was not necessarily always the case. The parallel with 'palanquin' (v. 9) suggests some elaborate portable couch is meant here.

Of Solomon. The possessive is marked by the *šel* particle attached to the name. Solomon's name appears here for the first time since 1:5, and after being used in 3:9, 11, will not reappear until 8:7, 12. As noted,[1] Solomon's appearance three times in these six verses calls for our attention. A basic question would have to be why someone as notoriously lascivious as Solomon should appear in an account of pure holy love, or even of pure sexual love between a man and a woman. Some commentators merely excise the name. Others, like Hirschberg,[2] remove the name by identifying the word as a form of the verb *šālam*, 'to make whole or complete' (the word 'peace', *shalom*, is also from this root), so that the word becomes something like 'a consummation gift'.[3] This seems difficult to defend in the light of the modifier 'king' in vv. 9 and 11. It appears that the same argument that was used for the inclusion of the name in 1:5 is valid here: this is an appeal to the

---

[1] *Cf.* Introduction, pp. 19–21.
[2] H. H. Hirschberg, 'Some Additional Arabic Etymologies in Old Testament Lexicography', *VT* 11, 1961, p. 380.
[3] See below on 6:13, *Shulammite*, pp. 154f.

beauty and status of the royal class, as an example of the best (*cf.* 1:9).

The escort of *sixty mighty men* drawn from the *mighty men of Israel* recalls the personal bodyguard of David (2 Sa. 23:8–39), whose duty it was to defend the royal persons. Song 6:8 mentions *sixty queens*, the only other use of this figure in the Song. The proposal that these were five from each of the twelve tribes of Israel or ten from half the tribes is sheer supposition.[1]

Israel. This is the only time this name is used in the Song. Its presence is an indication that the poem dates prior to the death of Solomon in 931 BC. After that time 'Israel' referred to the Northern Kingdom which was in rebellion against the Davidic monarchy.

8. *Girt with swords* (AV *hold swords*; ASV *handle the sword*; NEB, JB *skilled swordsmen*; NIV *wearing the sword*). The term is used in 3:4, 'I held him', and there indicates the encircling clutch of her arms; the corresponding idea of the sheath of the swords 'belted on' is best expressed by the RSV. Delitzsch suggests 'held fast by the sword' *i.e.* 'skilled', but that idea is better expressed in the next colon.[2]

Swords. Either the short eighteen-inch dagger-like weapon (*cf.* Jdg. 3:15f., 21) fastened to the *thigh*, or the larger iron swords adopted from the Philistines after David subjugated them.[3]

Expert in war (NIV *experienced in battle*). The verb implies more than theoretical knowledge. They have practical experience as well.

Alarms (AV, ASV *fear*; Heb. *paḥaḏ*) generally means some external, objective danger, here either roving bands of outlaws who would relish capturing a wealthy bridal train, or perhaps some wild animals that would attack a lone traveller but not a large party.[4] NEB *demon of the night* is unsubstantiated. There

[1] The presence of military motifs is not unusual in ancient Near Eastern love poetry. *Cf.* the Commentary on Song 1:9. In the Egyptian love poetry (Simpson, p. 305 no. 15, p. 317 no. 33), Prince Mehy, the royal warrior and his armed guard appear. *Cf.* Introduction, p. 28, n. 1 and p. 37, n. 2.

[2] Delitzsch, p. 63. His translation spoils the parallelism. But *cf.* Dahood II, p. 227.

[3] 1 Sa. 17:51; 2 Sa. 8:1–12; 24:9. See Yadin, pp. 174f., 208f., 334–337, 340f., 344, 384f.

[4] *Cf.* Dahood I, pp. 81f. and II, pp. 104, 331, for cognates from Ugaritic 'pack' of wild dogs or jackals.

is much legendary material associated with demons, but the Old Testament gives no credence to these tales.[1]

9. *Palanquin* marks the distinction from the word translated 'litter' in v. 7, which is missed by NIV *carriage*. The word (Heb. *'appiryôn*, LXX *phoreion*) is of uncertain derivation and occurs only this once in the Old Testament. The similarity in sound of the Hebrew and Greek words suggests to some commentators that the Hebrew term is derived from the Greek. Ugaritic *apn*, a two-wheeled cart, or the Sumerian carriage made for the god by the king, may be in mind here. Others argue for a Sanskrit, Akkadian or Egyptian origin for the word, but to date no definitive answer can be given. The context seems to require some sort of portable sedan-chair that could be either wheeled or carried, constructed of the finest materials. Delitzsch suggests there are two different vehicles here: the one in which the Queen is being carried (v. 7), and the palanquin in which Solomon waits. JB *throne* reflects this idea.

Wood of Lebanon. The Lebanon mountain range in the north-west part of the land served as a natural barrier between Phoenicia and Israel/Syria. The timbers from Lebanon were in great demand all over the ancient Near East.[2] Cedar and cypress for construction timber and finish panels were most in demand.

Most of the translations fail to catch the poetic parallelism in the verse. Following the Hebrew, the bicolon reads:

> A palanquin made for himself the king,
> Solomon from the wood of Lebanon.

This is a classic example of ancient Near Eastern poetry, with the caesura coming before, not after, 'Solomon'.

10. *Posts* (AV *pillars*), frequent in the Old Testament, appears in the Song only here and at 5:15. The word can mean either columns (of a building, *e.g.* Jdg. 16:25, 29; 1 Ki.

---

[1] *Cf.* Pope, pp. 435–437, and Gaster, pp. 769–771, 812f. Gaster argues that this phrase means 'nightmares', but swords are not much help against these.

[2] *Cf.* 1 Ki. 4:33; 5:7–11; 6:14–19; 7:1–8. Extra-biblical accounts include the campaign records of Pharaoh Ramses II (*c.* 1301–1234 BC), and the Egyptian 'Tale of Two Brothers' which call this The Valley of the Cedars (*ANET*, pp. 25, 256). The Ugaritic Anat-Baal Cycle II, Col. 6 (*ANET*, p. 134) mentions the cedars of Lebanon. Ashurnasirpal II (883–859 BC) and Esarhaddon (680–669 BC) of Assyria both had Lebanon timbers shipped back to Assyria (*ANET*, pp. 276, 291).

7:2; of smoke/flame, Ex. 13:21), or poles (of a tent, Ex. 27:10). These were frequently elaborately decorated (1 Ki. 7:22), or as here, covered with an overlay of silver or other precious metal.

Back (NIV *base*; AV, ASV *bottom*; JB *canopy*; NEB *head-rest*; Pope *bolster*; Heb. *rᵉp̄îḏâ*). This word occurs only here in the Old Testament, although the root *rp̄ḏ* is found in Song 2:5 and twice elsewhere. LXX *anakliton* conveys the same root meaning, 'to lie back' or 'to stretch out'. Whether this is the part on which the occupant 'stretches out' or is the covering canopy which is 'stretched out' over the top is unclear from the context. *Gold* would, in the first instance, be the gold overlay on the back-rest, and in the second, some sort of gold cloth used for the canopy.

Seat (AV *covering*; Heb. *merkāḇ*) occurs only here and in Leviticus 15:9 where the meaning appears to be some sort of seat or saddle. The only other use of the masculine form (1 Ki. 4:26) has the same meaning as the common (50 times) feminine form. This is always translated 'chariot', and may be the seat or bench in such a vehicle. Here it is upholstered with *purple, i.e.* cloth, usually wool or linen, dyed with an expensive purple dye derived from a species of shellfish found along the Phoenician coast. The colour is usually associated with royalty or the aristocracy.

The next colon is difficult, although the general sense is apparent. The interior of the palanquin (AV, ASV *the midst thereof*; RSV *within*; JB *back*; NEB *lining*) was *inlaid*, JB (AV, ASV *paved*; LXX *lithostrōton*; Heb. *rāṣap̄*) *with love*. The verb occurs only this once in the Old Testament, but the noun occurs eight times in the feminine form and once in the masculine. The masculine form at 1 Kings 19:6 and the feminine at Isaiah 6:6 are used of live coals. The other seven references are translated 'pavement'. Something like 'mosaic' that catches and reflects the light as if it were on fire may be implied here.

Lovingly (AV, ASV *with love*). Most translators take this as expressing the motive with which the decoration was carried out, but the Heb. *'ahᵃḇâ* frequently conveys the idea 'love-making' (*cf.* Song 2:4). NEB *its lining was of leather* follows the suggestion that *'ahᵃḇâ* is cognate with the Arabic *'ihāb* 'hide' of an animal. JB *ebony* assumes an unsubstantiated emendation of the text. Inlay and decoration on beds is familiar from the ancient Near East. At Ugarit, samples of beds inlaid with erotic scenes have been found. Perhaps this is what is being described here.

Daughters of Jerusalem, cf. 1:5. JB omits this colon. NEB detaches it from v. 10 and links it in parallel with the first colon in v. 11. The crux of the difficulty is the use of the prefix *mi*. Although it normally means 'from' or 'away from', it sometimes means the source of an action or event, and can be translated 'by'. It is to be so understood here.

11. *Go forth . . . and behold* (NIV *come out . . . and look*; JB *come and see*; NEB *come out and welcome*). This combination recurs at Song 1:6–8; and 7:12 (*cf.* 3:3). The two imperatives are directed towards the *daughters of Zion.* This expression, which occurs only here in the Song, is used by Isaiah (3:16f.; 4:4) in exactly the same way, and the singular 'daughter of Zion' is used 23 times, usually of the nation. Here it is in parallel to the *Daughters of Jerusalem.*

King Solomon. Cf. 3:7, 9.

Crown, not the royal crown used in the coronation/consecration ceremony, but a 'diadem' or 'wreath' made either of branches (like the laurel wreath of the Olympic games), or of precious metals and stones (Ps. 21:3), that is a symbol of honour and joy (*gladness*). The crowning by *his mother* indicates that this is a celebratory crowning, for the royal crowning was carried out by the divine representative, the High Priest.[1] According to the rabbinic materials, 'a bridegroom is compared to a king' and until the destruction of Jerusalem by Rome in AD 70, 'crowns' were worn by ordinary brides and bridegrooms.[2]

The coupling of *the day of his wedding* (only use in Old Testament) with *gladness* (NEB *joy*; 'celebration' and 'mirth' are also attested meanings of Heb. *śimḥa*) underscores the freedom and willingness of the marriage partners.

b. Beauty and desire (4:1–15)

The long unit 4:1–15 divides neatly after v. 7 with the *inclusio* 'you are beautiful, my love' delineating the first section, and the Lebanon motif in 4:8, 15, the second. Although no clear

[1] The Old Testament gives two detailed accounts of the coronation ritual: 1 Ki. 1:32–48, and 2 Ki. 11:11–20. *Cf.* the discussion in R. de Vaux, *Ancient Israel* (McGraw-Hill, 1961), pp. 102–107.
[2] Pirke deRabbi Eliezer, ch. 16, and Babylonian Talmud, *Soṭa* 49a.

pattern of vocabulary usage can be discerned, there are some interesting parallels between this section and the previous unit, 3:6–11, that help explain the relationships developed in this third major section of the Song.

The language of the Song now becomes increasingly erotic, as the descriptions of the lover and beloved are developed and the consummation of their love concludes the section (4:16 – 5:1). The sensuality evoked here goes far beyond what any allegory or typology requires, and makes it, in Fuerst's words, 'beyond the bounds of credibility' that the book was intended to be understood that way.[1]

1. *You are beautiful, my love.* Repeated here and in 4:7, this expression combines two ideas from 1:8f. of the girl's beauty, and the close companionship they share. This precise wording is found in 1:15. The same two Hebrew words are found in reversed order but with the same sense in 2:13, and in 6:4 they appear for the last time with an emphatic pronoun 'you' between them.

Now the girl's beauty is spelt out in the first of two extended analogies. From 1:15 the comparison of her *eyes* as *doves* is repeated, but with the addition of *behind your veil* (AV *within thy locks*).

Veil (Heb. *ṣammâ*) occurs in the Old Testament only at Song 4:1, 3; 6:7, and Isaiah 47:2. In the Song passages the LXX translates *siōpēsiōs* 'silence' or 'taciturnity', but in Isaiah as *katakalymma*, 'veil' or 'covering'. AV *locks* may be based on the Arabic *ṣm*, 'hair', but the Hebrew is more probably closer to the Aramaic *ṣᵉmam*, 'to veil'.

The introduction of the veil at this point in the Song underscores the marriage aspect. Normally girls and women wore head-dresses but not veils, except for special occasions.[2] Engagements (Gn. 24:65) and the actual wedding celebration (Gn. 29:23–25) were two of these occasions.

The last bicolon of 4:1 is repeated again at 6:5.

Hair. The imagery indicates that the beloved does not have her whole head covered with the veil, but that her long black locks ripple and tumble freely. Most Palestinian goats have long wavy black hair. The movement of a large flock on a

[1] Fuerst, pp. 184f.
[2] *Cf.* Gn. 38:13–15, where Tamar, Judah's daughter-in-law 'put on a veil' and was taken by Judah to be a harlot. *Cf.* Song 1:7. See further R. de Vaux, *Ancient Israel*, pp. 30, 33–34.

114

distant hill makes it appear as if the whole hillside is alive (*cf.* 1:5; 5:11).

Moving (NIV *descending*; AV *appear from*; ASV *lie along*; JB *frisking*; NEB *streaming down*; Heb. *šegālšû*). This word occurs in the Old Testament only here and at 6:5 in an identical context. The rabbinic literature uses the root of boiling water. Other writers use it in the sense of 'streaming' or 'trailing down'. The suggestion that *šgš* (and the Ugaritic *šgt*) means 'snow' fails to catch the imagery of the verse.[1]

Gilead, the high plateau east of Galilee and Samaria, is noted for the high and rugged cliffs which climb over 3,500 feet from the floor of the Jordan Valley. They present a beautiful but mysterious aspect in the shimmering heat of the afternoon.

2. The *flock* imagery continues, now with the girl's teeth likened to a flock of newly-washed, newly-shorn sheep. *Shorn* occurs only here and at 2 Kings 6:6, where Elisha 'cuts' a stick to retrieve a lost axe-head from the river.

Come up, as in 3:6 of the procession from the desert. Note the contrast here of the newly-washed sheep and the dusty caravan. In this state, the pink of the sheep's skin shows through the clipped wool and adds a warm, live lustre.

The last half of the verse with its *twins* picturesquely defines the symmetry and perfection of her teeth. The imagery is obvious, but the precise meaning is not. 'Bear twins' is the usual translation, but multiple births and the survival rate of the lambs to the extent suggested here is an obvious exaggeration.[2] The verb (Heb. *tā'am*) occurs only here and at 6:6, but a related noun (Heb. *ta'ôm* or *tô'am*), occurs eight times (Gn. 25:24; 38:27; Ex. 26:24 (twice); 36:29 (twice); Song 4:5; 7:3). The meanings may include the 'bearing of twins', but such a specific meaning is not necessary. 'Twinning' or 'matching' catches the sense equally well, *i.e.* each ewe has her matching lamb, so each upper tooth has its matching lower tooth – none is missing.[3] A common picture in the ancient Near Eastern

---

[1] Pope, p. 459.

[2] See J. J. Finkelstein, 'An Old Babylonian herding contract and Genesis 31:38f.', *JAOS* 88, 1968, pp. 30–36. On p. 34 he indicates an 80% survival rate was the average. In a recent BBC discussion a shepherd's comment, 'we lost only five this season', suggests that the mortality rate was usually considerably higher.

[3] See Finkelstein, p. 35, n. 20. As far as it is possible to ascertain, multiple births among ewes were very infrequent in the ancient Near East.

love poetry is of teeth 'like pomegranate seeds' (*cf.* Simpson, p. 312, no. 28), and one poem compares the beloved's teeth with the notches in a flint knife-blade.

3. The description of her beauty continues with comments on her face. Cosmetics were common in the ancient Near East. Here it is a crimson or scarlet dye used as a lip colour (*cf.* Jos. 2:18).

And your mouth (Heb. *miḏbār*). AV *speech* and JB, NEB *words* follow the LXX *lalia* and the common meaning of the Heb. root *dḇr*. Delitzsch notes the form used here means the mouth as the 'instrument of speech'.[1] The ordinary word for mouth (Heb. *pî(k)*) is a monosyllable, and too short for the poetic metre here.

Lovely (AV, ASV *comely*; NEB *delightful*; JB *enchanting*) occurs in Song 1:5; 2:14; 6:4 (as well as in Pss. 33:1; 147:1 and Pr. 17:7; 19:10; 26:1).

Cheeks (AV, ASV, NIV *temples*; NEB *parted lips*; Heb. *raqqâ*). The Hebrew word occurs only here (and in the parallel text in 6:7), and three times in Judges 4:21f.; 5:6, where Jael killed the Canaanite general, Sisera, by driving a tent-peg through his 'temple'. No particular reason is evident why the 'temples' should be considered objects of beauty, or why the pomegranate figure should be used for the 'brow'. The term means more broadly 'the side of the face' *i.e.* cheeks (LXX *mylon*), for which the red skin of the fruit is an apt comparison.

Veil. Cf. 4:1.

Halves (AV, ASV *piece*; NEB *cut piece*) *of a pomegranate*. Most commentators take the word 'slice' or 'piece' to indicate the interior of the pomegranate with its juicy red flesh, hard white seeds and yellowish membranes, and then have trouble dealing with this image. It sounds like a description of an advanced case of acne. Nothing in the word, however, demands the inside of the fruit. It means simply 'piece' (of cake, 1 Sa. 30:12; of a millstone, Jdg. 9:53), and could mean the outside surface as easily as the inside. The blush-red smoothness of the pomegranate skin fits the imagery far better. The fruit of the pomegranate (*Punica granatum*) was widely used for food and as a decorative motif on clothing or buildings (Ex. 28:33–34; 1 Ki. 7:18). Pomegranate wine had a reputation in Egypt as an aphrodisiac, where, as in Mesopotamia, pome-

[1] Delitzsch, p. 73.

granates were used in love potions.[1] *Cf.* 8:2.

4. *Neck, cf.* 1:10; 7:4.

Like the tower of David is not the present-day tower just inside the Jaffa Gate of Jerusalem, since that structure dates from no earlier than the Herodian period. More likely it is the tower mentioned in Nehemiah 3:25 'projecting from the upper house of the king at the court of the guard'.

David. Cf. Introduction, pp. 19–21 and Subject Study: Lover (Beloved), p. 65.

Built for an arsenal (AV, ASV *armoury*; JB *fortress*; NIV *with elegance*; NEB *winding courses*; Heb. *talpîyôt*; LXX *thalpiōth*). The word is completely unknown apart from this occurrence. LXX assumes it to be a proper name 'Tel Pivoth' (merely transliterating the Hebrew), but no such site is known. NIV is unsubstantiated. Most translators and commentators assume some link with the Arabic verb *tlp* 'to perish' (or 'a cause of perishing' *i.e.* a weapon) or the verb *tlh* which in the Piel means 'to hang up for display'. NEB follows the suggestion that the noun is derived from a root *lpy* which means 'arrange in courses', *i.e.* 'layered',[2] and here refers to the layered necklace the girl wears.

Thousand, in Hebrew as in English, is frequently a round number, not necessarily arithmetically exact. *Cf.* 5:10.

Bucklers (Heb. *māgēn*; LXX *thyreos*). The Greek word describes the large rectangular 'door-shaped' shield which covers the whole body. It is used twelve times to translate the Hebrew *māgēn* which, more correctly, is the smaller round shield carried by officers and light infantry. The Heb. *ṣinnâ* is more accurately translated by *thyreos*.[3] NIV *shields* is suitable here, but the failure to distinguish between the *māgēn* here and the *šeleṭ* in the last colon is confusing.

Shields (Heb. *šeleṭ*). Most translators equate this word with

[1] *Cf.* Simpson, p. 304, no. 12, lines 7–8; p. 309, no. 18, lines 14–17; p. 312, no. 28, lines 1–9, 22–33. 'The sister and brother make [holiday],/[swaying beneath] my [branches];/high on grape wine and pomegranate wine are they,/ and rubbed with Moringa and pine oils . . ./' (lines 6–9). One rabbinic tradition notes that Solomon's crown (*cf.* 3:11) was patterned on the calyx end of the pomegranate fruit.

[2] See A. M. Honeyman, 'Two Contributions to Canaanite Toponymy', *JTS* 50, 1949, pp. 50–52, and S. J. Isserlin, 'Song of Songs iv, 4: An Archaeological Note', *PEQ* 90, 1958, pp. 59–61.

[3] See Yadin, pp. 134, 418f. for the rectangular shields, and pp. 340f., 360, 368, 411, 420, for the round shields.

the small round shield (*māḡēn*), preserving a close parallelism in the bi-colon. The word occurs only seven times in the Old Testament and the precise meaning is not obvious.[1] The occurrence of the word in the Qumran Scroll, 'The War of the Sons of Light and the Sons of Darkness', supports the idea of some offensive weapon, perhaps a javelin or an arrow.

Warriors (JB *hero*; AV, ASV *mighty men*) is the same word used twice in 3:7. The image in the verse is one of splendour and glory, perhaps with the multifaceted necklace she is wearing (*cf.* v. 9) reminiscent of the complex of arms and weaponry displayed triumphantly from the tower.

5. The idea of symmetry introduced in v. 2 is here repeated of her breasts which are likened to twin gazelle fawns (*cf.* 2:7) grazing (or 'resting', *cf.* 1:7) among the lilies (*cf.* 2:1). See 1:3; 2:16; and 6:3.

6-7. The first half of v. 6 appears also in 2:17. See p. 102 for commentary. Many commentators argue that it is an unnecessary repetition at this point. It seems to fit better with the concept of v. 5 than with what follows. Verses 6b and 7 would then form a separate thought unit.

Delitzsch, Seerveld and Lehrman attribute v. 6 to the girl, since these are her words in 2:17, but the shift to the first person in v. 6b is not sufficient reason for this, especially if v. 6a is the concluding thought to v. 5. The seventh verse is clearly the lover's speech.

The mountain of myrrh and the hill of frankincense; *cf.* 1:13 and 3:6. Attempts to identify these as geographic references founder on the fact that neither myrrh nor frankincense is indigenous to Palestine – both were imported spices from far distant lands. Delitzsch's identification of these with the temple mount in Jerusalem where 'incense ... ascended up to God every morning and evening'[2] is likewise far-fetched, even though 'hill' (Heb. *giḇ'â*) is often used of a cultic centre. This is merely a continuation of the description of the physical charms of the girl, and the lover's desire and intention to

---

[1] LXX is far from consistent, using 6 different Greek words for the one Hebrew word: 2 Sa. 8:7 'ornaments' (bracelets) *chlidōn*; 1 Ch. 18:7 'collar' (necklace) *kloios*; 2 Ki. 11:10 'three-sided shield' *trissos*; 2 Ch. 23:9 *hoplon*, in the singular a large shield, but in the plural, as here, usually arms or instruments of war generally; Je. 51:11 and Ezk. 27:11, 'quiver' (for arrows) *pharetra*; and here, Song 4:4, 'javelin' *bolis*.

[2] Delitzsch, p. 78.

possess them. See 5:1 for further development of this. Song 1:13 is the source of the image.

The first colon of v. 7 is an exact repetition of 4:1. The feminine form makes it clear that the lover is addressing the beloved.

No flaw (AV, ASV *spot*; JB *blemish*) *in you, i.e.* no physical or moral shortcoming which would detract or mar her beauty. The word is used only eighteen times in the Old Testament, ten in Leviticus and four in Numbers and Deuteronomy, generally in describing the perfect sacrificial animals which were required (*cf.* Mal. 1:12–14).

8. RSV, NEB, NIV follow LXX translating the first word in the colon *with me* (Heb. *'ittî*) as a verbal form (Heb. emended to *ᵉtî*, an imperative from the root *'atâ* 'come'). The normal verbal form *come* (Heb. *tābô'î*) at the end of the colon serves for the whole line. The emendation is unnecessary, as the repetitive 'with me' is good style and makes perfectly good sense here.

Of more importance is the translation of the preposition *min*. The most common meaning is 'from', and most versions translate it here *from Lebanon*. If Solomon is the speaker, this is understood to mean his request to the Shulammite to come with him from Lebanon to the city. But Shunem in Galilee is already a long way from Lebanon which is in the opposite direction from Jerusalem. It makes no sense to go to Lebanon first – unless she is fleeing from the king. A more plausible option is to take *min* in the sense of 'in'.[1] Thus the invitation is to go with the lover into the secluded slopes of the 'valley of the cedars' where they can be alone and undisturbed (see p. 111, n. 2).

Bride (JB *promised bride*; AV *spouse*), occurs in five consecutive verses beginning here, and then in 5:1. It is found 28 times elsewhere in the Old Testament. The focus of the word is on the married status of the woman, particularly on the sexual element presupposed in that status as 'the completed one'. *Cf.* Hosea 4:13f.; Isaiah 62:4f., and commentary on Song 7:1.

Depart (NIV *descend*; NEB *hurry down*; JB *lower your gaze*; AV, ASV *look*; Gordis *leap*; Pope *come*; Heb. *šûr*). Two separate roots with identical form lie behind the variety of translations. One means 'journey' or 'descend', the other, 'gaze on' or 'look at'.

---

[1] See Dahood, I, p. 106; II, p. 148.

The latter is preferable.

Amana is usually taken to be a mountain in the Anti-Lebanon range, but its exact location is uncertain. It is probably the hill in which the Amana River, which flows through Damascus, has its source (Heb. *ro'š*, 'head', 'peak', 'top', 'source'). The contrast between the muddy lower Jordan and the clean waters of the Amana is the issue in the Naaman story in 2 Kings 5:12 (see *Macmillan Bible Atlas*, map no. 8). *Senir* and *Hermon* are the Amorite and Hebrew names for the tallest peak (over 9,200 ft.) in the Anti-Lebanon range. The Lebanon and Anti-Lebanon (Mount Hermon) ranges lie some 15 miles apart on opposite sides of the Litani-Hasbani (Biqaʿ) valley.

Lions and *leopards* were known in Palestine from prehistoric times (1 Ch. 11:22; Is. 11:6f.; Je. 13:23; Ho. 13:7; Am. 3:4). Both species were thought to be extinct in Israel, but since 1974 the leopard has been sighted (and photographed) many times. The reason for the introduction of these wild animals at this point in the Song is unclear. Pope (pp. 475–477) discusses several options. One, which is supported by the Sacred Marriage Ritual texts, is the observation that the lion was often associated with Inanna/Anat, the Akkadian/Canaanite goddess of love.

9. After the break of v. 8, vv. 9–15 return to the description of the beloved's beauty and its effect on her lover, leading up to the climactic consummation of 4:16 – 5:1.

Ravished my heart (NEB, NIV *stolen my heart*; NEB mg. *put heart into me*; Heb. *libaḫtînî*). This is one of the causative uses of the Piel. The verb has been variously interpreted as 'to take heart' or 'to lose heart', *i.e.* 'to stir him up' or 'to devastate him'. 'Ravish' expresses the latter view. The former idea 'arouse' or 'excite' fits the context better, so that the idea 'aroused my passion' surfaces.[1]

---

[1] The most persuasive argument for this understanding of *lbb* comes from the Mesopotamian literature. A series of magical texts invoking male potency uses the term 'rising of the heart' (Sumerian *ŠÀ.ZI.GA*, Akkadian *niš libbi*). These are not simply 'love incantations', for they are recited by women, and are directed only towards men. The contexts of the term *ŠÀ.ZI.GA* prove that the incantation was intended to produce prolonged sexual excitement in the male, leading to extended intercourse. See R. D. Biggs, *ŠÀ.ZI.GA Ancient Mesopotamian Potency Incantations: Texts from Cuneiform Sources*, Vol. II (J. J. Augustin, 1967), especially pp. 2f. A briefer note that arrives at similar

My sister, my bride. Cf. 4:8 on *bride*. 'Brother' and 'sister' as terms of endearment between lovers is well attested in the literature from the ancient Near East.[1] There is no incestuous relationship being discussed here. This is simply conventional lovers' talk to express the closeness and permanence they desire in their union. In Song 8:1 the free expression of familiarity between siblings expresses the girl's feelings.[2]

A glance of your eyes (AV, ASV *one of thine eyes*). 'Glance' does not appear in the Hebrew text, but is an attempt at explaining the masculine form 'one' used with the feminine form 'eyes'. Since the beauty of her eyes has already appeared as a theme of the Song (*e.g.* 1:15; 4:1), the meaning of the passage is clear in spite of the obscure syntax.

One jewel of your necklace (JB *pearl*; AV, ASV *one chain of thy neck*). This is the only Old Testament use of the singular form here translated 'jewel', although the plural appears in Proverbs 1:9 and Judges 8:26. A related form is the name Anakim (Nu. 13:33; Dt. 9:2; Jos. 15:14) used of the 'giants' (*i.e.* 'long-necked ones' or 'those you have to bend the neck to see') in the land prior to the settlement under Joshua. The term used here probably means some sort of long pendant on her multi-stranded necklace (*cf.* Song 1:10).

10. *How sweet* (AV, ASV *how fair*; NIV *how delightful*). NEB *how beautiful* is closest to the normal meaning for the Hebrew *yāp̄eh*. *Cf.* Song 1:8 and p. 86, n. 1.

Love (NEB, LXX *breasts*). See on 1:2, 4.

Sister, bride, cf. vv. 8f. above.

The third colon of this verse is identical with the second colon of 1:2, and the last colon reflects the opening motif of 1:3. The aromatic anointing *oils* helped replace the natural

conclusions without examining the *ŠÁ.ZI.GA* material is N. M. Waldman, 'A Note on Canticles 4.9', *JBL* 89, 1970, pp. 215–217.

[1] See, *e.g.*, Kramer, pp. 97–104 for some Mesopotamian texts, and Simpson, p. 302, no. 9; p. 303, no. 12; p. 310, no. 21; p. 312, no. 28; and M. Lichtheim, *Ancient Egyptian Literature: A Book of Readings*, Vol. II (Berkeley U.P., 1976), pp. 182–193 for Egyptian examples. The apocryphal book of Tobit 7:15; 8:4, 21 contains some rabbinic examples. JB renders v. 21 as 'I am your father and Edna is your mother. We are your parents in future as we are your sister's' (*i.e.* our daughter, your wife). See below, on Song 5:1.

[2] A similar motif is found in one of the Egyptian love poems. 'I'll kiss him in front of his crowds,/I'll not be ashamed because of the women./But I'll be happy at their finding out/that you know me this well.' Simpson, p. 320, no. 36, lines 17–20.

skin oils lost to the heat and dryness of the climate; they were more than just *perfumes* (NIV, JB, NEB).[1]

Any spice (JB *all other spices*; NEB *any spices*; AV *all spices*; ASV *all manner of spices*). The noun is plural and the particle is normally 'all', although in comparisons, as here, 'every' or 'any' is a suitable translation. *Spices* (Heb. *bᵉśamîm*) is specifically the balsam tree (shrub), then the sweet-smelling oil it produces, and finally perfumes in general. The sense of the colon is not that her *perfumes* are better than any others, but that to her lover even her everyday anointing oils smell better than the most exotic perfumes.

11. *Lips.* Cf. 4:3; 5:13; 7:9.

Distil nectar (JB *distil wild honey*; NEB, NIV *lips drop sweetness like the honeycomb*; AV, ASV *drop as the honeycomb*). The verb (Heb. *nāṭap̄*) occurs 17 times in the Old Testament, eight of them of 'dropping words', *i.e.* 'preaching' or prophesying.[2] The other nine uses describe dripping water (rain), myrrh, wine, or, as here, 'honey'. Proverbs 5:3 parallels 'dripping honey' with 'oily speech', the seductive blandishments of the harlot. Many commentators interpret this verse in the Song as if the beloved's words were sweet, but this is really no more satisfactory than a strict literalness – dribbling honey from the mouth is not particularly attractive. This is an obvious metaphor for the sweetness of her kisses.

Honey (Heb. *nōp̄et*) is specifically that which drips of its own accord from the honeycomb, as distinct from *dᵉḇaš*, 'honey', in the next colon which is more generally 'sweetness' and includes date-syrup or grape-syrup as well as bee's honey removed from the comb. The inclusion of *dᵉḇaš* in the list of 'firstfruits' (2 Ch. 31:5) indicates that this was not wild (or 'found', *cf.* 1 Sa. 14:25–27) honey, which would not be eligible as an offering (*cf.* Lv. 2:11), but was the 'work of the hands' (*cf.* 2 Sa. 24:24) from domesticated bees.

Bride. Cf. 4:8.

Milk and honey are standard symbols of the fruitfulness of

---

[1] One of the Cairo Love Songs (Simpson, p. 311, no. 26), reads 'I wish I were her washerman,/if only for a single month,/then I would be entranced,/ washing out the Moringa oils/in her diaphanous garments . . ./

[2] Ezk. 20:46; 21:2; Am. 7:16; Mi. 2:6 (3 times), 11 (twice). Jb. 29:22 should be included here also, for it speaks of 'dripping words'. Verse 23 illuminates the origin of this use of the word 'they waited for me as for the rain'. In Ezekiel and Amos, *nāṭap̄* occurs in parallel with *nāḇa'*, 'prophesy'.

the land of Palestine.[1] Milk also is a common motif in the ancient Near Eastern love poetry, particularly from Mesopotamia where Dumuzi, the shepherd, is the best of the marriage partners because 'His cream is good, his milk is good,/. . . His good cream he will eat with you', and 'Make yellow the milk for me, my bridegroom . . . I will drink fresh [?] milk with you . . ./The milk of the goat, make flow in the sheepfold for me,/ With . . . cheese fill my holy churn . . . , Lord Dumuzi, I will drink fresh milk with you.' From Egypt come these lines 'Because of hunger/would you then leave me?/or because you are thirsty?/Take then my breast:/for you its gift overflows.'[2]

Heb. *rîaḥ* is translated 'fragrance' in 1:3, 12; 2:13; 4:10; and 7:13, but *scent* here and at 7:8.

Garments (NEB *dress*; Heb. *śalmâ*) is not the common word for clothing (Heb. *beḡeḏ*, used over 200 times in the Old Testament but never in the Song). The *śalmâ* is the outer garment (*cf.* Ru. 3:3) which served both as a cloak for day and a cover while sleeping (Ex. 22:26f.). This latter usage gave rise to the use of the word for a bed-covering, specifically the sheets of the wedding bed on which the 'tokens of virginity' were found (Dt. 22:17). In the context here, some sort of sleep-wear (négligé?) may be implied. References to the royal robes of Psalm 45:8 are misleading here, for the psalm uses *beḡeḏ* there.

Lebanon. See 3:9; 4:8, and *cf.* Hosea 14:7.

12. This verse marks the first occurrence of the *garden* in the Song, but this theme, which will reappear in 4:15f.; 5:1; 6:2, 11; 8:13, has already been introduced in 1:8 with 'my vineyard'. The image of the garden behind its walls and with the gate *locked* suggests the unapproachableness of the area to all but those who rightfully belong. Metaphorically the 'garden' is used as a euphemism for the female sexual organs (See Subject Study: Garden, pp. 59f.) and here, *a fountain sealed* and *a garden locked* speak of virginity. The couple, while approaching consummation of their love, still have not reached that level of intimacy. Note the recurrence of the bride expression for the fifth consecutive verse (*cf.* 4:8). It will not reappear until 5:1 when the consummation occurs.

Spring. NIV, ASV, AV follow Hebrew, differentiating Heb. *gan* 'garden' in the first colon from Heb. *gal* in the second. RSV,

---

[1] *E.g.* Nu. 13:27, and *cf.* the Egyptian 'Story of Si-Nuhe' lines 80–92, *ANET*, pp. 19f.

[2] Kramer, pp. 56, 62; Simpson, p. 298, no. 1. See below on Song 5:1.

NEB, JB follow the ancient translations, emending to *gan* in the second. The noun *gal* is derived from the verbal root *gll* 'to roll, flow', and takes on the meaning 'heap up' (as waves or stones), or 'spring' of water. The latter idea sustains the parallel with the last part of this colon.

Fountain (Heb. *'ayin* 'eye'), *i.e.* the place of flowing tears or, as here, the place where the earth 'weeps'. To 'seal' a spring was to enclose it and protect the water for the rightful owner; Hezekiah did this when he had the tunnel dug from the Virgin's Spring at Gihon to the Pool of Siloam to safeguard Jerusalem's water supply.[1] Proverbs 5:16 uses this imagery to describe the sexual life shared by husband and wife, and the context here (*cf.* v. 13) has obvious sexual overtones.

NEB transposes v. 12 to follow v. 14, but there is no compelling reason for the shift.

13. *Your shoots* (AV, NIV *plants*; NEB *two cheeks*; Heb. *šᵉlāḥayîk*). The word occurs only ten times in the Old Testament. The root *šlḥ* means 'to send out' (*e.g.* a messenger, an arrow, shoots, *etc.*), and the noun form normally is translated as 'weapons', either javelins or swords. Most commentators follow the imagery of Isaiah 16:8 where the metaphor of a vine whose 'shoots spread abroad' (Heb. *šᵉluḥôt*) is used. Nehemiah 3:15 mentions the 'wall of the Pool of Shelah (Heb. *šelaḥ*) of the king's garden, as far as the stairs that go down from the City of David'. This is probably the Pool of Siloam (*cf.* above on v. 12 and p. 123, n. 1), *i.e.* the pool of the 'sending out' of the water from the Virgin Spring (Gihon). Thus the word 'Shelah' is taken to mean the conduit itself, cut out with 'tools' ('weapons'), and *šᵉlaḥ* in this sense means 'canal'. Hirshberg takes this one step further, linking *šᵉlaḥayik* with the Arabic *šalk*, 'vagina'.[2] Pope renders the word 'groove', but with the same obvious symbolism that Hirshberg explicates. *Cf.* Song 5:4.

Orchard. The Heb. *pardēs* is an Old Persian loan-word, usually translated 'paradise', which in the Avestas means an enclosed garden, usually of circular shape. The word occurs in the Old Testament only here, at Nehemiah 2:8 (of the king's 'forest') and in Ecclesiastes 2:5 where Solomon boasts of having made 'gardens and parks' in which he planted 'all kinds of fruit trees'. There is no need to argue, as most

---

[1] *Cf.* 2 Ki. 20:20, and *Macmillan Bible Atlas*, map no. 114.
[2] Hirshberg, 'Arabic Etymologies', *VT* 11, 1961, pp. 379f.

commentators do, that the presence of this word demands a post-exilic date (after 536 BC) for the Song. The Persians appear in the written annals of Shalmaneser III in the ninth century as a settled people, and hence must have been in the territory as early as 1000 BC, possibly as early as 1300 BC.[1]

Pomegranate. Cf. 4:3 and p. 117, n. 1.

Choicest fruits (NEB *rare fruits*; JB *rarest essences*; AV *pleasant fruits*). RSV adds 'all', as if fruits other than pomegranates were intended, as do JB and NEB. More probably the intention is to indicate that the 'pomegranates' are all the best. *Cf.* 7:13.

Henna and nard. Cf. 1:12, 14, for these as symbols of beauty and sensuality.

14. The list of perfumes and spices continues. Some of these have been introduced earlier: *nard*, 1:12; *frankincense*, 3:6; *myrrh*, 1:13; and the *chief spices*, 4:10; others appear now for the first time. This is the only Old Testament mention of *saffron*, the dried, powdered pistils and stamens of the *Crocus sativus*, a small crocus native to Asia Minor. A single ounce of spice requires over 4,000 individual blossoms.

The *calamus* (Heb. *qāneh*) is simply a 'stalk' or 'reed'. Two distinct types of plants are so identified. The 'giant reed' (*Arundo donax*) with lance-shaped leaves and sturdy, straight stalks that grow as tall as eighteen feet, and as much as three inches in diameter at the base, was commonly used in the ancient Near East as a measuring rod. Our English word 'canon', an authoritative standard (*e.g.* the Scripture), is derived from this use. The second plant, and the one probably meant in this context, is the so-called *sweet cane* (NEB) (*Andropogon aromaticus* or *Calamus aromaticus*), a wild grass that has a gingery smell and taste, and from which a ginger-oil can be extracted. Others identify this plant with a type of sugar cane (*Saccharum biflorum* or *Saccharum officinarum*, both of which are indigenous to Palestine), but these were not used for perfumes or spices as the context here seems to demand.

Cinnamon is the bark or the oil distilled from the bark of the *Cinnamonum zelanicum*, a medium-sized tree native to south-east Asia. It was one of the ingredients in the holy oil (Ex. 30:23–29), and was also thought to be something of an aphrodisiac (*cf.* Pr. 7:17). Cassia (Ps. 45:8) is a cheaper substitute,

---

[1] A. T. Olmstead, *History of the Persian Empire* (Univ. of Chicago Press, 1948), p. 22, and *cf.* W. F. Albright and W. O. Lambdin, *Cambridge Ancient History* 1:4:iii.

sometimes used to adulterate the pure product. The second-rate material is ignored by the Song, which uses only the pure and best.

Aloes (Heb. *'hl*, 'odoriferous tree' BDB, p. 14, probably a Sanskrit loan-word). There are three possibilities here. Most identify this as either the 'eaglewood' (*Aquilaria agallocha*) or the sandalwood (*Santalum album*). These are not native to the area, but come from the Far East. Nor are they normally used as perfumes. The wood itself is aromatic, and, because insects were repelled by it, it was commonly used to make insect-proof cabinets and boxes. NEB *incense-bearing trees* is based on this idea. More likely, what is intended here is the *Aloë succotrina*, a spicy drug extracted from the pulp of the leaves of a large shrub native to the island of Socotra at the southern end of the Red Sea. This spice was used, along with myrrh, as a major embalming ingredient by the Egyptians. Joseph of Arimathea and Nicodemus used a large quantity of this mixture in the preparation of Jesus' body for burial (Jn. 19:38–42). Proverbs 7:17 lists this as one of the perfumes in the harlot's bed – perhaps anticipating the 'death' which comes from consorting with harlots (*cf.* Pr. 7:21–27). These negative aspects are missing from the Song.

All these exotic spices have erotic connotations in the love poetry generally, and are not out of place here. Even if the lovers did not actually possess quantities of these expensive items, they serve well as symbols of the rarity and beauty of the beloved.

15. *A garden fountain* (AV, ASV *a fountain of gardens*; JB *fountain that makes the garden fertile*). The Hebrew 'gardens' is plural, perhaps to indicate that the spring waters many gardens.

Living water is running water, not drawn from a cistern or well with a bucket, but 'flowing' of its own accord. The *Lebanon* range is the source of the Jordan River, which, in its upper reaches, flows rapidly and noisily with beautiful crystal-clear water.

The imagery is not of the wide-ranging activities of the girl, but of the abundance of her beauty and fruitfulness when the sealed fountain is opened and the locked garden unbolted.

c. Consummation (4:16 – 5:1)

The third major division of the Song comes to a climax with these two verses. They form the exact middle of the Hebrew text, with 111 lines (60 verses, plus the title, 1:1) from 1:2 to 4:15, and 111 lines (55 verses) from 5:2 to 8:14. These two verses contain five lines of text, but they also contain the climax of the thought of the poem. Everything thus far has been moving towards this consummation. From this point on, everything moves towards the consolidation and confirmation of what has been pledged here. The sister/bride now becomes the 'consummated one' (see on 6:13 – 7:5), as lover and beloved extend to each other the fullness of themselves.

16. *Awake.* The injunction that concludes sections 1, 2 and 4, *do not awaken love until it please* (2:7; 3:5; 8:4), here turns positive as she invokes the wind to awake, for love has pleased to stir.

The *north wind* and *south wind*, as Pope correctly notes, is merely parallelism, with no specific significance such as Delitzsch attached to them, *i.e.*, that the alternating cool and warm breezes stimulated the growth of the garden.[1] Nor is it necessary to see any particular sexual significance in the use of *come* (Heb. *bōʾ*), even though that word is used frequently to mean penetrate sexually (*e.g.* Gn. 38:8, 16: Ezk. 23:44).

Blow, as in 2:17; 4:6, of the stirring of the breeze.

My garden. Pope assumes that the first four cola of this verse are spoken by the lover, with the last two spoken by the beloved. This seems to be an unnecessary complication. The girl speaks here of her own person (*cf.* 1:6 *my vineyard*), which in the last two cola is also *his garden* to enter and enjoy. Taking this as the girl's request retains the parallelism with 2:7; 3:5; and 8:4 which are also her words.

Fragrance (JB *sweet smell*; NEB *perfume*; AV, ASV *spices*; Heb. *bāśām*, as in 4:10, 14; 5:1, 13; 6:2; 8:14). *Cf.* 4:10 on Heb. *rîaḥ*.

Wafted (Heb. *nāzal*, v. 15) is used here with the sense of spread gently to attract her lover.

My beloved. Cf. 1:2 and Subject Study: Lover (Beloved).

[1] S. N. Kramer, 'Cuneiform Studies and the History of Literature: The Sumerian Sacred Marriage Texts', *PAPhS* 107, 1963, pp. 485–515. Tablet CT XLII no. 13, line 8 reads, 'I the queen of heaven took along the light breezes' as part of the sacred marriage ritual, but nothing much seems to be made of this in the subsequent narrative.

Let him come. It is her express wish that he come to take possession of and enjoy *his garden*, *i.e.* herself (*cf.* Introduction pp. 37–39) in all her intimate delights.

5:1. His response is as joyous and willing as is her request, and the full intimacy now enjoyed is the culmination which they both desired. What follows in this verse is a complex set of *double-entendres*, with a number of words having openly erotic implications.

RSV and JB render the verbs in the first four cola with the simple present tense, *I come*, indicating action in progress, while AV, ASV, NIV and NEB use the English present perfect tense, *I have come*, suggesting action begun in the past and continuing into the present. Either is a possible rendering of the Hebrew perfects, but RSV is preferable in this context.[1]

I come is his response to 4:16c.

My sister, my bride. The last occurrence of this combination was in 4:12 – the 'locked garden'. Here, for the first time in the Song, the 'garden' is opened and entrance invited and fulfilled. From this point, she is no longer the 'bride'; she is the 'completed one' (*cf.* 4:8). The connotation of 'psychophysical closeness',[2] *i.e.* as sexual partner in marriage, suggests the rendering 'my dear wife'.

I gather (NEB *have plucked*). The word occurs only here and in Psalm 80:12 where it refers to plucking fruit from behind a broken wall. But this is not stolen fruit. In rabbinic Hebrew, the term is used specifically of plucking figs, which in the ancient Near East had definite erotic and sexual links. See above on 2:13. Pope suggests 'eat' as the proper translation in spite of the fact that myrrh is not meant to be eaten.[3] (Wine, mixed with myrrh and gall, Mt. 27:34, was offered to Jesus at the crucifixion, apparently as some sort of anaesthetizing drug.)

JB translates *balsam* where the other versions use *spices*. Cf. 4:10.

Eat and *drink* in the next two cola complete the progression.

Honeycomb and *honey* (Heb. *ya'ar* and *d⁽e⁾bāš*). *d⁽e⁾bāš* occurs in 4:11 with *milk*, and the meaning in both these places is clear. It is more difficult with *ya'ar*, which occurs 59 times in the

---

[1] *Cf.* GK, sec. 106, i, m, n.
[2] *Cf.* W. E. Phipps, 'The Plight of the Song of Songs', *JAAR* 42, 1974, pp. 82–100, especially p. 83. See above, p. 121, n. 1.
[3] Pope, pp. 504f.

Old Testament, including Song 2:3 'brambles'. Apart from 1 Samuel 14:26, and here, the word is always translated 'forest' or 'thicket', or some synonym for these (*e.g.* Dt. 19:5; 1 Sa. 22:5; 2 Ki. 2:24, *etc.*). In 1 Samuel 14:26, Jonathan dipped his staff into the 'honeycomb' and ate. It may be the complex cell-structure of the comb is what is in mind here, but it is equally likely that 'thicket' is still the most appropriate translation, as Jonathan's staff penetrated the thicket where the hive and comb were hidden. The ancient Near Eastern love poetry frequently uses both the image of honey and of the 'thicket' as euphemisms for the female genitalia.[1]

Wine. See Subject Study: Wine, pp. 66f., and commentary on 1:2; 2:4.

Milk. See on 4:11.

The last bicolon of the verse has posed many problems for commentators. The basic issues are to whom the words are addressed, and by whom they are spoken. Some marginal notes in one of the LXX manuscripts indicate the words are addressed to the companions at the wedding feast, by the bridegroom. Most commentators have followed this lead; but, as Delitzsch notes, such an invitation extends to all the guests the privilege of enjoying the favours of the bride, which elsewhere have been reserved for the bridegroom alone. To make any sense in this context, the words must be addressed to the couple by the onlookers and guests.

The expression *drink deeply* normally means 'become intoxicated' with wine (*e.g.* 2 Sa. 11:13; Je. 51:39), but is used in other ways. Isaiah 49:26 characterizes the captors of Israel as 'drunken with their own blood as with sweet wine' (ASV). For this verse, the NEB *drink until you are drunk with love* catches the meaning well.

Lovers (Heb. *dôḏîm*, plural) here means 'lovemaking'. *Cf.* Subject Study: Lover (Beloved), pp. 64f.

Thus the third division of the poem ends with the couple's companions and guests rejoicing with them and encouraging them to drink their fill of ecstasy and joy in each other's arms – and bed.

---

[1] Some representative examples are: Lambert, p. 113, quoting from tablet K 7924, obv. 3, 'In your vulva is honey'; Kramer, 'Cuneiform Studies', p. 496, Inanna 'picks a sweet "honey-well", puts it about her loins'; Kramer, p. 104, 'The brother brought me into his house,/Laid me down on a fragrant honey-bed./My precious sweet, lying by my "heart"'.

IV. LOST – AND FOUND (5:2 – 8:4)

This long section marks the working out of the relationship established in the previous chapters. The low-key opening lends a sense of subdued contentment after the joyous abandonment of 5:1. Again, as in the second major section of the Song (2:8 – 3:5), there is a request/denial/search/find sequence in the relationship between the lovers. And again, as there, the resolution of the problem becomes possible only as the protagonists recognize the mutual responsibility each has to the other (*cf.* 1 Cor. 7:3–5). Here we are given the beloved's perspective. Of the 111 lines, 80 in this section are the words of the girl. This is really *her* book.

a. The break (5:2–8)

The most common approach to this section is to take it as a dream sequence. Delitzsch comments, 'to sleep while the heart wakes signifies to dream, for sleep and distinct consciousness cannot be co-existent'.[1] Others argue that only by understanding this as a dream can the rapid shifts of emphasis or the seemingly inexplicable reactions of the protagonists be justified.

But such an understanding is not the only possibility. The opening colon may indicate the status of near-sleep – those drowsy minutes when the mind is still alert to outside stimuli, but one is never really sure that the things one hears then are really taking place. Pope remarks that these comments would 'suit very well the condition of one expecting or hoping for a tryst with a lover'.[2] That may well be, but the reaction of the girl in v. 3 is not one which would be expected in such a situation.

A much more realistic approach to this section is that proposed by Glickman.[3] This section, particularly vv. 2 and 3, records the tender approach of the lover and the unexpected apathy and indifference of the beloved to his overtures. It was a temporary lapse in their relationship (v. 6), but certainly a

---

[1] Delitzsch, p. 91.   [2] Pope, p. 511.

[3] S. C. Glickman, 'The Unity of the Song of Solomon', unpublished Th.D. Thesis, Dallas Theological Seminary, 1974. A summary of his arguments and their development is presented in S. C. Glickman, *A Song for Lovers* (IVP/USA, 1976), pp. 60–65, 182–185.

common one between husband and wife, and, if continued, bears the seeds of the disintegration of the relationship. Here, as elsewhere, the Song is realistic and unselfconscious in recording and describing human responses.

2. The unit begins with an emphatic pronoun *I* (Heb. *ʾanî*), which elsewhere in the Song serves as a formula to introduce different aspects of the beloved's relationship with her lover/husband.[1] In this unit the construction occurs four times (vv. 2, 5, 6, 7, 'I slept', 'I arose', 'I opened', and 'Sick with love am I').

Slept . . . awake. Both verbs are participial forms, indicating the continuing state of the girl as the section opens. Apart from 7:9, this is the only use of 'sleep' in the Song; but the 'awake' here is the same word which appears in the refrain at 2:7; 3:5; 8:4, and in 4:16 and 8:5 of rousing to activity.

Heart frequently in the Old Testament means simply the physical organ (*e.g.* Ps. 38:10), but more often is the seat of the emotions (*e.g.* Pr. 15:13; Song 3:11) and the will (*e.g.* Ex. 35:21; 36:2), as these reflect the rational function we ascribe to the brain and intellect (*cf.* Ps. 90:12; Pr. 18:15).[2] The Song uses the word only three times: here, 3:11 and 8:6 (but *cf.* 4:9 for the verbal form).

Hark. Cf. 2:8.

Beloved, see Subject Study: Lover (Beloved), pp. 64f.

Knocking occurs only three times in the Old Testament. In Genesis 33:13 the word is used of driving flocks beyond their endurance, and in Judges 19:22 of the rabble who abused the Levite's concubine in Gibeah. In those contexts the sense is importunate and violent solicitation, but that hardly seems suitable here, although the piling up of endearing addresses in the next colon is certainly importunate.

Sister. The permanency of the relationship (*cf.* 4:9), suggested by 'sister' and anticipated by the lover in his request, is suddenly called in question by her response in the next verse. Apart from 8:8, where the normal meaning of the word appears, this is the last time the term is used in the Song. *Cf.* 4:9.

My love. Cf. 1:9; 2:2.

My dove, first used as a pet-name in 2:14, occurs here and

[1] *E.g.* Song 1:5; 2:1, 5; 6:3; 7:10; 8:10.
[2] A brief summary can be found in *TDNT* 3:606–607, and a more extensive treatment in H. W. Wolff, pp. 40–58.

131

in 6:9 with the added qualification *my perfect one* (AV, ASV *undefiled*; NIV *flawless*). This latter expression is used in Genesis 25:27 in the sense of 'peaceful' or 'quiet', and in Psalm 37:37 in parallel with the 'righteous' or 'upright' man. The best-known occurrences are in Job 1:1, 8; 2:3. The AV *undefiled* suggests 'virgin', but that connotation is absent from the Hebrew. Ethical and moral blamelessness is more the idea. Delitzsch (p. 93) suggests 'wholly devoted' to the beloved, but the context seems to demand *her* devotion to her lover.

The last two cola are in strict parallel, although the precise meaning of *qᵉwuṣṣôt*, *locks* (NIV *hair*) is not certain. The word occurs only here and at v. 11. BDB, p. 881, likens it to the Arabic *ḳṣṣt*, 'the hair over the forehead'. A masculine noun, apparently from the same root, means 'thorns' or 'thorn-bush'. The rabbinic commentary *Bereshith rabba* on Genesis 27:11 identifies Jacob as 'smooth-headed', *i.e.* 'bald' (Heb. *qērēaḥ*) and Esau as 'curly-haired' (Heb. *qawwās*).

Dew/drops of the night (NEB *moisture*; NIV *dampness*; Heb. *rāsîs*). The cool Palestinian nights produce heavy dew which during the long summer dry-season provides the necessary moisture for the vineyards. This is the only use in the Song of these two words. The verb *filled*, AV (NEB, NIV *drenched*; JB *covered*; Heb. *mālaʾ*) occurs again at v. 14, 'set' with jewels. That image, 'bejewelled with dew', would be an interesting one here.

Whether this verse is describing a midnight rendezvous of the lovers, or the return home of the beloved after fulfilling his duties elsewhere, is not specified in the context; but the latter seems more likely.

3. *Garment* (AV *coat*; NEB *dress*; JB *tunic*; NIV *robe*; Heb. *kuttōnet*; LXX *chitōn*). The word is used of Joseph's coat (Gn. 37:3), of the high priest's robe (*e.g.* Ex. 28:4), and of official robes (Is. 22:21). It is also found in Genesis 3:21 of the skin coats made for Adam and Eve, and this use reflects the basic idea of the word. It is the garment worn next to the skin, not the 'garment' of 4:11 which served as a bed-covering, nor the common *beḡed* which was used to describe clothing in general. Delitzsch's comment (p. 93), 'she lies unclothed in bed', catches the precise meaning of the colon.

Bathed (NIV *washed*) *my feet*. The routine of rinsing the feet was necessary after walking in the dusty streets and paths in open sandals. *Cf.* John 13:1–17.

After each of these excuses she asks *must I . . . ?* (NIV, NEB), a better rendering than RSV *how could I . . . ?* (Heb. *'êkākâ*). This form occurs only here and at Esther 8:6, although the similar form *'êkâ* with the same meaning appears in Song 1:7 and frequently elsewhere in the Old Testament. Often it is found in songs of mourning or lamentation, and here reflects a petulant unwillingness to act rather than the impossibility of action. Pope (p. 515) suggests this may 'represent a bit of coy pretense intended to tease the eager male', but the negative implications of the 'must I' seem to make this unlikely. Rather she appears unwilling to put herself to any trouble even for her lover.

Feet (Heb. *reḡel*) normally has its common meaning, but on several occasions is a euphemism for the genitals (*e.g*, 'wash your feet' and 'lie with my wife' are used as parallels, 2 Sa. 11:8, 11; *cf.* Dt. 28:57; Ru. 3:3–9; Is. 7:20). Whether or not this is the meaning here is open to question, although there is certainly sufficient evidence for this sort of *double entendre* in the next verse where her description of her lover's action and her own response to it continues.

4. *My beloved. Cf.* 1:13.

Put (AV, ASV *put in*; JB, NIV *thrust*; NEB *slipped*) is the very common Hebrew verb *šālaḥ*, used nearly 900 times in the Old Testament, but only this once in the Song. The meaning is to send, let go, stretch out, *etc.* (*cf.* 4:13, the related noun, translated 'shoots'). NIV and JB *thrust* best preserve the meaning.

The construction with the preposition (Heb. *min*) following the verb has produced a variety of translations and much difficulty for commentators. The Hebrew *min-haḥōr*, 'from the hole', is rendered in RSV *to the latch*; AV and ASV *by the hole of the door*; NEB *through the latch-hole*; JB *through the hole in the door*; NIV *through the latch-opening*. The basic meaning of the preposition is 'from' or 'away from', *i.e.* indicating either source or direction. 'Through' in the sense of 'by means of' (*e.g.* 'wine', Is. 28:7), and a partitive use ('two of/from every kind', Gn. 6:19) are also frequent, but all the translations suggested for the word here are unsupported. There is, however, growing evidence that *min* is frequently used in parallel with Hebrew *bᵉ* 'in' or 'into', and that meaning is more satisfactory here.[1]

---

[1] See especially Dahood, I, p. 106; II, p. 148; III, p. 160, on Pss. 18:6; 68:26; 118:26. A number of other biblical and extra-biblical references are

The word translated *latch-hole* (NEB), or expanded to *hole of the door* (AV, *etc.*; Heb. *ḥôr*) occurs only six other times in the Old Testament.[1] An examination of these passages makes it plain that the meaning of the noun is normally a cave or cave-like hole. Most commentators on this passage take the word to mean a hole bored through the door to provide access to the latch or lock, but there is nothing in the context that supports this idea. The words demand the meaning inserting something into a hole of some sort, but exactly what or where is unspecified.

Hand (Heb. *yāḏ*), like 'feet' in v. 3, normally means simply the physical hand, but also like 'feet' it is sometimes used with other meanings. In at least three places (1 Sa. 15:12; 2 Sa. 18:18; Is. 56:5), *yāḏ* is translated by 'monument' or 'pillar'. Surviving examples of such 'monuments' are normally tall stone pillars, rounded at the top, some of which bear inscribed hands raised in worship.[2] The Canaanite cult was a sexually-oriented fertility cult, and the presence of these 'pillars' or monuments in the form of phallic representations suggests a possible link between the use of *yāḏ* for 'monument' and the next development.

It is now established beyond serious question that *yāḏ* is occasionally used as a euphemism for the male copulative organ, both in the Ugaritic literature and at Qumran.[3] Several scholars have suggested this meaning for certain Old Testament texts as well. Isaiah 57:8 is certainly to be understood this way;[4] Isaiah 57:10; Jeremiah 5:31; 50:15 may also be

---

cited there. *Cf.* Pope, p. 518, for a discussion of Pr. 17:23 and 21:14 where *min* and *bᵉ* are used in parallel statements.

[1] 1 Sa. 14:11; 2 Ki. 12:9; Jb. 30:6; Ezk. 8:7; Na. 2:12; Zc. 14:12. The form *ḥûr* with the same meaning occurs at Is. 11:8; 42:22.

[2] *E.g.* the Hazor Stele, *ANEP*, p. 365, no. 871; and the Nut Stele, *ANEP*, p. 183, no. 543. In Ezk. 21:19, RSV translates 'signpost', *i.e.* a 'hand' to show the way, although there is no evidence to show that this was in fact 'hand-shaped'.

[3] *UT*, p. 409. The reference here is to text no. 52, 'The Birth of Dawn and Dusk, and the Seven Good Gods of Fertility'. The most readily available translation is probably in Gaster, pp. 406–435, especially pp. 427–429, and p. 428, n. 2. The Qumran reference is in the 'Manual of Discipline' 7:12–15, where various penalties for indecent exposure, *etc.* are listed. For further discussion of this whole question, see M. Delcour, 'Two Special Meanings of the Word *yḏ* in Biblical Hebrew', *JSS* 12, 1967, pp. 230–240. Further evidence is preserved in Lucian, *The Syrian Goddess* (*De Dea Syria*), xvi, xxviii, xxix.

[4] Even Delitzsch, *Isaiah* 2, p. 375, in 1877 commented, 'The Arabic furnishes several analogies to the obscene use of the word; and by the side of Ezek.

examples of this usage.[1] Ugaritic also has a verb *ydd* meaning 'to love' which may lend its meaning to the Hebrew word.

None of this is decisive, of course, but as Cook notes,[2] the *double entendre* by nature is 'so delicate as to leave some doubt about its presence at a specific point'. Nevertheless, this appears to be one text where the erotic meaning is present. If *yād* does mean the male member here, *ḥôr* is its female counterpart.[3]

My heart (JB *the core of my being*; NEB, AV *bowels*; Heb. *mēʿeh*, *cf.* 5:14, *belly*). The basic meaning of the word is the internal organs generally (2 Sa. 20:10; Ps. 22:14), or the digestive tract (Jon. 2:1f.). But several texts use the term to refer to the procreative organs, either male (*e.g.* Gn. 15:4; 2 Sa. 7:12) or female (*e.g.* Ru. 1:11. In Gn. 25:23; Ps. 71:6; and Is. 49:1, *mēʿeh* is used in parallel with *beṭen*, the common word for *womb*). The focus of the *thrill* is specifically sexual.

Once her desire has been aroused, further gratification is essential and the 'search motif' which is common to the ancient Near Eastern love poetry is an outworking of that desire.

5. There are several parallels in the next four verses with 2:10 – 3:5, and we are left again with the distinct impression that these are deliberate *double entendres* on the part of the poet. Note the lover's invitation to 'arise' (2:10, 13) and her response in 3:2. Following the arousal of her love in v. 4, and reflecting on her coldness of v. 3, she attempts to rectify that situation. The 'I' here and in v. 6 is the emphatic form which begins v. 2. *To open*, a common Old Testament word, in the form used here often means 'surrender' (*e.g.* 2 Ki. 15:16; Is. 45:1).

Hands and *fingers* are here used in simple parallelism. Compare v. 4.[4]

Dripped. Cf. 4:11; 5:13, 'distil'.

Myrrh. Cf. 1:13. 'Liquid myrrh' is either that which flows out by itself from the tree (so Delitzsch, p. 95, taking the

---

xvi. 26 and xxiii. 20, where the same thing is affirmed in even plainer language, there is nothing to astonish in the passage before us'.

[1] See Delcour, *JSS* 12, 1967, p. 234. For similar explicit use in the Mesopotamian literature, *cf.* Kramer, pp. 64, 105.

[2] A. Cook, *The Root of the Thing: A Study of Job and the Song of Songs* (Indiana U.P., 1968), pp. 110, 123. *Cf.* C. Exum, *ZAW*, 1973, pp. 50–51.

[3] *Cf.* above, p. 129, n. 1.

[4] See U. Cassuto, *Biblical and Oriental Studies* 2 (Magnes Press, 1975), pp. 43f., 49, for discussion of this idiom in the Ugaritic and Hebrew literature.

verbal form, Heb. *'ābar*, in the sense of 'overflowing'), or a mixed unguent of a creamy or oily consistency.[1] In either case, it is present in sufficient quantity to adhere to the door-lock. There is nothing in the passage to indicate by whom the myrrh was placed, whether the lover who left it as a token of love, or the girl who, in her response, took time to prepare herself for the encounter.

6. The intention of the first colon of v. 5 is fulfilled here, but not with the result she expected. Her lover/husband, rejected, had *turned* aside (*i.e.* had 'taken a different direction') and disappeared. For earlier uses of the verb *'ābar*, see 2:11; 3:4; 5:5.

Soul (NEB, NIV *heart*; Heb. *nepeš*), *cf.* 1:7; 3:1ff.; and 6:12. *My soul failed* suggests a fainting spell. Rachel's death is described this way (Gn. 35:18).

When he spoke (NEB *when he turned his back*; JB *at his flight*; Heb. *bᵉdabᵉrô*.) The variant translation of JB and NEB is based on the suggestion that this is an occurrence of the relatively rare (eight or ten times) root *dbr*, meaning to turn away or subjugate.[2] The context here seems to require the less common translation, so the colon could be rendered, 'I nearly died when I found he had gone'.

The search/find motif from 3:2 is again introduced, this time elaborated by her report that she 'called' repeatedly, but got no answer. The final colon appears here for the first time. RSV and NEB inserted this line at 3:1d, but the Hebrew text lacks it there.

7. The first line here repeats 3:3, but before she has the opportunity to pose the question she did there, she becomes the victim of those whose duty was to protect the city and its citizens. No reason for their reaction is given in the text, although many commentators suggest their violent treatment was occasioned by her refusal to stop her frantic activity when challenged.

Beat and *wounded* are close synonyms, although the latter is used only three times in the Old Testament (*cf.* Dt. 23:1; 1 Ki. 20:37), and has the specific sense of bruise or crush.

---

[1] *Cf.* Hirschberg, *VT* 11, 1961, p. 377.

[2] Possible texts suggested for this root include 2 Ch. 22:10; Jb. 19:18; Pss. 18:48; 47:4; 75:6; 116:10; 127:5; and Is. 32:7. Arabic *'dbr*, 'turn back', 'relent', may be cognate. The common meaning 'speak' is attested nearly 1,150 times in verbal forms and nearly 1,500 times as a noun.

The *mantle* (AV *veil*; NIV, JB, NEB *cloak*; Heb. *rᵉdîd*; LXX *theristron*) is still another item of clothing distinct from those mentioned in 1:7; 4:3, 11; and 5:3. The Greek garment identified by the LXX translation is a light-weight summer cloak. The Hebrew verbal root from which the noun is derived means 'to beat out' or 'make flat' (*e.g.* a gold-leaf covering 'beaten out' on the cherubim in the temple, 1 Ki. 6:32), and so to make a thin covering for something. There may be a subtle play on words here with the 'beating' in the previous colon and this word here. The term appears elsewhere only in Isaiah 3:23, where it is included in a list of clothing and ornaments which the women of Israel would have taken away in the days of the exile. Pope (p. 527) suggests an Akkadian derivation from a word *dudittu* (or *tudittu*) which was a jewelled ornament worn on the breast. It was one of the gifts presented to a bride at her wedding. The letters *d* and *r* are very similar in Hebrew, and could easily have been confused by a copyist. Akkadian *radādu* is cognate to Hebrew *rādad*, 'to beat down, subdue'. Whether this is an item of clothing or a piece of jewellery makes no difference to the sense of the passage.

The final colon recapitulates the opening colon of the verse again with a potential play on words evident. *Walls* probably means simply the city walls, *i.e.* the territory the watchmen were assigned to guard, but the Song uses the word 'walls' elsewhere only in 8:9f., where it is used as a euphemism for the girl whose 'breasts were like towers'. If the *rᵉdîd* was a loose cloak that was removed by the watchmen, they may be pictured here as gazing on the 'wall', *i.e.* the girl in her state of semi-nakedness.

8. The first colon is a repetition from 2:7 and 3:5, and will re-appear at 8:4. In those places it serves to introduce the final verse of a major section of the Song. Here, however, the balance of the verse is different, and no major unit is ended. LXX adds here as the second colon 'by the gazelles or hinds of the fields' as in the two earlier texts, but the Hebrew does not have that colon.

The variety in translation is due to the difficulty of handling the two particles *'im*, 'if', which after an oath or adjuration normally becomes an emphatic negative: 'certainly not';[1] and *ma*, '*what*' (see on 3:6) *will you tell him* (NIV); (RSV *that you tell*).

---

[1] *Cf.* GK, pp. 471f.

The issue is to decide whether the girl is asking the city-girls to tell her lover something, or whether she is begging them *not* to tell him. If there is any similarity with the 2:7 and 3:5 passages, the latter seems to be the preferred translation.[1] NIV is correct in the third colon, but with the repetition of 'tell him' destroys the sense of the last colon.

Recognizing that 'love' (Heb. *'ahᵃbâ*) should be translated 'love-making' here (*cf.* on 1:4; 2:4; 3:10, and Subject Study: Love, pp. 60–63) avoids the difficulty. She challenges her companions: 'What are you going to tell him? That I am worn out (Heb. *ḥalâ*, 'become weak, ill, exhausted') with love-making?' *i.e.* 'that I don't want any more?' The question is almost rhetorical. 'Don't be foolish. How could I not want more?'

b. A leading question (5:9)

A single comment by the city-girls serves to set the stage for an elaborate description of the physical charms of the lover.

9. The verse has posed serious difficulty to most interpreters. The repeated colon reads literally, 'What is your love [or 'lover', or 'love-making'] from (a) love [or 'lover', or 'love-making', Heb. *ma-dôdēk midôd*]?'

If *mi* with *dôd* is to be taken as a partitive, the translation becomes 'more than another lover'.[2] There are numerous Old Testament references where the *mi* construction is partitive, *e.g.* Genesis 3:1, 14; 37:3; Deuteronomy 7:7; Psalm 45:3, *etc.* If, on the other hand, as Delitzsch suggests, the *mi* construction is comparative, the rendering of JB and NIV is more correct. These versions interpret the colon to mean the beloved is 'better' than other lovers, and the city-girls are interested in 'how' this is so. The implication seems to be that he is better at 'love-making' than others; but this idea does not seem to fit either with the girl's chaste behaviour (4:12), or with response to the question in the next section. Neither approach is entirely satisfactory.

[1] GK, p. 443, n. 1, draws a parallel here with Arabic *mâ taqûlû* 'say now', and translates 'will you not tell him?', *i.e.* 'I charge you that you tell him'.

[2] L. Waterman, '*dwdy* in the Song of Songs', *AJSL* 35, 1919, pp. 101–110, attempted to prove that *dôdî* was a proper name 'Dodai' (or 'David'), so the verse reads 'What is thy Dodai in comparison with David?' He rejected the addition of 'another' as 'inadmissible'. Although the article has much valuable material, its conclusion has gained little support.

The use of *most beautiful of women* here and in 6:1 (NIV) may be a somewhat mocking rehearsal of the lover's words in 1:8, and her response praises her lover's beauty in extreme terms.

c. A joyous response (5:10–16)

Love songs describing the physical beauty of the beloved are common in the ancient Near East, but most of them describe the female. Such detailed description of the male, as here, is seldom recorded.[1] This section is of particular interest, for it records what was apparently the epitome of male physical beauty, just as the lover's description of his bride (4:1–5; 6:5–7; 7:1–5) preserves the ideal of female beauty.

The two most detailed accounts, here and 7:1–5, share many common features: an orderly progression from head to foot (vice versa in the case of the description of the girl); animal comparisons (ravens, doves, 5:11f.; gazelles, 7:3); geographic comparisons (Lebanon, 5:15; 7:4); flowers and spices (5:13; 7:2); springs and pools (5:12; 7:4); the work of architects (5:15; 7:4), goldsmiths and jewellers (5:14; 7:1); *etc.* The emphasis in these two poems is on colour, form, beauty and strength.[2]

10. Her praise song opens with a general description of her lover. He is *radiant* (JB *fresh*; NEB *fair*; AV, ASV *white*; Heb. *ṣaḥ*). The word appears only four times in the Old Testament. Comparing these references indicates the meaning is 'dazzling' or 'shimmering'.[3] Either idea fits the gold/ivory/jewel references.

Ruddy (Heb. *'adôm*) occurs eleven times as an adjective, always with the meaning 'red' or 'ruddy'. The verbal form

---

[1] In the Egyptian Love Songs, there are occasional references to the man's beauty: 'Most beautiful youth who ever happened' (Simpson, p. 304, no. 13); 'Lover excites my desire with his voice' (p. 316, no. 32), but even where these songs are addressed to the lover, they generally reflect the girl's own feelings and reactions. Elaborate descriptions of the girl's physical charms are common. *Cf.* Simpson, pp. 315f., no. 31, and Kramer, pp. 63f., 95. Where the lover is described in these poems, it is usually in terms of his strength to carry on warfare or to lead his people (Kramer, p. 64), not his physical beauty, although Inanna does comment on Dumuzi's 'lapis lazuli beard' and his 'mane-like hair' (Kramer, pp. 73, 99). *Cf.* also P. Craigie, 'The Poetry of Ugarit and Israel', *TB* 22, 1971, pp. 3–31, especially pp. 11–15.
[2] See Wolff, pp. 70–72.
[3] Je. 4:11 'a hot wind from the desert', *cf.* Is. 18:4. Is. 32:4 records that in the Messianic age the stammerer will speak 'readily and distinctly'; perhaps 'dazzling words' is what is meant there.

occurs another ten times (*e.g.* Is. 1:18). Most commentators take this simply as the normal complexion of a healthy young man, but Pope (pp. 531f.) suggests some sort of cosmetic which was applied to the face or body. The Hebrew noun *'ādām*, 'man', is a more likely source for the term here, in which case, her lover is 'manly'.

Distinguished (AV, ASV *chiefest*; NEB *a paragon*; JB *to be known*; NIV *outstanding*; Heb. *dāḡûl*, *cf.* 2:4; 6:4, 10). The verbal form occurs only here and at Psalm 20:5 and in the Song 6:4, 10, with the meaning 'look' or 'behold', and the derived meaning of something conspicuously visible, *e.g.* a 'banner' or 'bright star'. *Cf.* the discussion of the root at Song 2:4.

Ten thousand is not to be understood literally, but simply as a 'very great number'; *cf.* 4:4. Her lover is the superlative one in a huge multitude, and she now proceeds to detail how this is so.

11. The description of his hair as *black as a raven* is the only figurative use of the word 'raven' in the Old Testament. In every other instance, it refers simply to the bird (*e.g.* Gn. 8:7; 1 Ki. 17:4). This simile precludes the possibility that the first colon is describing him as blond. The *head* of *finest gold* must refer to the face and neck, not to the hair.

The two words translated *finest gold* are both poetic words occurring relatively infrequently in the Old Testament (nine or ten times each), and in this combination, only in this verse (*cf.* 5:15). The precise meaning of the second of these (Heb. *pāz*) is not certain. The traditional translation 'pure gold' (*i.e.* 'refined gold') is possible, but most recent lexicographers have identified this as 'chrysolite' (Gk. 'golden stone'), *i.e.* any one of several yellow or green-yellow semi-precious gem-stones (*e.g.* topaz, *etc.*). 'Chrysolite' is now used technically of magnesium iron silicate ('olivine'), which is a pale green crystalline mineral, but the ancient use of the name is much broader.

The expression is uncommon in the Old Testament, the closest equivalent being in the Aramaic portion of Daniel (Dn. 2:32) where Nebuchadnezzar's image is described in similar terms. Pope (pp. 535f.) has an extended discussion of the numerous images of gods found in various ancient Near Eastern excavations, and suggests that this passage is similar to others describing these gods. Such a cultic explanation is possible, but unlikely. In light of the discussion of v. 10 above, this expression more probably means simply that his features are exquisitely sculpted and his complexion a golden tan. *Locks* (of hair), *cf.* 5:2.

Wavy (AV, ASV *bushy*; NEB, JB *like palm fronds*; Heb. *taltallîm*, LXX *elatai*) occurs only here in the Old Testament. The Greek *elatai* (sing., *elatē*) has a variety of meanings, including the silver fir tree, the pine, sea-weed, or the covering on the buds of the date-palm. Akkadian and Arabic cognates are also used in this latter sense. The precision of the image is unimportant. Delitzsch notes that the 'freshness and flexibility of the abundant long hair of the head' is what is described here.

12. *Eyes like doves. Cf.* 1:15; 2:4 (Heb. *yônâ*). The addition of the Hebrew *k* 'like' (missing from 1:15) suggests the picture of these birds darting about.

Springs (AV *rivers*; ASV, NEB *brooks*; NIV *streams*; JB *pool*; Heb. *'apîq*) is another word whose precise meaning is uncertain. The root is used in the sense of 'enclosed' or 'restrain', so the noun is probably something like 'enclosure' or 'channel' (of a river). The imagery suggests the doves perched 'on' (Heb. *'al*) the banks, so his eyes are deep-set in their sockets.

The last half of the verse is obscure. The sense appears to be describing the contrast of the iris with the white of the eye (*cf.* 4:1), both *fitly set* (NIV *mounted like jewels*) in the face. This last expression occurs only here in the Old Testament (Heb. *millē't*), although the verbal root *mālē'*, 'fill', 'be full', is common. JB *at rest on a pool*, and NEB *as they sit where it [water] is drawn*, follow the rabbinic understanding that the required meaning is something like a pool or watering place.[1] RSV, NIV, AV and ASV link the word with Heb. *millû'â*, used in Exodus 28:17, 20; 39:13, *etc.*, of a setting for jewels. *Cf.* Song 5:14.

13. *Cheeks* is used elsewhere in the Song only at 1:10 where the girl's beauty is described.

Beds (Heb. plural) *of spices*. This exact expression occurs again at 6:2 in parallel with 'his garden' (*cf.* 4:16). Ezekiel 17:7, 10 are the only other Old Testament uses of the word 'bed'. There it also clearly means 'garden plot'. On 'spices' (Heb. *bāśām*), *cf.* 4:10, 16; 5:1.

Yielding fragrance (AV *sweet flowers*; ASV *banks of sweet herbs*; NIV *yielding perfume*; NEB *chests full of perfumes*; JB *banks sweetly scented*; Heb. *migd'lôt merqāḥîm*, LXX *phyoysai myrepsika*). RSV and NIV follow LXX, reading the Hebrew as *m'gadd'lôt* from a root *gdl*

---

[1] *Cf.* Gordis, p. 91.

141

meaning 'to grow' or 'make strong'. The Hebrew *mig̱dᵉlôt* is properly 'towers' (*cf.* Song 4:4; 7:4; 8:10), here used in the sense of 'stronghold' or 'treasure-chamber' (as NEB). This is the only Old Testament use of *merqāḥîm*, but the verb *rāqaḥ*, used eight times (and other related nouns used about six times), describes the art of mixing ointments and perfumes (*e.g.* Ex. 30:25; 2 Ch. 16:14; Ec. 10:1).

His lips are lilies. Cf. 4:3 and 2:1.[1]

Distilling liquid myrrh. Cf. 5:5 for a slightly expanded version of this expression. *Distilled, cf.* 4:11. *Liquid* (Heb. *ʿōḇēr*) occurs in 2:11; 3:4; 5:5, 6, and here. Delitzsch understands this to describe the words the lover speaks, but the frequent use of the 'kissing' image in the Song (*e.g.* 1:2) suggests this as a better interpretation here.

14. *Arms* is more correctly *hands* (AV, ASV, NEB, JB, Heb. *yāḏ*), but, as Jeremiah 38:12 indicates, the term can be used for any part of the arm.[2] The Hebrew plural form here forbids the meaning discussed in 5:4.

Rounded gold (NIV, NEB *rods of gold*; AV, ASV *rings* (mg. cylinders) *of gold*; JB *golden, rounded*; Heb. *gᵉlîlê zāhaḇ*). The Hebrew *gᵉlîl* occurs only four times in the Old Testament: 1 Kings 6:34; Esther 1:6; Isaiah 9:1, and here. None of these references is particularly helpful, although the Esther reference to 'silver rings' may provide a clue.[3] The Hebrew root *gll* ('to roll') suggests a circular form, perhaps a rod or cylinder. 'Galilee', the 'circle of the Gentiles', is also derived from this root. *Gold* is the common Old Testament term for the precious metal, and is a different word than that used in v. 11.

Set (Heb. *mālaʾ*). *Cf.* v. 12.

Jewels (AV, ASV *beryl*; NIV *chrysolite*; NEB *topaz*; JB *jewels of Tarshish*; Heb. *taršiš*). No certain identification of this gemstone is possible, although the parallel with 'gold' suggests a

---

[1] *Lilies* is used in the titles of Pss. 45, 69 and 80, apparently as the name of the tune to which they were sung. The latter two are sombre evaluations of the state of the nation in difficulty, and the idea of a deep colour, 'the blues', makes sense here. *Cf.* Kidner, p. 44.

[2] *Cf.* 'The Legend of Keret' Krt A line 157, 'He washed from hand to elbow', *ANET*, p. 144. *Cf. UT*, p. 251, *yrhs.ydh.amth* 'His hand to the elbow'.

[3] M. Dahood, 'Ebla, Ugarit, and the Bible', in G. Pettinato, *The Archives of Ebla* (Doubleday, 1981), p. 313, identifies Eblaite *gú-li-lum* = 'bracelets' as a 'well-attested noun', and quotes this verse in the Song as 'His hands are golden bracelets studded with gems'. This rendering may suggest the idea of 'precious clasping' by these arms as the meaning of the passage.

yellowish-coloured stone, possibly topaz or beryl (*cf.* 5:11). Tarshish is one of the ancient names for Spain, so that the JB translation could be taken as 'Spanish jewels'.

Body (AV, JB, NEB *belly*; Heb. *mēʿeh*). *Cf.* 5:4 'heart'. The following modifiers demand the outer part of the trunk, not the internal organs as at 5:4. Pope (p. 543) suggests 'loins' as including back as well as belly.

Ivory work (AV *bright ivory*; JB *a block of ivory*; NEB *a plaque of ivory*; NIV *polished ivory*). 'Ivory' (Heb. *šēn*) is the common Old Testament word for 'teeth' (*cf.* Song 4:2; 6:6). Ezekiel 27:15 mentions 'ivory tusks [Heb. *qarnôt šēn*, 'horns of teeth'] and ebony' as trade items. This is probably what is intended here and in 7:4. The second word in this construction is the Heb. *ʿešet*, used only this once in the Old Testament, although a related verb is found once in Jeremiah 5:28, and a feminine plural adjective occurs once in Ezekiel 27:19. A comparison of these texts suggests the meaning 'polished', 'smooth', or 'shiny' for the word.

Encrusted (ASV, AV, NEB *overlaid*; NIV *decorated*; JB *covered*; Heb. *ʿālap*) occurs in the sense 'cover' only here and at Genesis 38:14 of Tamar's veiling herself. The word is used elsewhere only four times with the sense 'faint' or 'lose consciousness' (Is. 51:20; Ezk. 31:15; Am. 8:13; Jon. 4:8). The link between these two meanings is obscure, unless the idea of 'fainting' suggests 'being wrapped up in oneself'.

Sapphire (Heb. *sapîr*, LXX *sappheiros*) is not our modern 'sapphire' which is a blue corundum (aluminium oxide coloured with titanium), but the azure-blue *lapis lazuli* (NEB) (sodium aluminium silicate), which is a much softer, less durable mineral. The true sapphire was uncommon in the ancient Near East, while lapis lazuli was prevalent. Various attempts at literalizing this description only result in ludicrous pictures, as Delitzsch's 'branching blue veins under white skin' (p. 105). This whole section is purely poetic hyperbole.

15. *His legs*, or more properly 'thighs', here includes the whole leg from thigh to ankle. The word is used only this once in the Song, but appears eighteen times elsewhere, twelve of them in the Pentateuch of the 'heave offering', *i.e.* the right shoulder of the sacrificial animal which was the priest's rightful portion (Lv. 7:32, 34).

Columns (AV, ASV, NIV, NEB *pillars*); *cf.* 3:10.

Alabaster (AV, ASV, NIV, NEB *marble*; Heb. *šēš*) occurs only here, and in 1 Chronicles 29:2 and Esther 1:6 as marble or alabaster. Another thirty-eight times it is translated 'fine linen' or 'silk'. Colour or texture would be the common feature linking these very different translations.

Bases (AV, ASV, NEB, JB *sockets*) is frequent in Exodus and Numbers of the socketed bases into which the framing of the tabernacle was put.

Finest gold, NEB (Heb. *pāz*). *Cf.* 5:11.

Appearance (AV *countenance*; ASV, NEB *aspect*). *Cf.* 2:14.

Lebanon. *Cf.* 3:9; 4:8; 7:4.

Choice (AV, ASV *excellent*; JB *unrivaled*; NEB *noble*; Heb. *baḥûr*). 'Select' or 'stately' is preferred. Delitzsch translates 'distinguished'.

Cedars. *Cf.* 1:17.

Pope comments on the incongruity of describing a 'mere man' in terms of the majesty of Lebanon. Delitzsch uses the verse to support the identification of the lover as Solomon rather than the 'sunburnt shepherd'. Yet the force of the whole unit is that in the girl's eyes her lover (be he king or peasant) is beyond comparison.

16. *Speech* (AV, ASV, NIV *mouth*; NEB *his whispers*; JB *conversation*; Heb. *ḥēk*, 'palate'). *Cf.* 2:3. Here the 'palate' includes the whole mouth as the source of speech. In the description *most sweet* (NIV, NEB, JB *sweetness itself*), the Hebrew plural 'sweets' is used as an intensive and serves to focus the emphasis on the predicate.

Altogether desirable (NEB *wholly desirable*; AV, ASV, NIV *altogether lovely*; JB *altogether lovable*). Another plural form here, 'desirables', reinforces the emphatic structure: 'everything about him is delightfulnesses'.

This is (NEB, JB *such is*) *my lover* (Heb. *dôḏî*); *cf.* 1:13 and Subject Study: Lover (Beloved), pp. 64f.

My friend (NEB *my darling*). A common Old Testament word, *rēa* expresses companionship and friendship without the overtones of sexual partnership. *Cf.* Psalm 45:14. There is refreshing candour in her identifying her lover as also her 'friend' – friendship goes far deeper than mere sexual compatibility and excitement. Happy is the husband or wife whose spouse is also a friend.

Daughters of Jerusalem. *Cf.* 1:5.

144

d. A second question (6:1)

The Jerusalem women respond to this paean with another question.

1. NIV, NEB and JB destroy the exact Hebrew parallelism by translating Heb. *'anâ* as *where* in line one and *which way* in line three. The two verbs are respectively 'go away' (Heb. *hālak*; *cf.* 2:10, 11; 4:6) and 'turn aside' or 'slip away' (Heb. *pānāh*). The latter, used only here in the Song, is a different word from that used in 5:6.

Fairest among women. Cf. 1:8; 5:9 for the other two uses of this phrase in the Song.

NEB *that we may help you to seek him* catches the force of the last colon. Her ardour has convinced them he is worth looking for and they are now willing to join her. On this seek/find motif, see the Introduction, p. 38, and the Commentary on 3:1–5.

e. A curious response (6:2–3)

These two verses are a difficult section for most commentators. Pope and others stress the cultic elements linking this with garden tombs and the death of the god.[1] Delitzsch *et al.* turn to Christological allegory and take the 'historical fact . . . idealized . . . as a figure of a higher Loveliness which was therein as it were typically manifest' (p. 108).

What these interpretations overlook is that if the 'garden' was a known haunt of the lovers and she was aware of his retreating there, she would not have wasted time going into the city nor asking for help from the Jerusalem women. She would have gone directly to their rendezvous. This unit is more probably her conscience-stricken recollection of her lover's approach to her bed (5:2f.), and her refusal to accept him. Now she remembers their relationship and commitment to each other.

2. *His garden.* This may, of course, be a literal garden, but on the analogy of 4:10 – 5:1, it is more likely a reference to the physical person of the beloved. (*Cf.* Subject Study: Garden, pp. 55–60.)

Bed of spices. Cf. 5:13.

---

[1] Pope, pp. 553–557; Kramer, pp. 100, 127–131.

Pasture. RSV, JB and ASV incorrectly add *his flock* which is not in the Hebrew text. NIV *to browse*, AV *to feed* are more accurate. *Cf.* 1:7f.; 2:16 for this construction. NEB *to delight* in the garden is a good interpretative insight, although not a technically accurate translation.

Gather (NEB *pick*) *lilies.* This is the only use of this verb in the Song, but lilies are mentioned frequently. *Cf.* 2:1f., 16, and p. 102, n. 1, for the specific erotic connotation of this picture.

3. The first colon is a recapitulation in a slightly different form of 2:16. It will re-appear in 7:10. The second colon condenses the last bicolon of v. 2.

f. The lover overwhelmed (6:4–10)

The lover, in spite of his rejection in 5:3, is still the lover. He has not abandoned his beloved in her selfishness, but now openly expresses his continued adoration of her beauty and character.

Many of the comparisons in this section have already appeared in the Song, but several new similes do occur. The unit opens and closes with the *inclusio* 'terrible as an army with banners', and reveals the lover's awe at her beauty.

4. *You are beautiful.* This description is used both by the Jerusalem women (*e.g.* 6:1) and the lover (1:15; 4:1).

My love is the feminine form of the word translated in 5:16 as 'companion' or 'friend' (*cf.* 1:9 and 4:1).

Tirzah was an ancient Canaanite city in Samaria which served as the capital of the secessionist Northern Kingdom for some fifty years during the reigns of Jeroboam and his successors until Omri established Samaria as the capital about 879 BC (1 Ki. 14:1–20; 16:8–26). The exact location of the city has not yet been established, but most authorities identify it with Tell el-Farah (North), about seven miles north-east of Shechem on the main road toward Beth-Shean. The site is one of great natural beauty with extensive gardens and groves encouraged by its abundant water supply (one of the best in Israel). The site also had great strategic importance until its destruction in the ninth century. The mention of Tirzah in this connection may give some indication of the date of the Song. It seems unlikely that a southern (Judean) king would use this site as a simile for beauty, especially since the first fifty years after the division of the Solomonic kingdom were marked by mutual hostility between the fragments of the united monarchy. A Solomonic date for this part of the Song is most likely. Pope's attempt to make this a form of the verb *rāṣâ*, following the LXX, and translating the colon, *Fair you are my darling, verily pleasing*, is ingenious, but unconvincing, and his proposal requires the excision of *as Jerusalem*.

The parallel between the two cities – one the capital, the other a northern 'garden city' – is in keeping with the royal/rural elements in this unit.

Comely (NEB, NIV *lovely*; JB *fair*). *Cf*. 1:5; 2:14; 4:3.

As Jerusalem. This is the only use of the name in the Song that is not accompanied by the phrase 'daughters of'. In Lamentations 2:15 the city is called 'the perfection of beauty, the joy of all the earth'.

Terrible (NIV *majestic*; JB and NEB delete this colon, although NEB note adds 'majestic as the starry heavens (*see verse 10*)'; Heb. *'ayummâ*). The adjective occurs only here and at Habakkuk 1:7 where it is used of the Babylonian armies. A related noun means 'terror', 'dread', or 'awe', and suggests this form may be translated 'awe-inspiring' or 'splendid'.[1]

As an army with banners (Heb. *kannidgālôt*) is more difficult. The Hebrew text does not contain the word for 'army', but simply reads 'as bannered'. The context suggests that it is the cities which are thus bedecked, and the introduction of 'armies' here is superfluous. In the light of the discussion of *dḡl*, meaning 'to look upon' (*cf*. 2:4), this colon is rendered simply 'splendid to look upon'. The expression is repeated in 6:10. *Cf*. 5:10.

5–7. The opening colon is straightforward. Her eyes have been noted as very beautiful and seductive several times already (1:15; 4:1, 9), and the motif is carried out here. Her eyes (*cf*. 4:9) *disturb* (AV, ASV *overcome*; NIV *overwhelm*; NEB *dazzle*; JB *hold captive*; Heb. *rāhab*) her lover. The verb occurs only four times in the Old Testament, here, Psalm 138:3; Proverbs 6:3 and Isaiah 3:5.[2] Many commentators stress the elements

---

[1] S. D. Goitein, 'AYUMMA KANNIDGALOT (Song of Songs vi. 10)', *JSS* 10, 1965, pp. 220f., defends the meaning 'extraordinary', 'terrific', on the basis of numerous parallels from Arabic, Syriac, and Ethiopic. *Cf*. above, p. 91, n. 4.

[2] Derived nouns and adjectives are used another eight times, meaning 'pride' or 'strength'. The transliteration as a name *Rahab* in Pss. 87:4; 89:10; Is. 51:9, easily confused with the harlot Rahab (Heb. *rāḥāb*; *cf*. Jos. 2:1),

of fear or terror in the word, following Delitzsch 'placed in a state of paralyzing terror', but that idea seems out of place here. Psalm 138:3, 'Thou didst encourage me with strength in my soul' (ASV), sheds light on the meaning here, as does the LXX use of *anapteroō* for *rāhab̠*. The Greek word means to raise the feathers (of a bird), and metaphorically is used to mean 'put on the tiptoe of expectation' or 'to excite' and bring to a state of eager expectation. This is clearly the intent here – her glance 'turns him on' and makes him bold in his intentions.[1]

His description continues with a reprise of his words in 4:1–3 with only slight changes in wording: 'ewe' (Heb. *rahēl*) replaces 'flock' (Heb. *'ēder*) which includes both male and female animals, and *Mount* (NIV) is omitted this time before *Gilead*, as is the comment about her lips and mouth.

8. The enumeration of the *queens, concubines* and *maidens*, and the contrast with the uniqueness of the beloved (v. 9) is usually considered to be a reference to the huge harem of Solomon, none of whose 700 wives and 300 concubines (1 Ki. 11:3) was as attractive to the king as the lady of the Song. The relatively small numbers, *sixty* and *eighty*, are supposed by Delitzsch to indicate this episode took place early in Solomon's reign before his harem grew to its fullest number. More probably, no particular harem is being considered. Note the text does not say 'Solomon has' or 'I have', but it is a simple declaration: *There are . . .* , and my beloved 'is unique' (v. 9, NIV).

Queens occurs in the Song only in these two verses, and elsewhere in the Old Testament only of Esther and Vashti (25 times in Esther) and of the Queen of Sheba in 1 Kings 10 and 2 Chronicles 9. The Aramaic equivalent is used twice in Daniel 5 of the wife of Belshazzar. The word is never used of the wives of Judean or Israelite kings.

Concubines in ancient Israel were not mere bed-partners. They were actually 'wives' (*cf.* Jdg. 20:3–5), albeit of secondary rank, with certain protections and privileges that set

---

would be better avoided and simply translated 'proud'. The parallel with 'serpent' in Jb. 26:12f. and 'reptile' in Is. 51:9 has led many commentators to see some mythological elements here, *i.e.* 'Rahab' as a primordial chaos monster, but the Old Testament itself gives no evidence of such an identification. The biblical links between the Edenic serpent and the sin of pride are sufficient explanation for rejecting the mythological idea.

[1] Pope translates 'drive me wild', following Waldman's rendering 'sexually aroused'. *Cf* above, p. 120, n. 1.

them apart from those outside the wife/concubine categories.

Maidens, unmarried women (Heb. *ʿalomôt*), *cf.* 1:3. The increasing numbers, *sixty, eighty, unnumbered* and the decreasing order of rank, *queens, concubines, maidens*, serve as a dual foil to the uniqueness of the beloved.

9. None of the translations captures the lilt of the Hebrew of the opening clauses here. 'Unique [Heb. 'one'] is she, my dove, my undefiled; unique is she to her mother.' This motif is found in an Egyptian poem which begins, 'One, the lady love without a duplicate/more perfect than the world', continues with a detailed description of the lady's physical attractions (as here and in 7:1–9), and closes: 'When she comes forth, anyone can see/that there is none like that One'.[1]

My dove, my undefiled is a reprise from 5:2.

Flawless (AV, ASV *choice*; JB, NIV *favourite*; Heb. *bārâ*). RSV follows BDB, p. 141, taking the Hebrew in its more common meaning. The other versions select the secondary meaning of the verb root. This understanding becomes the primary one in later Hebrew. These descriptions do not mean that the beloved was an only child, but simply that she was the favourite of the mother. As Pope notes, 'it is no special distinction to be a favourite only child' (p. 570). NEB *devoted to the mother who bore her* has found little support.

Maidens (AV, ASV *daughters*; NEB *young girls*) is the Hebrew *bānôt*, not *ʿalomôt* as in v. 8. AV is most accurate. *Cf.* 2:2. In the Song, the word is usually found with 'Jerusalem', *e.g.* 1:5.

Happy (Heb. *ʾāšar*) is more accurate than *blessed* (AV, ASV, NIV, JB) which is more precisely the Hebrew *bārak*, a cultic term not used in the Song.[2] Some suggest *ʾāšar* has the connotation 'envious desire', but 'congratulations' seems more in keeping with the idea of expressing happiness. This is the only use of the term in the Song, and it occurs only fifteen times in the Old Testament.

Queens and *concubines*, as in v. 8, but without the numbers.

Praise (Heb. *hālal*) is frequent in the Old Testament of 'praise to the LORD ("halleluia")', but is also used of people

---

[1] 'The Chester Beatty Love Songs (The Songs of Extreme Happiness, First Stanza)', Simpson, pp. 315f., no. 31. This is a series of seven songs spoken alternately by the boy and the girl in which the first and last words of each successive song is either the next number (from one to seven), or a play on the sound of the appropriate number.

[2] *Cf.* Introduction, pp. 42–44, and p. 28, on Psalm 45:2.

(*e.g.* Gn. 12:15; Jdg. 16:24; Pr. 31:28) and places (Ezk. 26:17) in the sense of 'boast about'. This latter idea illuminates the parallel with 'happy' above.

10. *Who is this?* (AV, ASV *Who is she?*). As in the identical expression in 3:6, the form is feminine, and the answer, although unspecified, must be the girl.

Looks forth (NEB *looks out*; JB *arising*; NIV *appears*; Heb. *hanniŝqāp̄â*) *like the dawn.* The verb form is participial from the root *ŝqp̄* which means to 'look down on something' or 'overhang'. It occurs twenty times in the Old Testament, only this once in the Song. A number of times it is used of someone looking out a window (*e.g.* Jdg. 5:28; 2 Sa. 6:16, *etc.*) which seems to be the sense here, except that this is hardly the verb one would expect with 'dawn'. Pope lists a number of parallels in other literatures where the sense 'superiority' is evident in the word, but this too is a difficult concept to relate to the 'dawn'. Delitzsch suggests the sense 'rising up from the background', and the NIV *appears* continues this idea; while it cannot be adopted certainly, this understanding has fewest problems.

Dawn (Heb. *ŝaḥar*), *cf.* 1:5. There is no word in this verse for 'dusk', hence little possibility of the Ugaritic cult meaning being found here. Nor does the context allow the sense of 'swarthy' here.[1]

Fair (NEB *beautiful*; Heb. *yāp̄eh*), as in 6:4; *cf.* 1:15; 4:1.

Moon (Heb. *lᵉḇānâ*, the milky/white one) is a rare word, occurring only here and in Isaiah 24:23; 30:26, in each case in parallel with 'sun' (Heb. *ḥammâ*, 'heat', the 'hot one'). This is the full moon as opposed to the 'new moon' (Heb. *ḥōdeŝ*).[2]

Bright (AV, ASV *clear*; JB *resplendent*; Heb. *bārâ*). *Cf.* v. 9, *flawless.*

Terrible as an army with banners. This is an exact repetition of the last colon of 6:4, and rounds off the lover's description of his beloved.

---

[1] *Cf.* above, p. 134, n. 3.

[2] An extensive treatment of the problems of terminology and the role of the moon in the ancient Near Eastern cults is given by C. R. North, '*chādhāsh*; *chōdhesh*', *TDOT* 4, pp. 225–244.

g. The beloved's excited anticipation (6:11–12)

These two verses pick up a number of themes introduced earlier. Now she expresses her surprise and excitement at the joyous reception her lover has accorded her.

11. *I went down* is the girl's confession that she has followed her lover to the garden (*cf.* 6:2).

Nut orchard (NIV *grove of nut-trees*; Heb. *ginnat*). This particular form occurs only here and in Esther 1:5; 7:7f., where it is used of the palace garden where state banquets were held. *Cf.* 4:12 and Subject Study: Garden, pp. 56f. The *nut* (Heb. *'ĕgôz*) is properly 'walnut', although in late Hebrew it is used of nuts generally. This is the only Old Testament use of the word.[1]

Blossoms (AV *fruits*; ASV *green plants*; NIV *new growth*; JB *what was sprouting*; NEB *the rushes*; Heb. *be'ibbê*). The root *'ēb* occurs only here and in Job 8:12. NIV and JB have the better renderings.

Valley (NEB *stream*; Heb. *naḥal*) occurs only here in the Song, but is frequent elsewhere in the Old Testament, usually with the meaning of the deep, narrow valleys that carry the torrents of water in the rainy season, but which are dry channels most of the year.[2]

Vines. Cf. 2:13.

Budded (AV *flourished*; Heb. *pāraḥ*), used in the Song only here and in 7:12, is a common word elsewhere in the Old Testament, and is one of the specifically agricultural words the author of the Song delights in using.

Pomegranates. Cf. 4:3 and p. 117, n. 1.

In bloom (AV *budded*; JB, NEB, ASV *in flower*; Heb. *hēnēṣû*). The word occurs only four times in the Old Testament (Song 6:11; 7:12; Ec. 12:5; Ezk. 1:17). A related word is translated 'flower' in 2:12. The root means to shine or sparkle. See 7:12 for repetition and expansion of this idea.

12. Commentators are unanimous that this verse is the

[1] Pope, pp. 574–579, has an extensive section tracing the Ugaritic parallels and the explicitly erotic connotations associated with nuts and nut-trees in the fertility rituals. Delitzsch, pp. 114–116, argues the passage refers to the garden-pools along the Solomonic aqueducts between Jerusalem and Etam, about seven miles south-west of Jerusalem on the Bethlehem/Hebron road. *Cf.* Josephus, *Antiquities of the Jews* viii.7.3.

[2] See previous note and Pope, pp. 574–582, for a summary of cultic activities in 'valleys'. *Cf.* Subject Study: Garden, pp. 57–59, and Is. 57:3–10, esp. vv. 5f.

most difficult in the Song and one of the most difficult in the Old Testament to make sense of.[1] Various proposals to emend the text, simply to remove the verse, or to ignore the problem have marked the efforts of translators and commentators from the LXX to now. The words themselves are all common, all but the last used well over 100 times each in the Old Testament, but the syntax is elusive.

Before I was aware (NIV *before I realised it*; JB *before I knew*; NEB *I did not know myself*; Heb. *lō' yāda'tî* 'I did not know'). *Cf.* 1:8. NEB links the next word *napšî* with the first two, but this rendering leaves the next verb standing alone, and requires elaborate emendation to make any sense of the rest of the verse.

My fancy. (AV, ASV *my soul*; JB, NIV *my desire*; NEB *she made me feel*; Heb. *napšî*). This is the last use of this word in the Song (*cf.* 1:7; 3:1). The RSV is a little less definite than the JB and NIV, but that ambiguity is good here, allowing the idea 'imagination' to emerge.

Set me (AV *made me like*; JB *hurled me*; Heb. *sāmatnî*; *cf.* 1:16). If *napšî* is the subject of the clause, there is no need to take this literally. Rather the meaning is clearly she 'feels' this way.

Chariot (NIV *royal chariots*; NEB *myriads*; Heb. *merkābâ*). The Hebrew text has no preposition here, the initial *me* being an integral part of the noun. The word, which occurs only here in the Song, is used over forty times elsewhere in the Old Testament of various types of two-wheeled vehicles: war-chariots (1 Ki. 10:29); state-chariots (Gn. 41:43); cult-chariots (2 Ki. 23:11; Is. 66:15) or simply vehicles for general travel (Gn. 46:29). Two closely related words are used in Song 1:9 and 3:10.

Beside my prince (AV *of Ammi-nadib*; ASV *my princely people*; NIV *among the royal chariots of my people*; JB *as their prince*; NEB *reigning over the myriads of his people*; Heb. *'ammî-nādîb*). Again, no preposition is indicated in the Hebrew text. The first word, 'my people', is very common in the Old Testament, but occurs only here in the Song. The second is found about twenty-six times in the Old Testament but in the Song only here and in 7:2 – 'queenly' maiden. Where the words are used in combination, as here (and in *e.g.* Nu. 21:18; Pss. 47:9; 113:8), those

---

[1] *E.g.* Roland Murphy, 'Toward a Commentary on the Song of Songs', *CBQ* 39, 1977, pp. 491f., remarks that this verse is the most obscure in the Song, and 'has resisted all attempts at translation'.

described are the leaders of the people, *i.e.* the 'princes'. NEB's emendation to a third person form is unwarranted. AV follows LXX in taking these two words as a proper name. Several individuals bore this name in the Old Testament, but none is prominent enough to be the source of this comparison.

Several commentators draw attention to the Egyptian 'Prince Mehy' who appears in a couple of the love songs as a royal lover in a chariot.[1] The precise meaning of the verse is not clear. Perhaps there is some merit in Fuerst's suggestion that there is some idiomatic meaning we cannot recover.

h. A request, a question, and a reply (6:13 – 7:5) (Heb. 7:1–6)

The Hebrew and Greek texts number 6:13 as the first verse of ch. 7, so that ch. 7 contains 14 verses rather than 13 as in the English versions. The numbering of the English versions is followed here. The next eighteen verses are very frequently linked together by the commentators, who identify the women of Jerusalem as speaking in 6:13a, the lover as speaking in 7:1–9, and the beloved responding in 7:10 – 8:4. But closer examination suggests a better division of the unit. The onlookers (wedding guests?), who would stay for several days to celebrate, urge the bride to put in an appearance and join the festive dance. She demurs with a question, 'Why me?' (6:13b), and they reply (7:1–5) with their praise of her beauty. Her lover/husband then joins in with his adoration (7:6–9) and she renews her commitment to him (7:10 – 8:4).

13. The request and the question are brief and both raise problems of interpretation. *Return* (NEB, NIV *come back*; Pope *leap*; Heb. *šûbî*), repeated four times, emphasizes the urgency of the entreaty. Pope's proposal, emending to *sêbî* from the verb *yšḇ*, is based on the Arabic cognate 'to leap'. The request then is for her to begin the dance. The more usual understanding is the call to come back to the garden of her fancies.[2]

---

[1] See Simpson, p. 305, no. 15, and p. 317, no. 33. Chariots also appear in *e.g.* p. 321, no. 38, and p. 322, no. 39. Similarly, in the Mesopotamian love lyrics (*cf.* above, p. 98, n. 2), 'the wagon of her lord' is mentioned. See also M. Civil, 'Išme-Dagan and Enlil's Chariot', *JAOS* 88, 1968, pp. 3–14. *Cf.* Song 3:9.

[2] Gordis, p. 95, suggests 'halt' or 'stay' as the meaning here. *Cf.* 'Some Hitherto Unrecognized Meanings of the verb *SHUB*', *JBL* 52, 1933, pp. 153–162.

That we may look (NIV, NEB, JB *gaze*; Heb. *wᵉneḥᵉzeh*). This verb *ḥāzah* occurs in the Song twice, both times in this verse, and both times in the plural. The sense is to see with insight and understanding, not just 'gaze on' or 'look at', which is expressed by a different verb (*cf.* 1:6; 2:14). This verb is used frequently of the prophetic visions.[1] Here the onlookers meant to verify by examination the beauty they have had described to them. Delitzsch's identification of these onlookers as the 'daughters of Jerusalem' is unlikely, since the verb form in the next colon is masculine: *Why should you look?* These are the 'friends' who speak to the lover in 5:1e.

O Shulammite (NEB *Shulammite maiden*; JB *maid of Shulam*; Heb. *haššûlammît*). This is the only place in the Old Testament this word appears. It is variously rendered as a proper name 'Shulamith' (so Delitzsch), or as in JB as the name of the place from which the girl comes (*cf.* Introduction, p. 47). Neither view is entirely satisfactory, nor has won general acceptance. The presence of the article *ha-* (or the preposition *ba-*) in the second instance precludes this being her name. On the other hand, no certain reference to an identifiable site appears anywhere in the literature. The most likely site is Shunem (Heb. *šûnēm*), near Mount Tabor in Galilee's Esdraelon Valley about nine miles west of Megiddo (Jos. 19:18; 1 Sa. 28:4; 2 Ki. 4:8), from which town Abishag, David's last nurse/wife came (1 Ki. 1:1–3). By New Testament times the town was being called 'Shulem', but the evidence for this shift is late, and attempts to identify this town as the beloved's home are sheer speculation.

Albright's suggestion[2] that Shulamith's prototype is really the Assyrian war-goddess Shulmânitû is ingenious, but hardly convincing.[3] This identification provides a clue which some commentators have adopted, that 'Shulammite' is 'Solomon's lady' and the name is simply a feminine form of the name Solomon.

---

[1] *E.g.* Is. 1:1; 2:1; 13:1; La. 2:14, *etc.* In about twenty instances the noun *ḥōzeh*, 'seer' (or 'see-er') is used of the prophets themselves, *e.g.* 2 Sa. 24:11; 2 Ki. 17:13; 1 Ch. 21:9; Am. 7:12, *etc.*

[2] W. F. Albright, 'Archaic Survivals in the Text of Canticles', in D. W. Thomas and W. D. McHardy (eds.) *Hebrew and Semitic Studies Presented to Geoffrey Rolles Driver* (O.U.P., 1963), p. 5 and the bibliography there in nn. 2, 6.

[3] The Ugaritic Anath, the virgin/wife/warrior/avenger of Baal, is her counterpart in Canaan.

Yet another idea, proposed by Hirschberg,[1] is that the root *šlm* in this context has the meaning 'To give a consummation gift' to a bride the morning after the wedding. The 'Shulammite' is then the 'consummated one', and what follows is a response to her question 'What do you see in one who is no longer virgin?'

The final colon also presents a major interpretative problem. *Dance* (AV *company*; JB, NEB *dancers*; Heb. *kimḥōlat*) in its various forms occurs some fourteen times in the Old Testament, but only here in the Song. The meaning is clearly 'dance' or 'dancing', not 'dancer'. The exact choreography is not recoverable, but the sense of celebration and joy in association with victory in war (Ex. 15:20; 1 Sa. 18:6), religious ecstasy (Ex. 32:19; Jdg. 21:21; Pss. 149:3; 150:4), or simply joyous celebration (Je. 31:13), suggests some sort of vigorous group activity with antiphonal singing and instrumental accompaniment.

Two armies (NIV *Mahanaim*; JB *two rows*; NEB *the lines*; Heb. *hammaḥᵃnāyim*). Again, the precise meaning is elusive. Suggestions of some sort of sword dance or celebration of bloody military victory seem out of place here.[2] Wetzstein, in his article on Syrian marriage customs,[3] identifies this as one of the dances in the wedding celebration. The Hebrew word is used over 200 times in the Old Testament, with the common meaning 'hosts' or 'armies' (*e.g.* Ex. 14:20, *etc.*). The NIV rendering of it as a proper name identifies the site in Gilead where Jacob met the angel on his return to Canaan (Gn. 32:2).[4] This Mahanaim was an important city in early Israelite history (*cf.* 2 Sa. 2:8; 17:24–27), and was one of the cities of refuge established by Joshua (Jos. 21:38), but there is no indication that the city was famous for its contribution to the art of the dance, Delitzsch's 'dance of the angels' (p. 121), notwithstanding. The best rendering seems to be 'the dance of the two groups (hosts)', or the 'counterdance' (so Fuerst, p. 193), reading the Hebrew as the proper name of a *dance*, not of a *place*. Her question then becomes, 'Why do you want to look at me when there are so many others in this dance?' Both these questions

---

[1] *VT* 11, 1961, p. 381. *Cf.* above, p. 109, n. 2.
[2] *Cf.* Dahood, III, p. 358. Pope, pp. 601–614, has an extensive section on this understanding, but it seems to me 'he doth protest too much'.
[3] See Introduction, pp. 52f., and Delitzsch, pp. 170–172.
[4] See on Song 2:17, esp. p. 103, n. 2.

underscore the modesty of the beloved and her self-effacement that appeared as early as 1:6.

7:1. The reply to 6:13 follows in the next five verses. Most commentators and translations assign the whole unit 7:1–9 to the lover as he responds to her question, but the context (*i.e.* the plural forms in 6:13 and the last colon in 7:5) makes it clear that these five verses are spoken by the onlookers, not by the lover himself. His contribution – and a highly personal one it is – comprises vv. 6–9.

The companions respond to her question with a very explicit and erotic description of why she is the focus of their attention. Beginning from her feet and progressing upward to the crown of her head, they sing the praise of her beauty. Whether, as Delitzsch suggests, she removed her outer garments and danced in the light clothing of a shepherdess, or as Gordis argues (p. 96), she danced either naked or in diaphanous veils, she 'displayed all her attractions before them' (Delitzsch, p. 122).

Sandalled feet (NIV, NEB) were considered particularly attractive (*cf.* Judith 16:8f.). The Hebrew *pā'am* means either the foot itself or the steps of the dance.

Graceful (Heb. *yāpeh*), as in 6:10 and elsewhere in the Song, is rendered by most translators 'beautiful'.

Queenly maiden (AV, ASV, JB, NEB *prince's daughter*; Heb. *bat-nādîb*). As in 6:12, the meaning is not necessarily that the girl is of royal birth, but rather that she is of gracious and noble character and person.

Rounded thighs (NEB, JB *curve of your thighs*; AV *joints of thy thighs*; NIV *graceful legs*; Heb. *hammūqē yᵉrēkayik*). NIV avoids the clear meaning of the words. The word occurs only three times, here, Song 5:6, and Jeremiah 31:19 where the meaning 'turn' is obvious. Delitzsch's 'vibrations due to turning movements' is an awkward attempt at compromise. The expression, particularly as it is qualified in the last colon, clearly refers to the beautiful craftsmanship (*i.e.* the perfection) of her thighs.

The *yārak* (*cf.* 3:8) is not the leg as a whole, but is specifically the fleshy upper part of the thigh where the leg joins the pelvis (*cf.* Gn. 32:25–32; 46:26; Ex. 1:5; Jdg. 8:30), here likened to 'ornaments' (Heb. *ḥᵃlî*). This word occurs only three times in the Old Testament, here, Proverbs 25:12, and Hosea 2:13. The latter reference indicates these ornaments were used in the love-making that was part of the fertility ritual. The action

156

of the dance reveals the symmetrical beauty of her thighs.

Master hand (AV *cunning workman*; ASV *skilful workman*; NEB *skilled craftsman*). The Hebrew *'ammān* occurs only here in the Old Testament, but the verbal stem *'āmam* 'true', 'faithful' is common. Here the competent work of the artisan is used as a comparison.

2. The frank description continues as the onlooker's eyes continue their progress upward.

Navel (ASV *body*; Heb. *šarr*) occurs only three times in the Old Testament, here, Proverbs 3:8 (RSV *flesh*) and Ezekiel 16:4 where the umbilical cord is meant. Delitzsch notes this as the 'centre of the body' (p. 123), but the second colon refers to the 'belly' which is more correctly the 'centre'. The fact that the longer unit (vv. 1–9) does not use synonymous parallelism elsewhere suggests that no parallelism is intended here either. It is more likely, then, that the word should be translated 'vulva'.[1]

Rounded bowl (Heb. *'aggan hassahar*). The adjective occurs only here in the Old Testament.[2] *Bowl* or goblet (LXX *kratēr*) is also infrequent, occurring only here, at Isaiah 22:24, and Exodus 24:6. The word is used of large two- or four-handled metal or clay bowls. According to Isaiah 22:24, the *'aggan* was so heavy it could pull its hanging-peg from the wall, and shatter itself on the floor.[3] Admittedly, neither the navel nor the vulva is of large size, but the latter is more appropriate than the former.

Never lacking. Delitzsch treats this as an exhortation 'May [it] never lack . . .', *i.e.* as a plea for continued health. A simple declaration is more likely.

Mixed wine (AV *liquor*; ASV *mingled wine*; NEB *spiced wine*; NIV *blended wine*; Heb. *mezeg*). This is the only occurrence of this word in the Old Testament, although most commentators relate it to the Heb. *māsak* and its cognates; these are used

---

[1] Delitzsch rejects this as 'inconsiderate' and 'immodest' (p. 123), but the Arabic *sirr* is used of the 'secret' parts, and Lys (*cf.* above, p. 101, n. 3), develops this further. He argues for a root *šr* meaning a valley or a place to be farmed. The imagery of 'ploughing' as a euphemism for sexual intercourse is well-attested in the literature. *Cf.* Subject Study: Garden, pp. 59f., and Commentary on 5:1, esp. p. 129, n. 1.

[2] A related word *sōhar* occurs seven times in Gn. 39 and 40 of the 'round house', *i.e.* the prison in which Joseph was incarcerated.

[3] See J. Kelso, 'The Ceramic Vocabulary of the Old Testament', *BASOR Supplementary Studies 5–6* (New Haven, 1948), pp. 15f. and p. 47, fig. 2.

eight times of wine which is mixed either with water to dilute it or with spices and honey to strengthen it. *Cf.* Subject Study: Wine, pp. 66f., and Commentary on 8:2.

Belly (NIV *waist*; Heb. *beten*) is distinguished from *mē'eh* in 5:4, 14, in that it refers to the lower abdomen, below the navel, and is used specifically of the womb and the fetus carried there (*cf.* Jb. 3:3–11; 31:18; Ps. 139:13, *etc.*). Obviously the internal organs are not referred to here, but rather the rounded lower parts with their glistening wheat-coloured skin.

Encircled (AV, ASV *set about*; NEB *fenced in*; JB *surrounded*; Heb. *sûḡâ*). This is the only use of this word in the Old Testament, but an identical root meaning 'to move back' appears fourteen times. If *lilies* suggests intimacy (*cf.* 2:16; 6:3), there is continual upward movement suggested here, from her upper thighs to her pudenda, to her abdomen to her *breasts* (v. 3).

3. This is a reprise of the first two cola of 4:5.

4. The description of the beloved concludes with some earlier similes repeated and modified. Her *neck*, described as surrounded by beautiful jewelled necklaces in 1:10 and 4:4, is here praised for its own smooth *ivory*-coloured beauty (*cf.* 5:14). Her eyes, previously compared to the iridescent mauves and greys of the dove (1:15; 4:1, *etc.*), here are described as deep, clear *pools* (Heb. *berēkôt*). The word occurs some seventeen times in the Old Testament (*e.g.* 2 Sa. 2:13 of the 'pool of Gibeon'; Ne. 3:15 and Is. 7:3; 22:9, 11 of the Jerusalem water system in the Kidron valley). These 'pools' are not the springs themselves (*cf.* 4:12 'fountain'), but the deep reservoirs which the springs supply. The sense here is one of still, deep calmness rather than the sparkle and shimmer of flowing springs. AV *fishpools* is not likely, since those are relatively shallow but wide.

Gate. Ancient cities were built near a water supply. Ease of access to that meant one of the city gates would be near the point where water could be drawn (1 Ch. 11:17; Ne. 3:15f., 26).

Bath-rabbim (NEB *the crowded city*) is an otherwise unknown site, not mentioned in the Old Testament or other ancient literature. NEB takes the Hebrew literally, *the daughter of many*, but that makes little sense here. Most likely this is simply a proper name, parallel to *Heshbon*, or perhaps the name of one of the city gates at Heshbon. Recent excavations near Hesbon in Jordan, not far from modern Amman, have revealed the remains of large reservoirs near the city. This may be the origin of the simile.

Like a tower of Lebanon, i.e. solid limestone and 10,000 feet high, hardly seems an apt comparison for a lady's nose. The simile has given commentators no end of trouble. Prominent noses are not normally considered especially beautiful. Delitzsch (p. 127) took this to mean 'symmetrical beauty combined with awe-inspiring dignity', since it 'formed a straight line from the brow downward, without bending to the right or left'. This is hardly convincing. *Lebanon* (*cf.* 3:9; 4:8) is one of several words derived from the Hebrew root *lābēn*, 'to be white' (*cf.* 'frankincense', 3:6). It was probably the whiteness of the limestone cliffs that gave the mountain its name. This suggests that the imagery here is associated with the colour of her nose rather than its shape or size. Her face is pale, like the ivory tone of her neck, not sunburnt (*cf.* 1:6).

Tower. Heb. *migdal*, *cf.* 4:4; 5:13 'yielding'; 8:10.

Overlooking (JB *sentinel facing*) *Damascus.* The desert city, capital of Syria, lies on the eastern side of the Lebanon mountain range which dominates the western horizon.

5. The opening colon is variously translated; JB has *Your head is held high like Carmel*, NEB *You carry your head like Carmel* (Heb. 'your head upon you like Carmel'). The Old Testament has two sites named 'Carmel'. The best-known is the well-wooded mountain range that borders the southern edge of the Plain of Esdraelon and which served as a natural barrier to trade and military movement through Israel. The other Carmel is about seven and a half miles south-east of Hebron on the road to Arad. This site is on the edge of the Negeb, and, while suitable for grazing cattle, lacks the luxuriant vegetation of the northern site. The imagery in the text requires Mount Carmel to be the one in mind. This is the only mention of the site in the Song. Gordis (p. 96) understands 'carmel' to be a variant of the Hebrew *carmîl* 'crimson', here used in parallel with 'purple' in the next colon.

Flowing locks (AV, ASV *hair of thine head*; NEB *flowing hair on your head*; JB *its plaits*; NIV *your hair*; Heb. *dallat*). This Hebrew word is used eight times in the Old Testament, six (or seven) times of something which is 'poor' or 'weak'.[1] In Isaiah 38:12, Hezekiah on his miraculous recovery from his debilitating

---

[1] Gn. 41:19; 2 Ki. 24:14; 25:12; Je. 40:7; 52:15f.

illness, uses this word of 'pining sickness' (AV mg. 'thrum', *i.e.* the loose warp-threads left dangling after the cloth has been removed from the loom), or the sickness which leaves one limp and drooping. This provides a clue to the meaning here, not that the hair is lifeless and poor, rather that it hangs loosely and freely, and in effect makes her lover 'weak' with love.[1] JB *plaits* misses the image.

Like purple (NEB *lustrous black*), *cf.* 3:10. Earlier references to the lady's hair (*e.g.* 4:4; 6:5) indicate it to be black. 'Purple' is distinctly different, but probably indicates the lustrous highlights which shimmer and ripple as she moves, rather than, as Pope suggests, some sort of cosmetic or dye applied to her hair. NIV *royal tapestry* has no support.

A king (not *the* king as ASV and NIV). This is the only time the word is used without the definite article in the Song (*cf.* 1:4, 12; 3:9, 11). There is no reference here to Solomon. This is simply another use of the royal title for the lover.

Tresses (AV *in the galleries*; Heb. *bārhāṭîm*). The word occurs four times in the Old Testament, only this once in the Song, although a related word 'gutters' is found in Song 1:17. The root meaning is to run or flow, so that the picture here is of her hair having the appearance of running, rippling water. This is a common image in the love poetry.[2] NEB *Your tresses are braided with ribbons* is purely conjectural.

i. The lover's praise (7:6–9a)

After the detailed description of the beloved's beauty by the onlookers, the lover himself again adds his praise, speaking out of the remembering of the wedding night just past (*cf.* 1:8; 4:10).

6. *Fair and pleasant* (NEB *how beautiful, how entrancing*; JB *how beautiful, how charming*; NIV *beautiful . . . pleasing*). *Fair*, or *beautiful*, appears now for the last time (*cf.* 1:8) as the lover begins his final song of endearment. *Pleasant* (Heb. *nā'am*) occurs only this once in the Song and seven times elsewhere, although the

---

[1] *Cf.* C. Rabin, p. 212, for the *topos* of 'loosened hair' as a sign of the lover's fulfilment.

[2] The Egyptian poetry has several instances. Simpson, p. 299, no. 3 '. . . her brow a snare of willow,/and I the wild goose!/My beak snips her hair for bait,/ as worms for bait in the trap'; p. 301, no. 8, lines 17f., 'My arms are full of Persea branches/my tresses laden with salves'.

adjective *nāʿîm* is found in Song 1:16 and twelve times else-where. The usual meaning (in Ugaritic as well as Hebrew) is 'good' or 'gracious', but the parallelism here and in Song 1:16 seems to demand some term describing physical beauty.

O loved one (JB *my love*; NEB *my loved one*). These translations emend the Hebrew text to a vocative form, but as in 2:4f.; 3:10; 5:8, and the refrain at 2:7; 3:5 and 8:7, the meaning 'love-making' or 'love' in the abstract is preferable and more in keeping with the Hebrew text. (*Cf.* 1:4, and Subject Study: Love, pp. 60–63.

Delectable maiden (AV, ASV *for delights*; NIV *with your delights*; NEB *daughter of delights*; JB *my delight*; Heb. *battaʿănûgîm*). The verbal form *ʿanag* has the sense 'delicate, soft, delightful', and the noun *taʿănûg* has the meaning of luxurious, specifically erotic, delights (*e.g.* Ec. 2:8; Mi. 1:16). The sense of this last colon is a description of the delights of love-making remem-bered (4:16 – 5:1), and anticipated (7:10–12). Gordis (p. 97) quotes the rabbinic comment from Ibn Ezra on this verse: 'in all the world there is no such delight for the spirit and nothing as fair and pleasant as love'. Lehrman (p. 27) renders this 'how surpassingly delightful is love above all other pleasures'.[1]

7. AV and ASV correctly translate the demonstrative pronoun *this*, but most other versions ignore it. *Your stature* (RSV, NEB *you are stately*; Heb. *qômâ*) technically means 'height' from the verb 'arise' or 'stand up', but includes the idea of 'bearing' or 'carriage' which is 'compared' (*cf.* 1:9) to the *date palm* (Heb. *tāmār*, *Phoenix dactylifera*), a tall, slender tree that typifies grace and elegance, and is also a symbol of rejoicing and celebration (*e.g.* the use of palm-branches at Jesus' entrance into Jerusalem, Jn. 12:13).

Her *breasts*, which earlier are described as twin fawns (4:5; 7:3), are now compared to the *clusters* of fruit (Heb. *ʾeškol*, *cf.* 1:14). AV adds *of grapes*, picking up the imagery from the next verse, but there is no need to shift the image in this colon. The picture is not of multiple breasts as in the statue of Artemis of Ephesus[2] nor in their large size, as the 'cluster' of

---

[1] 'Coition, the centre of desire in the poem, is veiled by circumlocution, by metaphor, or by roundabout description of the delights of love play'; here in 7:6 there is a term 'heavily weighted toward physical lovemaking' – A. Cook, *The Root of the Thing: A Study of Job and the Song of Songs* (Indiana U.P., 1968), p. 110.

[2] See *IBD*, p. 123.

grapes from the valley Eshcol which required two men to carry it (Nu. 13:23f.), but rather of the 'sweetness' the heavy, dark fruit provided.

8. *I say* (AV, ASV, NIV, NEB *I said*; JB *I resolved*, Delitzsch *I thought*). The sense of the verb is immediate (*i.e.* present or just present), rather than in some distant time as Delitzsch suggests, 'retrospectively'. In order to harvest dates, one needs to climb the tree; but the reward, the honeyed sweetness of the fruit, is worth the effort. Lehrman (p. 27) puns here 'the king tells her to what heights he would go to obtain her love'.

Lay hold (JB *seize*; NEB *grasp*; Heb *'aḥaz*). The verb frequently has the sense of violent grasping (*e.g.* Jdg. 1:6; 12:6), but does not necessarily have that angry connotation. The same verb is used in Song 2:15; 3:4, 8.

Branches (AV *boughs*; NIV *fruit*; JB *clusters of dates*; NEB *fronds*; Heb. *sansinnâ*). This is the only use of this word in the Old Testament. Gordis (p. 97) links the word with the Akkadian *sinninu* 'the top-most branches of the palm'. Most commentators identify her breasts as the object of his grasping, but this word suggests rather her hair (v. 5), in which he is willing to be entrapped, as the thing he will grasp in their embrace.

Oh, may . . . is probably too strong, as the AV *shall be* . . . is not strong enough. The Hebrew *nā'* added to the verb expresses a wish or desire. In the previous verse the beloved's *breasts* are compared with the sweetness of the dates; here the image changes to the fruit of the vine (*cf.* 2:13; 6:11). The intention is not, as Delitzsch suggests, to describe them as grape clusters that 'swell and become round and elastic the more they ripen' rather than being 'of a long oval form with a stony kernel' as dates are. The parallel with v. 7 suggests rather the different, but delicate, sweetness of the grape contrasted with the heavy sweetness of the date-honey.

Scent (AV, ASV *smell*; NIV *fragrance*; Heb. *rîaḥ*) is used elsewhere in the Song of the beloved's perfumes (1:3, 12; 4:10f.), or of the fragrance of the plants of the garden (2:13; 7:13).

Breath (AV *nose*; Heb. *'ap*), *cf.* 7:4. The word normally means 'nose' or 'face' (*e.g.* Gn. 2:7; 3:19, *etc.*), or 'nostrils' (Gn. 7:22), frequently as these flare in anger (Ps. 30:5; Zc. 10:3). Since neither the normal translation nor 'breath' seems entirely satisfactory here, Pope proposes some 'more distinctly feminine zone than the nose or the mouth'. Ugaritic *ap* is used of both the mouth and nose, but also of the nipple of the breast and of the 'opening' of the city gate. Akkadian *apu* also means an 'opening'. These parallels suggest 'nipple' as a possibility here, or even more intimately, the 'opening' or 'entrance' *i.e.* the vulva (*cf.* Pope, pp. 636f.).

Apples (NEB *apricots*), *cf.* 2:3, 5.

9a. A number of difficult problems are posed by this verse. ASV, NIV, JB and many commentators (*e.g.* Gordis, Pope, Delitzsch, *etc.*) link the first colon with the preceding verse. The suffix on the first noun, *your kisses*, is feminine, indicating that the girl is still being described.

Kisses (AV *roof of thy mouth*; ASV *thy mouth*; NEB *your whispers*; JB *your speaking*; Heb. *ḥikēk*) is interpretative, for this common word means simply mouth or palate. *Cf.* Song 2:3; 5:16.

Best wine. The words she used in her opening wishes (1:2) are now turned back on her by her lover. The construction is superlative.

j. Consummation – again (7:9b – 8:4)

What begins in the last two cola of v. 9 continues through the first four verses of ch. 8, and capsulizes the fourth major division of the Song. The girl, who has been the object of the attention of the assembled crowd, now responds with a re-affirmation of her commitment to her lover/spouse. In the second and third cola of v. 9 there is an abrupt switch as the beloved speaks. RSV and NEB emend these two cola to feminine forms, and include these lines in the lover's address to his beloved, but, as Delitzsch notes (p. 133), vv. 9b and 10 both contain the title *lᵉdôdî*, 'my beloved', which elsewhere in the Song is always used of the male. This suggests that emendation is not necessary and that the ASV, JB and NIV are correct in splitting the speech after the first colon.

9b. All but one of the words (*dābab*, 'glide') in these two lines are common, but as is frequently the case, it is difficult to make certain sense in translation. The Hebrew 'going to my beloved smoothly, gliding (over) lips of sleepers', is rendered very differently in the English versions. ASV is closest to the Hebrew. JB and NEB *flowing* is permissible for the Hebrew *hālak* (*cf.* Pss. 58:7; 105:41), although 'go' or 'walk' is the more common rendering. *Go down* (AV, ASV, RSV) is more correctly the Hebrew *yārad* as in 6:2, 11.

Smoothly (AV *sweetly*; NIV, JB *straight*; Heb. *mêšārîm*) appears elsewhere in the Song only at 1:4 where Gordis translates 'for thy manliness' (*cf.* p. 76, n. 1). The word appears only in the plural form (twenty-one times) and is usually translated 'uprightness', 'equity' or 'righteously'. Delitzsch (p. 132) remarks that wine 'which tastes badly sticks in the palate, but that which tastes pleasantly glides down directly and smoothly'.

Gliding (NIV *flowing gently*; AV *cause . . . to speak*; JB *as it runs*; Heb. *dābab*) is unknown in Hebrew apart from this use.[1] AV reflects some rabbinic interpretations, but there is no support for this proposal in the ancient literature. Delitzsch suggests 'ruminate', *i.e.* 'enjoy the after-taste' which would fit nicely with the preceding idea. Nothing certain, however, can be established yet for this term.

Lips and teeth (AV, ASV *lips of those that are asleep*; JB *the lips of those who sleep*; Heb. *śiptê yešēnîm*). AV, ASV, JB read the latter word as a plural participle from the verb *yšn* 'to sleep'. RSV, NEB, NIV emend to *wešēnîm*, changing the initial letter to the conjunction 'and' (Heb. *w*), and reading the rest of the word as the plural form of *šēn* 'teeth'. This latter reading appears to make better sense in the context, but Gordis (p. 97) translates 'stirring the lips of sleepers (with desire)'. In either case the erotic connotation is present.

10. *Cf.* 6:3. NIV *belong* is interpretative, but leaves a rather negative sense. RSV *I am my beloved's* is more accurate. Here the second colon changes.

Desire (Heb. *tešûqâ*) occurs only here and in Genesis 3:16; 4:7. The meaning is of strong desire that impels to action.[2]

11. Her response to his desire is couched in terms he had directed to her in 2:10–14. The stroll into the *fields* (NIV *country-side*), *i.e.* the open country, is with the intention of spending

---

[1] The word has not yet appeared in the Ebla texts, but it does occur as a proper name at Ugarit, *UT* no. 636. The Akkadian *dabābu* 'plot, plan', and the Arabic *dabûb* 'tale-bearer', may be cognate, but do not clarify the Hebrew meaning.

[2] Susan J. Foh, 'What is Woman's Desire?', *WTJ* 37, 1975, pp. 376–383, argues that the force of the word is negative – a desire to dominate and rule, but that seems out of place in this context. For a more positive view, see M. Woodson, 'He loved me – He loved me not', *CT* 19, 1974, pp. 8–10. Woodson treats the Genesis passage as meaning that the woman's desire is for more attention from her husband. The effect of the curse is to divide the husband's interests so that the wife is constantly frustrated in her desire for the renewal of the Edenic closeness. Such an interpretation of *tešûqâ* makes excellent sense in this context.

the night (*lodge*) there together.[1]

Among the henna bushes, NEB. Other versions have *villages* (Heb. *kōp̄er*). The lexicons list at least four different nouns with this form and spelling. The verbal root means to cover or seal something (*e.g.* Gn. 6:14), and is used most frequently of 'atonement', *i.e.* 'covering' sin. The nouns, however, vary considerably. In 1 Samuel 6:18; 1 Chronicles 27:25; and Nehemiah 6:2, *kōp̄er* is translated *village*, *i.e.* 'unwalled village' in contrast to 'walled' cities. But twice before in the Song (1:14; 4:13), *kōp̄er* is used of the copper-coloured cosmetic dye extracted from the henna-plant. This shrub, which grows wild in Palestine, is covered in spring with fragrant whitish flowers growing in clusters like grapes. In view of the parallel in vv. 11f. with the perfume/vineyard/field motifs from earlier in the Song (*e.g.* 1:13f.; 2:11-17; 4:12-16, *etc.*), NEB *henna bushes* is preferred over the other versions.

12. JB *in the morning* is interpretative. The Hebrew text means simply 'start early', often with the overtone of eager expectation, as here.

Vineyards. Cf. Commentary on 1:6 and 2:15. The personal metaphor is lacking here, although the erotic element is evident from the context. The motif of budding vines is repeated from 6:11, but here it is expanded, with the third colon repeating the image from 2:13, 15. On the *blossoms*, see above on 2:13, pp. 99f.

The fourth colon is a reprise from 6:11.

The gift of *love* is to be bestowed there in the garden/vineyard. The ancient versions render this 'breasts' as in 1:2, 4; 4:10. See discussion on 1:2.

13. The *mandrake* or 'love apple' is a pungently fragrant plant that has long been considered an aphrodisiac – not that these lovers needed any additional stimulation, but the use of such items has long been a part of the lore of love-making. The word occurs only here, and four times in Genesis 30:14-16.

Over our doors (JB, ASV *at our doors*; NIV, NEB *at our door*; AV *at our gates*; Heb. *'al-p̄etāḥênû*). The noun occurs some 164 times in the Old Testament, most often in the Pentateuch of the door of the tabernacle, and frequently of gates of cities (*e.g.* 1 Ki. 17:10; Je. 1:15). The only metaphorical uses are Hosea

---

[1] *Cf.* 1:13 for the only other use of this verb in the Song. It is frequent elsewhere in the Old Testament.

2:15, 'a door of hope', and Micah 7:5, 'guard the doors of your mouth'. Pope (p. 650) argues that the reference here is to the girl's sexual charms; on the basis of the next word this is possible, although there is no clear use of the noun with this meaning. Nor is the suggestion that the reference is to a shelf over the door, where produce was stored or where fertility charms were displayed, any more satisfactory.

Choice fruits (AV *pleasant fruits*; ASV *precious fruits*; NIV *every delicacy*; NEB *rare fruits*; JB *rarest fruits*; Heb. *kol-mᵉḡāḏîm*). This rare word occurs earlier in 4:13, 16 where it is used of the girl's physical and erotic attractions. Here a similar meaning seems likely. *Cf.* Subject Study: Garden, pp. 59f.

New as well as old. Those already known and those yet to be discovered, all of which she has kept for her beloved. *Cf.* 4:16 and 7:10. The unequivocal devotion of the pair for each other is evident in this exchange.

8:1. *O that* (NEB, NIV *If only*; JB *Ah, why . . . not*) introduces a hypothetical wish directed to her lover, continuing into v. 2. She is not wishing that they were literally brother and sister, but that they had the freedom of public expression of their love. What was not in good taste even for husband and wife was perfectly permissible between brother and sister.[1] This is the only use in the Song of the common word *brother*. In 1:6 the expression used is 'my mother's sons'.

Met you (AV, ASV, NIV, NEB *found*; Heb. *māṣā'*) was used seven times previously in 3:1–4 and 5:6–8 where the search motif is developed.

2. The Hebrew text is relatively straightforward (ASV *I would lead thee and bring thee into my mother's house, who would instruct me*), but many commentators and translators follow the LXX in adding *and into the chamber of her that conceived me* (KJV, *cf.* NEB), from the parallel passage in 3:4.

Because the first two words in the Hebrew, *lead* and *bring*, have similar meanings, they are probably to be taken in apposition. But Gordis deletes 'lead' and NEB and Pope emend the text, assuming that some scribal error has crept in or that a

---

[1] This is a universal phenomenon. Simpson, p. 320, no. 36, records a similar wish in the Egyptian love poetry. 'If only my mother knew my wish,/she would have gone inside by now./O Golden Goddess, place him in her heart too,/then I'll rush off to the lover./I'll kiss him in front of the crowd,/I'll not be ashamed because of the women./But I'll be happy at their finding out/that you know me this well'.

section of one of the lines has been lost.[1]

The most difficult problem is the meaning of the Hebrew *tᵉlammᵉdēnî*. The verb is used nearly ninety times in the Old Testament, with the meaning 'teach' or 'learn'. The form here can be either second person masculine singular or third person feminine singular, and can refer either to the lover 'you will teach' or to the mother 'she taught'. The translations reflect the options: AV, ASV *who would instruct me*; JB *you would teach me*; NIV *she who has taught me*; NEB mg. *to teach me how to love you* (NEB text *for you to embrace me*).[2] If the feminine form is assumed, the teacher is the mother who has instructed her daughter in the 'facts of life', and it is to that 'schoolroom' she wants to return to show how well she has learned her lessons. If the masculine form is correct, her request is that her lover teach her the intricacies of love in the place where she had her first intimate contacts. In light of the last part of the verse, the feminine form is preferred: the art of preparing for love is best learned at home.

Spiced wine (NEB *mulled wine*). Wine is a frequent motif in the Song, but this is the only reference to 'spiced' (Heb. *reqaḥ*) wine. The precise meaning of the word is uncertain, but the general sense of compounding or mixing ointment or oil is found in Exodus 30:25–35. At Ugarit the *rqh* was the 'perfumer'. See Subject Study: Wine, pp. 66f., and Commentary on 5:1 and 7:2.

The juice of my pomegranates (NIV *nectar*). AV, ASV correctly read *pomegranate* here, although the form may be collective rather than strictly singular. If this expression is in apposition with the previous colon, 'pomegranate-wine' would be a suitable meaning. One of the Egyptian love poems identifies the beloved's breasts with the fruit of the pomegranate. The context here suggests a distinctly erotic connotation.[3]

3. This is a reprise of 2:6. The motif of the girl's longing for intimate contact is common in the ancient love poetry.[4]

[1] NEB *I would lead you to the room of the mother who bore me,/bring you to her house for you to embrace me* (mg. *teach me how to love you*); Pope, p. 653 'I would lead you to my mother's house, Bring you to the chamber of her who bore me'.

[2] The meaning 'conceived' can be obtained by deleting the *m* from the verbal form to get *tēlᵉdēnî* from the root *yld* 'to bear' rather than the MT *lmd* 'to teach'. See Gordis, p. 98 and Pope, pp. 658f. for more detailed discussion.

[3] *Cf.* 4:3 and p. 117, n. 1. See also, *e.g.*, Simpson, p. 298, no. 1, lines 11–13 and pp. 312f., no. 28.

[4] *Cf.* Kramer, pp. 63f., and Simpson, pp. 308f., no. 18, and pp. 316f., no. 32.

4. For the third time this refrain appears (*cf.* 2:7; 3:5), bringing to a close the fourth main section. Here the 'gazelles and hinds of the fields' are not mentioned, and the substitution of the Hebrew *mah* for the earlier *'im* used in oath-formulas is consistent. The form *mah* is generally considered to be a negative in this context (*cf.* GK, p. 443, n. 1) but the more normal meaning is 'what' or 'why'. Exum correctly notes that the refrain now becomes, 'Why do you arouse and waken love?' That love is *already* awakened (*cf.* 8:5) and needs no further stimulation from the onlookers,[1] and the unit which began with estrangement concludes with the lovers in each other's arms again.

V. AFFIRMATION (8:5–14)

Those scholars who see multiple sources for the Song[2] generally classify these last ten verses as a series of unconnected poetic units added to the collection by various editors or copyists. Admittedly, there are difficulties in any suggested grouping, but there are a sufficient number of links with the rest of the book to suggest the unity of this section and the main text. The third section of the Song (3:6 – 5:1) opens with these same words as this one and they both close with the consummation of love. Here we have a series of short references to, or comments from, all the participants in the Song – the companions, the brothers, King Solomon, the mother, the beloved, and the lover – as the commitment of the lovers to each other is re-affirmed and re-consummated.

a. Arousal (8:5)

The opening words of verse five are repeated from 3:6 and 6:10, but here the last half of the colon makes it clear that it is the beloved herself who is the object of this question in those earlier verses also.

5. *Leaning* (Heb. *rāp̄aq*) occurs only this once in the Old Testament, but it is common in the cognate languages, where the basic meaning is 'support' or 'take the elbow' of someone. There is no necessary suggestion of weariness here; the sense

---

[1] J. C. Exum, *ZAW* 85, p. 74.   [2] See Introduction, pp. 44f.

is rather of closeness and intimacy.

Apple tree (NEB *apricot tree*). *Cf.* 2:3, 5.

Awakened (AV *raised thee up*; NEB, NIV *roused*; Heb. *'wr*) is repeated from the chorus of 2:7; 3:5 and 8:4. No completely satisfactory explanation of this verse has yet been proposed, but as the Hebrew has all masculine endings in this section it is evident that the beloved is addressing her lover. Most commentators and many translations (*e.g.* JB, NEB) recommend changing these to feminine forms, but there is no support in the text for this change. Here, as elsewhere in the Song, the girl initiates the love-play.

b. Commitment (8:6–7)

These two verses have been the object of extensive discussion. Delitzsch and Pope have six and twelve pages respectively, and Pope has an additional twenty-page essay on love and death linking this passage (and the Song as a whole) with a funeral celebration. Such interpretation appears forced and unlikely.[1]

6. *Set me* (NEB *wear me*; NIV *place me*; Heb. *šûm*; *cf.* 1:6 and 6:12). NEB catches the ancient Near Eastern custom of wearing signet rings or cylinder seals on cords around the neck, but the force of the Hebrew verb here is more correctly rendered by the other versions.

Seal, *cf.* 4:12, occurs twice here. The engraved stone or metal seal was used to mark possession or ownership. Since they were, in part, the 'signature' of the owner, possession of another's seal was tantamount to having free access to all his or her possessions. The context here suggests that the girl wants to imprint her claim to her lover deeply and openly on him.

Your heart . . . your arm. The endings are masculine, as are

---

[1] Those who argue for the cultic interpretation of the Song take these verses in a distinctly Canaanite setting. *Death* 'Môt' (Heb. *môt* or *mawet*) and *flashes* 'Reshep' (Heb. *rešep*) are both important deities in the Ugaritic cult texts. Môt appears in conflict with Baal and Anath in the seasonal cycle of death and rebirth of the agricultural year, and Reshep is one of the fertility/pestilence gods who is linked with the Garden Motif, *cf.* p. 59, n. 2. See Pope, pp. 210–229, 668–678 for summary and bibliography. *Cf.* also U. Cassuto, *Biblical and Oriental Studies* 2 (Magnes Press, 1975), pp. 168–177, esp. p. 174; and Kramer, pp. 107–133, 154–161. Similarly, 'Rabim' and 'Nahar' (v. 7) are sometimes identified with the gods of the Sea and Underworld.

those elsewhere in this section. The beloved is speaking. The commentators have trouble with the use of 'arm' in this context, since signet rings are worn on the hands, not the arms. Some have argued 'bracelets' rather than 'rings' and taken 'arms' as parallel to 'fingers' on the basis of a line from the Keret Epic from Ugarit.[1] If this section is the girl's request to 'mark' her lover as hers, the problem with the picture disappears.

The third and fourth cola are among the best-known lines in the Song.

Strong (Heb. *'az*) occurs only here in the Song, but is frequent elsewhere in the Old Testament of an irresistible assailant or an immovable defender (Jdg. 14:18; Nu. 13:28).

Love, used here without any pronominal suffix (*cf.* 7:6), has the generic meaning. Love, as such, is *as strong as death*. Note that this is a comparative, not a superlative. Just as death is the fate of all – except those who are alive at the Lord's return – and when death summons, each one answers, so too, when love calls, that call is irresistible. The word of the gospel in John 3:16, through the hope of 1 Corinthians 15:51–57, finds its final glory in the marriage feast of Revelation 21:1–4.

Jealousy (NEB *passion*) is not to be understood in a negative sense ('the green-eyed monster'), but rather as an assertion of the rightful claims of possession. *Cf.* the cognate adjective in Exodus 20:5; 34:14, *etc.*

Cruel (NIV *unyielding*; JB *relentless*; Heb. *qašeh*) occurs some thirty-four times in the Old Testament, but only this once in the Song. The meaning 'hard' or 'obstinate' (vs. 'soft' or 'weak', 2 Sa. 3:39), *i.e.* 'inflexible', is best rendered with NIV or JB rather than the negative sense of the other versions.

Grave (JB, ASV *Sheol*; Delitzsch and Pope *hell*) is the abode of the dead. *Cf.* Proverbs 30:15f.

Flashes (AV *coals*). NIV and NEB treat the term as a verb *it burns*, or *it blazes* (Heb. *rešep*).

A most vehement flame (NIV *mighty flame*; NEB *fiercer than any flame*; JB *a flame of Yahweh himself*; ASV *a very flame of Jehovah*; Heb. *šalhebetyâ*). JB and ASV take the last syllable of the Hebrew as the divine name Yahweh, the LORD. The meaning could be 'love is a flame which has its origin in God'; while this is

---

[1] 'He washed his hands to the elbow, His fingers up to the shoulder'. *Cf.* Pope, pp. 521, 542, 666.

technically true, the fact that this is the only place in the Song a possible use of the divine name appears militates against this understanding of the final syllable. More likely, this is simply a use of a standard idiom for the superlative, as the RSV translates.[1]

7. *Many waters* (JB *no flood*; Heb. *mayîm rabîm*), and *floods* (NIV *rivers*; JB *torrents*; Heb. *neḥārôt*). The tenacious staying power of love is set against these tides and perennial rivers which are unable either to wash love away or put out its sparks.

The last half of the verse is rather unpoetic, and many commentators consider it to be a late addition or a corrupted fragment appended to verse seven. All the English versions follow the Hebrew text *all the wealth* (AV, ASV *substance*) *of his house* rather than the LXX 'all his life'. JB and ASV (and NIV mg.) read the pronoun as masculine 'he', *i.e.* the one who tries to buy love, while the other versions take it as neuter 'it' (*i.e.* the wealth) which would be scorned. Love is not for sale.

c. Contentment (8:8–10)

For many commentators the Song ends with 8:7. These last few verses are often relegated to the category of 'appendices' (JB). But even for those who take them as part of the Song proper, there are difficult problems. Most of the vocabulary is frequent in the Old Testament, but many words appear in the Song for the first time in these verses. Verses 8 to 10 seem to go together, but there is no universal agreement on this division. Nor is there consensus on the identification of the speaker/speakers, nor on the number of women being discussed in these verses. Delitzsch (pp. 151f.) argues that there are two women, the beloved who speaks here, and her younger sister who is being discussed. That is possible in v. 8, but causes difficulty in v. 10. Pope (p. 678) identifies the speakers as the brothers from 1:6 discussing the beloved, their sister. Gordis (pp. 99f.) rejects the brother hypothesis and attributes vv. 8f. to the suitors/companions who are addressing their 'sister', *i.e.* the beloved (*cf.* Introduction, pp. 38f., and Commentary on 5:1). No proposal has won the allegiance of the commentators, although it seems most probable that the brothers are speaking

---

[1] See Gordis, pp. 26, 99 for discussion, and *cf.* Je. 2:31 where 'gloom from Yahweh' is actually 'deepest gloom' (JB).

here, and the object of their attention is the heroine of the Song.

8. Responsibility towards a younger *sister* was clear in the ancient Near East, and may be reflected here. In any case, the young maiden has not, at least in their eyes, reached sexual maturity, and they are debating what will be done on the day she is *spoken for, i.e.* the day a man asks to marry her (*cf.* Ezk. 16:7f. for a similar use of this common expression). Since child marriage does not appear to have been common in ancient Israel, the implication is that she would be sexually mature before marriage.

9. Delitzsch suggests the *wall* signifies 'firmness of character', which will be enhanced by strong silver-covered *towers* (NIV; RSV *battlement*), and *door* signifies one accessible to seduction and therefore in need of 'strong *cedar*' (*cf.* 1:17; 5:15), reinforcing to safeguard her sanctity. However, these repeated *if* clauses are not contrasted, but are in apposition: both images stress the strength and security of her person.

10. Clearly it is now the beloved who speaks, picking up her cue from the words of the two previous verses. The shift to the singular pronoun in the emphatic form and position contrasts with the more hesitant beginning of the brothers' speech. RSV *was* is unsupported, and the meaning appears to be present, *I am* (AV, NEB, NIV, JB), rather than past. She gladly takes the *wall* image as her own and promptly proceeds to describe her *breasts* as *towers* (Heb. *migdālôt, cf.* 5:13 'treasure-chests'), more imposing and glorious than the crenelated battlements her brothers proposed. She is proclaiming her maturity and readiness for the love and marriage she has celebrated. *Cf* Ezekiel 16:7f., 10–13.

The last colon can be read either *then* or *thus* (NIV, Pope; NEB *so*), and the verb as either a simple statement *I was*, or a stative 'I became and continue to be'. In the former case the assumption is that the beloved is to be identified with the 'little sister' of v. 8, and that she is now grown up. In the latter case, the contrast is between the mature beloved and the still immature 'little sister'.

In his eyes. JB *under his eyes* is an interesting suggestion, but this rendering of the Hebrew preposition *be* has no support.

One who brings (ASV *found peace*; AV *found favour*; NIV, NEB *bringing* [who brings] *contentment*; JB *I have found true peace*; Heb *kᵉmôṣᵉʾēt šālôm*). The verb occurs nine times in the Song,

172

frequently as part of the search/find motif (*cf.* 3:1–4), and often has the connotation 'find by chance'. The emphasis is on the unexpected nature of the discovery.

Peace. Delitzsch develops a play on the words Solomon/ Shulammite/Shalom (Heb. *šālôm* = peace) as support for the idea that the lover in the Song is indeed Solomon. (*Cf.* Introduction, pp. 19–21.) Gordis offers four suggestions, concluding in his revised commentary ⟨p. 101) that the idea that she is a 'fountain of well-being' to her beloved is the preferred reading. However, a better sense for this line is obtained when *šālôm* is translated as 'completeness', 'harmony', or 'wholeness'. The central concept of the Hebrew term is one of unimpeded relationships with others and fulfilment in one's own undertakings. There is a clear reference here to the 'Shulammite' as the 'completed one' of 6:13.

d. Communion (8:11–14)

The closing section of the Song alternates between the beloved's final comments to the gathered friends and the lovers' gentle exhortations to each other.

11. The opening phrase here is reminiscent of the 'Song of the Vineyard' in Isaiah 5:1–7, which is also a love song.[1] Where that text is explicitly allegorical (*cf.* v. 7), this one is not, even though some traditional interpretation identifies the 'vineyard' with Solomon's large harem (*cf.* 1 Ki. 11:3).

Vineyard. See on 1:6 and 2:3, 15, and Subject Study: Garden, pp. 55f.

Solomon. See Introduction, pp. 19–21. The identification of the lover with King Solomon runs into difficulty with this section. The contrast here is with the rights of the king to administer his own possessions and the right of the girl to her own person. To confuse the lover and king vitiates the comparison.

Baal-hamon. The words can be translated 'Lord of a crowd', but of the ancient versions, only Vg. reads this way. Since this name is not attested elsewhere in the literature, a number of emendations have been proposed (see Pope, pp. 686–689), none of them convincing. Of known sites which may be in mind here, two are possible: Belmain (or Belmen), a Hellenis-

[1] *Cf.* G. L. Carr, 'Old Testament Love Songs and Their Use in the New Testament', *JETS* 24, 1981, pp. 97–105, esp. pp. 101f.

tic (third century BC) settlement on a secondary road about twelve miles south of Beth-Shan on the edge of the Jordan Valley, is probably not to be considered, since the time period is much too late for any reasonable date for the book. A better option is Belemoth (Khirbet Balama, modern Ibleam), about a mile south-west of Janin (ancient Beth-haggan, *cf* Subject Study: Garden, p. 56) in the Dothan valley. This site was occupied as early as the pre-conquest Canaanite period, and is mentioned in Judith 8:3 as the burial-place of Judith's husband Manasseh.

Keepers (JB *overseers*; NEB *guardians*; NIV *tenants*; Heb. *nōṭrîm*). The word occurs only nine times in the Old Testament, four of these in the Song (1:6 twice, here, and 8:12). The other five uses (Lv. 19:18; Ps. 103:9; Je. 3:5, 12; Na. 1:12) all have the negative connotation of holding a grudge or sustaining anger (*cf.* Song 1:6). This sense seems out of place here, although the concept of nurturing does fit.

A thousand pieces of silver (JB, NIV *shekels*; Heb. *'elep̄ kasep̄*). According to Isaiah 7:23, a thousand vines were worth 'a thousand silver [pieces]'. The term shekel is not in either of these texts, but since the shekel was the common measure of weight (and of coinage after about 500 BC), it is probably intended here. The common shekel weighed about 0.4 ounces (11.3 grammes) and the 'royal' ('heavy') shekel about 0.457 ounces (13 grammes), and at current silver prices would be worth around $3.00. The fee per tenant would, on this reckoning, be about $3,000.

12. *My vineyard, my very own. Cf.* 1:6; 2:15. The contrast is between Solomon's extensive properties (harem?) and the beloved's own person, of which she alone has the right of assignation.

Two hundred (shekels?) is probably to be understood in connection with the payment fee in v. 11, and is the percentage of the profit shared by the labourers. The king does not have the power to give the girl to any of his people, any more than he has to command her love.[1]

---

[1] This motif is found in the Egyptian love poetry. 'I found [Prince] Mehy in his chariot on the road/with his burly gang. . . . How foolish you are, my heart,/why would you stroll by Mehy?/If I pass beside him/I'll have to tell him my troubles./See, I am yours, I'll say to him,/and he'll shout out my name./But he'd pass me on to the harem/of the first man of his troop'. Simpson, pp. 317f., no. 33, lines 3–4, 9–16. *Cf.* above, p. 153, n. 1.

13. *Dwell* suggests permanent residence. NEB *sit* is more in keeping with the sense required here. The plural *gardens* indicates no specific garden, but that she is 'at home' in this setting. NEB *my bride . . . my garden* is interpretative, since neither the noun 'bride' nor the possessive pronoun 'my' is in the text.

Companions. Cf. 1:7. Probably not just the 'Jerusalem girls' but the whole group who had assembled for the celebration in 6:13 – 7:5.

Listening (ASV, AV *hearkening*; Pope *attentive*; NIV *friends in attendance*; Heb. *maqšîḫîm*) occurs only here in the Song, and means either 'listen carefully' or more broadly 'pay attention'. Whether *voice* is the object of this verb or of the verb *hear* in the last colon is a matter of debate. Gordis (p. 102) argues for the latter, and if *qsb* is, as suggested, more inclusive than 'listen', his suggestion has merit. The lover calls for her response to his presence (*cf.* 2:14).

14. His request draws an immediate response from his beloved, and her invitation is a reprise of many of the longings of earlier passages in the Song.

Make haste (NIV *come away*; NEB *come into the open*; Heb. *bāraḥ*) occurs only here in the Song. The word in its other sixty-five Old Testament uses usually means flight from enemies. Here she calls him to that rapid, abandoned flight *to* her. Some erotic imagery may also be present, for the idea of piercing or penetration occurs in Exodus 36:33 of bolts (Heb. *beriaḥ*), and in Isaiah 27:1 of the piercing serpent. This latter is a very common sexual symbol.

Gazelle, young stag. Cf. 2:9, 17.

Mountains of spices. Cf. 2:17; 4:6, 8, 10, 14; 5:13. The final invitation is to a continued celebration of the love and communion which the happy couple shares. The joys of physical union and mutual enjoyment are stamped with God's approval, for the Song of Songs is part of his holy Word.

175